A RICE VILLAGE SAGA

Also by Yujiro Hayami

ASIAN VILLAGE ECONOMY AT THE CROSSROADS (*with Masao Kikuchi*)

AGRICULTURAL DEVELOPMENT: An International Perspective (*with V. W. Ruttan*)

ANATOMY OF A PEASANT ECONOMY

ECONOMIC DEVELOPMENT: From the Poverty to the Wealth of Nations

Also by Masao Kikuchi

ASIAN VILLAGE ECONOMY AT THE CROSSROADS (*with Yujiro Hayami*)

A Rice Village Saga

Three Decades of Green Revolution in the Philippines

Yujiro Hayami
Professor of International Economics
Aoyama-Gakuin University
Tokyo, Japan

and

Masao Kikuchi
Professor of Agricultural Economics
Chiba University
Chiba, Japan

CAB INTERNATIONAL

00335010

BARNES & NOBLE
Lanham • Boulder • New York

IRRI
INTERNATIONAL RICE RESEARCH INSTITUTE, PHILIPPINES

First published in Great Britain 2000 by
MACMILLAN PRESS LTD
Houndmills, Basingstoke, Hampshire RG21 6XS and London
Companies and representatives throughout the world

A catalogue record for this book is available from the British Library.

ISBN 0–333–72617–0

First published in the United States of America 2000 by
BARNES & NOBLE
4720 Boston Way, Lanham, Maryland 20706

ISBN 0–389–21023–4

in association with
IRRI **INTERNATIONAL RICE RESEARCH INSTITUTE**
MCPO Box 3127, 1271 Makati City, Philippines

ISBN 971–22–0129–5

This book is printed on paper suitable for recycling and made from fully managed and sustained forest sources.

10   9   8   7   6   5   4   3   2   1
09   08   07   06   05   04   03   02   01   00

Printed and bound in Great Britain by
Antony Rowe Ltd, Chippenham, Wiltshire

Contents

List of Tables

List of Figures

List of Abbreviations

CLT	Certificate of Land Transfer
CPI	Consumer price index
DTI	Department of Trade and Industry
EP	Emancipation Patent
GDP	Gross domestic product
Hukbalahap (Huk)	*Hukbo ng Bayan Laban sa Hapon* (People's Army against Japan)
IA	Irrigators' Association
IDO	Institution Development Officer, for IA building
IRRI	International Rice Research Institute
MV	Modern varieties
MV_1	MVs from IR8 to IR34 and C4 varieties
MV_2	MVs from IR36 to IR62
MV_3	MVs from IR64 and newer
NFA	National Food Authority
NIA	National Irrigation Administration
O&M	Operation and maintenance in irrigation systems
OCW	Overseas Contract Worker
OL	Operation Leasehold in land reform
OLT	Operation Land Transfer in land reform
TFP	Total factor productivity
TSA group	Turn-out Service Area group, federated into IA
TV	Traditional varieties
UPLB	University of the Philippines at Los Baños

Preface

Bonsai – growing dwarfed trees in a dish – is a favourite art of the Japanese. The *bonsai* lover makes a lifelong effort to perfect the miniature shape of a tree or bush to reflect the spirit of the universe. The study of a single village in the Philippines since the 1960s that has been put together in this volume represents our effort to shape a *bonsai* of human society, however imperfect its present form may still be.

This study has been shaped during our association with the International Rice Research Institute (IRRI) since 1974, either as resident staff or as visiting scientists. The long-term maintenance of the village as our social observatory would not have been possible without our being allowed continuous use of IRRI's research infrastructure. We are particularly grateful to Randolph Barker, Head of the Agricultural Economics Department in the initial stage of our study, and to Mahabub Hossain, Head of the Social Sciences Division in its final stage, for providing encouragement and necessary support for this non-glamorous project. We also benefited from interactions with social scientists both inside and outside the IRRI within the academic community of Los Baños – Lourdes Adriano, Arsenio Balisacan, Gelia Castillo, Cristina David, David Dawe, Bart Duff, Jonna Estudillo, Robert Evenson, Grace Godell, Robert Herdt, Keijiro Otsuka, Sushil Pandey, Tirso Paris, Prabhu Pingali, Vernon Ruttan, Agnes Quisumbing, James Roumasset, Gerome Sison, Joyotee Smith, Anthony Tang and Thomas Wickham. One great advantage of our association with the IRRI is that we have been able to acquire correct scientific knowledge of rice plants and farming practices through interaction with natural scientists. Among many distinguished IRRI scientists from whom we have learned so much, we mention three distinguished names – Nyle Brady (soil scientist and former IRRI Director General), Gurdev Khush (plant breeder) and the late Shoichi Yoshida (plant physiologist). We must also recognize Michael Way, who helped to elaborate the title of this book through a series of enjoyable dinner conversations at the IRRI guesthouse.

Our field work has been critically dependent on the assistance of junior researchers in the IRRI's Social Sciences Division (formerly the Agricultural Economics Department). From beginning to end, Esther Marciano provided conscientious and dependable services in data collection and processing, and assisted us in establishing ourselves as insiders in the village community. The contributions of Luisa Bambo and Nellie Fortuna were equally valuable in the earlier stage of this project. Our sincere appreciation is extended to Milagros Obusan, Celia Tabien, Mena Serrano and Wally Tan, who supported us in the various phases of the field work. Violeta Cordova, Piedad Moya, Fe Gascon and Adelita Palacpac have been a major source of information on the reality of agriculture and rural life in the Philippines beyond our narrow observation. Efficient and reliable secretarial support from Mirla Domingo and Doris Malabanan has been invaluable, especially during the manuscript stages of this book.

Our final-round operations of this study were supported by the IRRI–Japan Shuttle Project, based on the Japanese government's special fund to the IRRI, and a research grant from the Japanese government through the Foundation for Advanced Studies on International Development.

Above all, our deepest gratitude goes to people in our study village called 'East Laguna Village' in this book. Their co-operation has been astonishing. Few have rejected our rather lengthy interviews, which sometimes involved sensitive questions. Indeed, we have learned more from these villagers than from the many books we have read. Whenever we have visited the village, something new has always struck us, reminding us how ignorant we were about their social and economic mechanisms. As such, this village has served the role of Socrates to us.

As a modest repayment to our debt of gratitude, '*utang na loob*', this book is dedicated to the East Laguna Villagers.

YUJIRO HAYAMI
MASAO KIKUCHI

Prologue: The Village Found

The sun was setting on the ridge of Mount Makiling. Our car was bumping over a gravel road with potholes created by the monsoon rain. We were weary after a day's journey. For a week, with a young assistant and a driver, I had been searching for a village in the rice belt along the coast at Laguna de Bay.

Since joining the International Rice Research Institute (IRRI) a month before, I had been preparing for a project involving comprehensive records of household economic activities using a suitable village as my social observatory. For this purpose I employed a young woman newly graduated from the University of the Philippines College of Agriculture, and began the search in September 1974.

I wanted a 'typical rice village' – modest in size with about a hundred households, clearly demarcated from other villages, not exposed too much to urban activities, and within commuting distance of no more than two hours from the IRRI so that I could visit it for constant checking of the records kept by my co-operators. However, contrary to what I had expected, such a village was difficult to find – they were either too large, contiguous with other villages, exposed to highways, or covered by special development projects supported by government or aid agencies.

While bouncing in the car I kept thinking 'perhaps there is no such a thing as a typical village'. 'That is the village,' the driver said suddenly. As I looked in the direction of his pointing finger, I glimpsed a grove of coconut trees at the end of the country road cutting across the green rice fields. As the car moved closer, I began to see houses among the palm trees. We drove into the village between houses with elevated wooden floors, bamboo walls and nipa-leaf roofs. These simple houses looked cool as they received the breezes blowing through the coconut leaves. 'Perhaps this is it', I muttered. Indeed, it did look exactly like the typical Philippine village I had in mind.

We were guided by villagers towards the house of the *barangay captain* (village headman). Mr Captain (as we have continued to call him even after his retirement from office) was at that time in his late forties. He was relatively tall by Filipino standards, with dark, rough skin sunburned from years of farm work. He was somewhat shy and reserved, and did not speak English, unlike many officials in Philippine villages. However, I soon found him to be a remarkably capable captain with a full grasp of the economic and social conditions of his village. The information he gave me about the village – 95 households, with a population of 549, most of whom were engaging in rice work, either as farmers or agricultural labourers, convinced me that this should be my project village. It was clearly separated from other villages by the sea of rice fields. I was glad to know that no special project was being undertaken in this village (although it was a great surprise to find later that a Japanese geographer had conducted a survey here eight years before).

In response to my appeal, Mr Captain cordially agreed to render co-operation and assistance. My assistant asked him if he could provide us with a list of villagers. To my astonishment, instead of giving us the written list, he named, for my assistant's transcription, all the names of the household heads and their status in terms of operational landholdings. He made surprisingly few mistakes compared with the data collected from the household survey that we conducted two months later.

Meanwhile, Mrs Captain tried hard to show the traditional Filipino hospitality. She rushed out to buy soft drinks and rice cakes, and said in correct English, 'Please help yourself'. She was a tiny person with inquisitive eyes and shiny, light-brown skin. She was elegant but not bashful like her husband, and looked so remarkably young that we doubted that she really had as many as seven children. I was told several months later that Mr Captain fell in love instantly when he saw her in another village singing a song with a guitar to orchestrate the work of rice transplanting by a group of young men and women. This I could easily imagine.

Such was the beginning of my link with this village. By no means did I anticipate that my association would continue for a quarter of a century, or, for that matter, that my assistant would marry a son of the Captain.

YUJIRO HAYAMI

1 Approach to a Village

Waves of modernizing forces, such as commercialization and new technology, have been pressing major changes upon rural communities in the Third World. Fears have often been expressed that these forces are destroying the traditional community institutions based on the principles of mutual help and income-sharing, thereby creating greater inequalities and a higher incidence of poverty in the rural sector. Such concerns have been expressed as a result of the development and diffusion of modern rice and wheat varieties since the late 1960s, popularly called 'the Green Revolution'. This book does not intend to add to debates on the economic and social consequences of the Green Revolution, on which prolific literature has been accumulated (Griffin, 1974; International Rice Research Institute, 1978; Lipton, 1989; David and Otsuka, 1994). By following the debates, however, we see the danger of trying to identify the effect of the Green Revolution or any one force of modernization without due consideration of its interactions with other forces. Such an approach has often resulted in a misunderstanding of the real causes of poverty and inequality (Hayami, 1992).

This study aims to give a microscopic view of the process by which agricultural production systems, village community institutions and rural people's economic well-being change under the pressure of those modernizing forces. The study is based on recurrent surveys of one village in the Province of Laguna, Philippines, since the 1960s.

Laguna Province lies along the southern coast of Laguna de Bay (the largest lake in the Philippines), south of Manila (see Figure 1.1). The strip of irrigated lowland along the lake is one of the most productive rice areas in the country. Relatively well-developed irrigation systems permit rice production in both wet and dry seasons in most rice fields. Because of the favourable environment, as well as Laguna's proximity to major agricultural research centres in Los Baños, including the International Rice Research Institute (IRRI) and the University of the Philippines at Los Baños (UPLB), farmers in the area were the earliest to adopt modern rice varieties and technologies, not only in the Philippines but also among tropical rice-producing areas of the world. Rice yields per cropping season in Laguna nearly doubled, from the level of 2–3 tons to 4–5 tons per hectare within less than twenty years since the release by the IRRI for wide dissemination in 1966 of IR8, the first high-yielding modern variety (MV).

The impact of this technological change on agrarian organization and rural life were, of course, important. However, in Laguna, many other

1

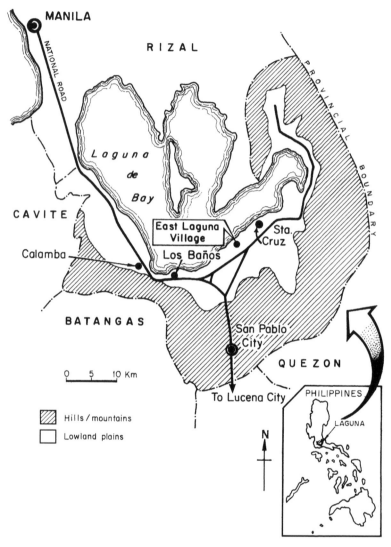

Figure 1.1   Map of the Province of Laguna, Philippines

factors also had significant socioeconomic influences. Land reform programmes implemented primarily for lowland rice areas under President
Ferdinand Marcos's martial law regime during 1972–81 converted traditional sharecropping tenancies to leasehold tenancies at a low, fixed, controlled rent. Rural villages in Laguna have been exposed rapidly to urban

economic activities facilitated by the completion of highways (notably the South Super Highway in 1977 and the Masapang Highway in 1978), and the increasing location of urban industries along those highways, especially on the west coast of Laguna de Bay. Meanwhile the population has continued to grow rapidly and the land: population ratio to decline sharply.

These factors have interacted with the adoption of new rice technology to cause major economic and social changes in Laguna, exemplified by the detailed historical accounts of a typical village to be found in this book.

VILLAGE PROFILE

Our study village (*barangay* or *barrio*) is one of thirteen in the Municipality of Pila. Henceforth, we shall call it East Laguna Village, because it faces the east coast of Laguna de Bay (Figure 1.1). Unlike the rapidly urbanizing west coast, the east coast of the lake, including this village, still maintains its traditional position as a rural area.

Economic Environments

The village is surrounded by wet rice fields. There is little difference in elevation between the rice fields and Laguna de Bay, so the fields are often flooded during the rainy season. Villagers live on slightly higher ground among coconut trees (see Figure 1.2). Their houses are hidden in the coconut grove, which looks like an island in a sea of rice fields – a landscape typical of the Laguna rice belt.

The *poblacion* (urban section or town) of Pila was developed in the early Spanish period. Within the municipality, East Laguna Village represents a newly developed area inhabited since the late nineteenth century. During the process of settlement, landlords who were living mainly in the *poblacion* gave settlers land parcels and advanced them credit for subsistence, on the understanding that they would enter into a sharecropping arrangement after a gratis period. According to national census data, the rice field area in the village increased from 36 hectares in 1918 to 94 hectares in 1960; no significant increase has been recorded since then. Originally, all the rice fields were rainfed, cropping only in the wet season. In 1958, a lateral of a national irrigation system was extended to this village. Since then, double cropping of rice has commonly been practised.

As in other rice-producing areas in the Philippines, absentee landlordism is pervasive, following the Spanish legacy. Even today, in this village, more than 60 per cent of the rice fields are owned by non-villagers, despite the

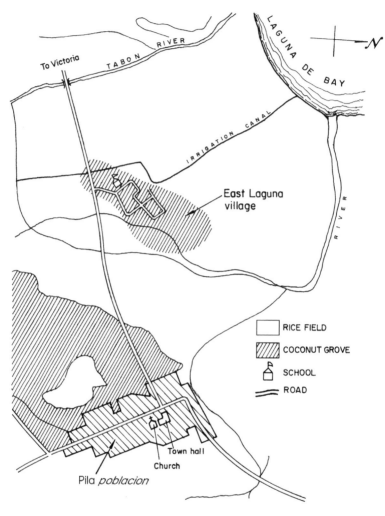

Figure 1.2   Map of East Laguna Village, Philippines

significant progress of land reform. However, unlike the inner part of Central Luzon where large rice *haciendas* prevailed before the land reform programmes, the long-settled areas along the sea and lake coasts around Manila have been characterized by small, scattered holdings of small to medium landlords. The 1976 survey recorded that all landlords except one owned less than seven hectares in this village, and the majority of them lived in the *poblacion* of Pila. This pattern has remained essentially unchanged up to the time of writing.

The coconut grove covers about sixteen hectares, of which about a third is owned by villagers and the rest by absentee landlords. Most villagers live under the coconut trees, with the consent of the absentee landowners. By custom, they are allowed to use the land under the trees for growing fruit and vegetables, and for raising livestock and poultry. In return, the villagers clear the underbrush. In October 1997 the grove held 266 houses, with a total population of 1209 people. About half of the houses are simple huts made mainly of bamboo and nipa leaves; a quarter are solid structures of concrete and lumber under a roof of galvanized iron; and the rest are a mixture of the two. Also located in the grove are a small Catholic chapel and an elementary school.

Rice farming is by far the most dominant enterprise in the village. Before a national irrigation system began to extend its service to this village in 1958, rice farming was limited to some six months under monsoon rain within the period May to November (see Figure 1.3). With irrigation and short-maturing varieties, rice is now produced over three to four months in both the wet season (June–November) and dry season (December–May). Seasonality is strong in employment and earnings from rice production.

Coconuts are only a minor income source for villagers, because few of them own coconut trees; even the harvesting labour is usually brought in from outside the village by the absentee landlords. Fishing and duck/pig raising are common sideline enterprises of the villagers. Self-employed non-farm activities, such as petty trade and cottage industries, as well as off-farm employment outside the village, are an increasingly important income source for villagers.

Villagers buy small daily needs from family grocery stores (*sari-sari*) in the village. They frequently go to a market and to shops in the *poblacion* of Pila, travelling a country road of about two kilometres on foot or by tricycle (a motorcycle attached to a wagon). For larger purchases, people go to Santa Cruz, the capital of Laguna Province, by *jeepney* (informal minibus) about eight kilometres away.

It is estimated that average per capita income per year in this village was about US$470 in the mid-1990s, about 40 per cent of the Philippine national average. With this income level, East Laguna Village would not be far away from the norm for lowland rice villages in the Philippines. Income distribution within the village was associated with the distribution of operational farmland holdings. In the mid-1990s, average per capita incomes in the households of large farmers holding more than two hectares

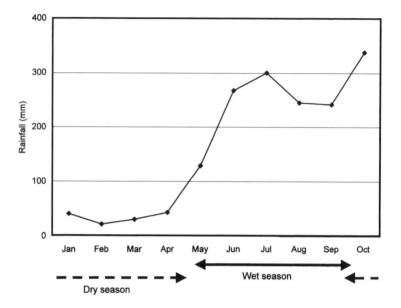

Figure 1.3 Rainfall pattern in Laguna (1979–95 averages measured at Los Baños)
Source: IRRI Agro-Climatic Unit.

of rice fields and small farmers below two hectares were about US$1300 and US$700 respectively, whereas those of landless agricultural labourers with no operational holdings was only about US$300, or less than US$1 per day. The majority of the villagers subsisted on incomes below the poverty line set by the Philippine government (see Chapter 10). Severe poverty and destitution were reflected in the fact that physical disability and sickness, obviously caused by malnutrition, were not rare to encounter.

Local Governance

East Laguna Village is a *barangay* (a Tagalog word for 'boat') or *barrio* (a Spanish word for 'section') which is chartered as the lowest level of local governance hierarchy in the Philippines, a step below *municipality*, and two steps down from *province*. However, its role as an administrative arm of the state is weak and it has remained largely as a 'natural village' or an autonomous community in which people happen to live together in a location and govern themselves according to traditional customs and norms through strong personal interaction rather than through legal coercion based on formal laws and professional policing.

The official governance structure consists of an elected *barangay captain* and a council of seven members elected for a term of three years, by which a secretary and a treasurer are appointed. This formal structure was determined by the Barrio Charter (Republic Act No. 2370 enacted in 1959, and Republic Act No. 3590, revised in 1963). This charter is a formalization of the grass-roots self-governance structure that has existed since the Spanish period, or even earlier. However, until very recently, the *barangay* had had few permanent fiscal means and no legal coercive power was needed for it to function as an effective governing organization. Village officials received no monetary compensation. Their activities, such as the solution of conflicts among villagers, and mobilization of villagers' labour for public works, followed traditional community procedures based on customs and norms, enforced by persuasion and consensus under the threat of possible social opprobrium or eventual ostracism against rebels. In this regard, the *municipality*, instead of the *barangay*, has actually acted as the lowest level of the state in local governance. Its officials, who include a mayor, council members, judges and police, all receive full-time salaries from the budget based on its own tax revenue and fiscal transfers from both central and provincial governments.

This structure began to undergo a major change with the passage of the Local Government Autonomy Act (Republic Act No. 7160) in December 1992 under President Fidel Ramos. With this Act, a permanent fiscal base was established for each *barangay* by granting a certain taxation autonomy, such as a business licence fee and real estate tax surcharge, and formalizing reallocation of central government revenue from the Bureau of Internal Revenue. With this fiscal base, a *barangay* is now able to pay its officials. It can also promote public work projects by paying a part of the cost in money. However, the impact of this reform on the village economy was small to negligible during our study period. Payments to the village officials have been token amounts for their voluntary services (and they are called 'honorariums'), unlike the professional salaries paid to the full-time municipality officials. This is illustrated by East Laguna Village with a *barangay captain*'s honorarium of only 1000 pesos per month, which is less than seven days' labour wage for manual farm work (a daily farm wage being about 150 pesos); and the secretary, treasurer and seven council members each received only 600 pesos in 1996. Although the *barangay* police was created with a chief and six policemen, it was inevitable that their activities could not go much beyond those of a voluntary night-watch group with their honorariums being as small as 350 pesos per person per month, less than three days' farm wage.

The *barangay* budget in 1996, with more than 70 per cent of its revenue coming from the Bureau of Internal Revenue, was so small that 60 per cent of expenditure covered the officials' honorariums even at such low rates, and only 20 per cent was used for economic development projects. With such a weak fiscal base, the *barangay*'s procedures for resolving conflicts and for constructing and maintaining the infrastructure continued to depend mainly on the traditional community mechanism of persuasion, consensus seeking, and social rather than legal compulsion.

Thus, while the 1992 reform of local governance has a potential for changing the nature of *barangay* in the Philippines drastically in the future, it is largely correct to regard East Laguna Village as a natural village or autonomous community for the period of our observations.

Social Structure

Since Laguna Province is located within the Southern Tagalog Region, East Laguna Village is predominantly inhabited by the Tagalogs – the second largest ethnic group (next to the Cebuanos) in the country, comprising about 20 per cent of the total population of the Philippines. Their language has been officially adopted as the national language of the Philippines. There are quite a few migrants from non-Tagalog regions, such as Bicol and Visayas, belonging to other ethnic groups, who settled in the village through marriage and circular migration (Chapter 3). However, there is no sign of significant discrimination against the non-Tagalogs. Although the Philippines is a multi-ethnic society with people speaking more than seventy different languages, cultural and social differences are not very pronounced, except among the mountain tribes and the Muslims in Mindanao.

By far the majority of households (80 per cent in 1997) in the village consist of nuclear families comprising one married couple and their children. It is customary that when children are married, they build a bamboo-nipa hut in the garden or in the vicinity of their parents' house rather than live under the same roof, although it is not uncommon for a newly-married couple to live in the parents' house for the first few years before they have their own children. Also, many old people live in their own houses separately from their children. Although living in separate houses, parents and grown-up children are usually in close relationships, and visit and help each other constantly. The traditional mode is that, after marriage, children move to their own huts and continue to make a living as employees in parents' and neighbours' farms, until they succeed to the farms after the parents' retirement. The process of succession usually involves implicit contracts for sharing incomes from the farms, with subtle variations in the terms of these.

Typical of the Philippines, as well as of other South-east Asian countries, the family structure in this village is 'bilineal' in the sense that family succession is not limited to the lineage of one particular sex; it is optional for children to follow the lineage of either husband or wife. Unlike the 'lineal' society of Japan, where a newly-married couple is identified as belonging to the husband's family and inherits the properties of the husband's parents alone, there is no social norm in this village that dictates differential belongings and inheritance rights between male and female lineages. The intergenerational family relationship is determined more by economic considerations than by social norms. For example, a newly-married couple may decide to live with the wife's parents because their farm is larger relative to the family labour available for farming than is the husband's parents'.

Inheritance of properties is, in principle, equal among heirs, as a pre-colonial indigenous tradition (Corpuz, 1977, p. 17). In practice, well-to-do children tend to receive less than their poorer brothers and sisters. Often, those who received a higher education and obtained stable, non-farm jobs forgo the right to inherit farm-related properties in the village. Generally, the one who continues to live with and take care of parents inherits a major share of the properties. There is little discrimination against women regarding inheritance. Nor is there any discrimination in economic activities beyond the natural division of labour based on the difference in muscle power. In this regard, women in Philippine villages are probably the most liberated among rural communities in the world.

There is no rule about who must live with old parents, but often it is an unmarried daughter or the youngest child. Thus, compared with a lineal family system with primogeniture, such as in Japan, intra-family relationships are relatively flexible and loosely structured.

Similarly, social relationships across different families and households in the village are also rather loosely structured, similar to those observed by John Embree (1950) for Thailand contrasted with Japan. First, the village is not so clearly demarcated from other villages with its geographical border being ambiguous, and entry to and exit from the village are free, involving no particular formality or courtesy. Second, village-wide co-operation in the construction and maintenance of the infrastructure, such as irrigation systems and roads, is rather thin. Indeed, Hiromitsu Umehara (1967), who studied this village during 1966–7 was puzzled by the observation that very few villagers participated in the rehabilitation of a country road connecting this village to Pila *poblacion*, despite its vital importance to the life of villagers. The same applies to the maintenance of irrigation systems (Chapter 6).

There is no rigid social hierarchy to command a village-wide collective action for augmenting and maintaining such infrastructure. Traditionally, East Laguna Village was a homogenous community consisting mainly of sharecroppers. They were strongly subordinate to landlords, who lived in Pila *poblacion* or nearby local towns, but they were fairly homogenous among themselves, both economically and socially. As land reform in the 1970s converted them into owner-farmers or leasehold tenants with land rents fixed at low rates, the subordination of villagers to absentee landlords was broken, but it consolidated a class differentiation between farmers who used to sharecrop rice lands, and landless agricultural labourers who staked out a living in wage employment for neighbouring farmers (Chapter 4). The income disparity between the two classes continued to widen as the Green Revolution resulted in significant yield increases (Chapter 5).

Yet the increased economic inequality has not resulted in distinct social class segmentations. Although leadership positions in the village, such as *barangay captain* and council members, tend to be held disproportionately by old settled families who are mostly large landholders, it is not unusual for small farmers and even landless labourers, as well as women, to be elected to office. Moreover, social norms on the rights and obligations of the leaders to command other villagers to obey in the organization of community work on the infrastructure are not established. Such a social structure, typical of villages in South-east Asia, is very different from that of traditional village communities in Japan, in which village officers were drawn from certain families with their rights and obligations *vis-à-vis* other villagers were clearly specified by custom, and their legitimacy as village elites depends on their dedication and leadership in maintaining the infrastructure, especially irrigation (Ohkama and Kikuchi, 1996).

The social structure of East Laguna Village also represents a sharp contrast to that of Hindu villages in India, where the community is rigidly segmented across hereditary castes (Wiser and Wiser, 1963; Srinivas, 1976). Rather, it is somewhat similar to that of non-Hindu tribes in the Himalayan foothills, where the community is relatively more homogenous and flexible with inter-class social mobility being allowed (Fürer-Haimendorf, 1980).

Characterization of this village community as 'loosely structured', however, does not mean that social interactions are thin and co-operation is low among villagers. Instead, close interactions and strong co-operation are visible in constant exchanges in services, gifts and small credits (in cash as well as in the form of rice and other daily needs), including collective work for such occasions as building bamboo-nipa huts (*bayanihan*). However, such collaboration is structured on an *ad hoc* personal basis among relatives and close friends rather than being based on established rules in the village. In this regard, a wide network of blood-based authentic relatives in the bilineal family system as well as of pseudo-relatives based on Catholic godparents–children and *compadre–comadre* relationships integrates villagers, with few exceptions. This personal network is further extended to economic transactions in the form of the regular-customer relationships (*suki*) in which, for example, a housewife always buys groceries from a particular personally-trusted store (Chapter 8). The network of personal relationships is consolidated by the strong sense of indebtedness in gratitude (*utang na loob*), by which one person doing a favour to another is assured of being reciprocated in the long run.

Village-wide customary rules also exist, though they are not as pervasive and compelling as in Japanese villages. For example, villagers who live in the coconut grove owned by landlords living outside the village are allowed to gather and consume coconuts that have accidentally fallen down from the trees, but are prohibited from deliberately causing them to fall. A villager is prohibited from letting his *carabao* pass through others' rice fields while crops are standing, but he is allowed to graze the *carabao* in anyone's field after the harvest. A farmer is prevented from rejecting anyone who wishes to collect fallen rice panicles (*pulot*) in his field after harvest. Such rules are fairly well observed, and violators are criticized as being shameless (*walang hiya*).

As the village of a Catholic country, almost all the inhabitants in East Laguna Village are baptized. There is a small chapel (*kapilya*) in the centre of the village, next to the elementary school. It is common to see the images of Christ and the Virgin Mary in villagers' houses. Social ceremonies, such as marriages and funerals, are performed by Catholic priests. The biggest annual event in the village is the *barrio fiesta* on 6 January to celebrate the village's patron saint. The *fiesta* is marked by a procession of young girls in their best dresses, often made specially for the day. All are invited to every villager's feast, involving an extravagant expense relative to the villagers' income.

However, it is not clear how strong a grip Catholicism has on the minds of villagers. According to Akira Takahashi (1972), authentic Catholic belief is strong among the urban middle to upper classes in the Philippines, but urban labourers tend to be attracted more to the new variants of Christianity (such as *Iglesia ni Cristo*), and rural villagers believe in Malayan animism alongside Catholicism. Umehara found in 1966 that few villagers attended regular mass on Sundays. His observation was consistent with ours in the past, though Catholic belief has seemed to be gaining power among villagers in recent years (Chapter 2).

Some have argued that *barrio fiesta* can be regarded as a Catholic dressing on the ceremony of animism praying to a native spirit for a good crop (Gorospe, 1966; Takahashi, 1972, p. 138). Indeed, the practice of charms, spells and taboos based on animism is rampant in the village. In the adaptation of pre-Christian customs and practices to Christianity, Philippine villages may not be so different from those in other regions of the world, including Europe. However, the major motive underlying the behaviour of the Filipinos, including the people in East Laguna Village, appears to be the aversion of shame *vis-à-vis* others within their personal network rather than the aversion of sin prescribed *vis-à-vis* one absolute God in Christianity. In this respect, Filipinos seem to be similar to the Japanese and many other Asians in belonging to the 'culture of shame' rather than the 'culture of sin' (Benedict, 1946).

Within this basic cultural similarity, the differences in social norms and community structures between Japanese and Philippine villagers appear to be based on traditional differences in relative resource endowments. In Japan, the danger of population pressure on limited land resources culminating in a subsistence crisis, especially for poor members in village communities, was already visible by the eighteenth century (Hayami, 1997, pp. 251–4). How to organize collective action to conserve and augment local commons and, in particular, irrigation systems, has thus become their central concern. Community norms have been developed to penalize free-riders in the enhancement and maintenance of the critical local infrastructure needed to increase output and employment at a pace consistent with population growth. Communities are 'tightly structured' in the sense that both geographical and social borders between one village and others are unambiguously demarcated, and that rights and obligations are clearly assigned to individual households relative to others within the village (Ohkama and Kikuchi, 1996).

In contrast, and typical of South-east Asia, East Laguna Village and its surroundings were traditionally more abundant in land resources before the 1950s. So the need to conserve and augment local commons had been low correspondingly. Also, until fairly recently, an option had been available for villagers to migrate to frontier lands for new land openings. Because the population was more mobile and the need to construct and maintain the local infrastructure by communal efforts was less compelling, villages in South-east Asia have been 'loosely structured' compared with those in North-east Asia. Even though relative resource endowments in the former have rapidly been approaching those of the latter in recent years, social norms have been slow to change.

Yet East Laguna Village has its own mechanism for guaranteeing subsistence to poor members in the same community. As in North-east Asia, village communities in lowland rice areas in South-east Asia are stratified according to claims to land property rights. The difference is that, instead of taking leadership in the construction and maintenance of local infrastructure vital for increasing output and employment under limited land resources, well-to-do members in Philippine villages tend to retreat from doing the work by themselves on their own farms. They employ poor neighbours even if they have sufficient family labour to perform farm tasks on their own holdings, while the better-off villagers develop patron–client relationships with landless tenants/labourers (Chapter 7). This system of sharing income through sharing work as a guarantee of subsistence to the poor seems to have established as a basic norm in the peasant communities in South-east Asia. Indeed, the rates of dependency on hired labour by small rice farmers in the Philippines, including East Laguna Village, are incomparably higher than those in Japan (Chapter 5). This work- and income-sharing norm was created under the traditional conditions of relative land abundance and high production risk inherent in rainfed farming, but it has continued to be maintained despite rapid decreases in land–labour ratios, and shifts from rainfed to irrigated farming systems (Chapter 6).

MODERNIZING FORCES

East Laguna Village appears to be as dormant under the shade of coconut trees today as it was when we first visited it in the 1970s. Under the surface, however, its economy and social organization have experienced dramatic changes. Besides the dramatic diffusion of modern rice technology, major forces that caused economic and social changes were (i) continued population pressure on limited land resources; (ii) implementation of land reform programmes; (iii) public investments in infrastructure, such as irrigation systems, roads and schools; and (iv) growing urban influences accelerated by improvements in transportation and communication systems.

Despite the closure of the cultivation frontier before 1960, the population of the village increased by as much as 3.7 per cent per year from 1966 to 1997, well above the Philippine national rate of 2.7 per cent. This extraordinary population growth in East Laguna Village has been the result of net immigration in addition to a high natural increase. The number of immigrants exceeded that of emigrants despite significant labour outflows from the village to urban areas. Large labour employment created by the construction of an irrigation system and the diffusion of new rice technology as represented by the adoption of MV encouraged labour migration to lowland rice villages from upland villages in the hills and mountains surrounding the rice belt along Laguna de Bay (Chapter 3).

With this high population growth, the availability of rice fields per capita in East Laguna Village decreased rapidly, from about a quarter of a hectare in 1966 to less than a tenth of a hectare in 1995. However, the effective crop area doubled as a result of the extension of a national irrigation system to the village in 1958. On the basis of this irrigation infrastructure, high-yielding MV diffused rapidly, resulting in significant increases in rice yields and labour employment from the late 1960s to the 1970s. But such major advances in rice production technology had no power to prevent the strong population pressure on limited land from increasing landlessness in this village. The number of agricultural labourers staking out subsistence from hired farm work increased sharply relative to the number of farmers (farm operators). The share of farmers' households among the total number of households in the village decreased from 70 per cent to 15 per cent during the period 1966–97, while that of landless agricultural labourers increased from 30 per cent to 60 per cent.

The sharp increase in landless labourer population was not only the result of increased land scarcity but was also promoted by land reform programmes in the 1970s. Traditionally, most villagers were sharecroppers, and they were later given leasehold titles through land reform. Strong protection of tenancy rights, with land rents fixed at lower-than-market rates resulted in a large income transfer from absentee landlords to tenants in the village. At the same time, land reform regulations resulted in an inactive land-rental market and narrowed the opportunity for landless agricultural labourers to become tenant farmers.

During the three decades of our study, the penetration of urban economic activities became increasingly visible. Urban influences accelerated, especially after improvements in the highway system in the late 1970s, which reduced travel time from Pila to Manila from more than three hours to about two. Correspondingly, the share of villagers' income from agricultural activities (including farm operation and hired farm work), in their total income decreased from about 90 per cent in the mid-1970s to less than 40 per cent in the mid-1990s. Landless labourers captured a larger share of this non-agricultural income increase than did farmers. In fact, the share of 'non-farm-worker households' whose major income source was non-agricultural activities, which had remained at zero until 1976, became observable in 1980 and increased to about 20 per cent of all village households by 1997. Villagers were able to capture the increased non-farm employment opportunities effectively with their improved education from a primary school established within the village as well as better access to secondary schools in the town.

APPROACH AND DATA

Our goal is to gain a concrete grasp of the total process of the way that the dramatic diffusion of modern rice technology has interacted with population pressure on limited land resources, the implementation of land reform programmes, the development of public infrastructure, and the penetration of urban economic activities to cause major economic and social changes in irrigated rice areas in the Philippines, with a view to developing insights on the modernization process of other developing economies which are under pressure from similar forces.

We have undertaken this task by means of an intensive study of East Laguna Village. By limiting our investigation to one village, the burden of detailed data collection over a wide range of economic and social variables can be reduced to a feasible amount. Moreover, close personal observations and interactions with villagers akin to the approach of anthropologists and sociologists are the only way to understand the nature and role of community institutions and norms that govern economic activities in the rural sector of the Third World.

Yet our approach is that of economists, applying standard economic logic even to the analysis of cultural and social phenomena, such as community norms and institutions, focusing on the influences of those factors on the village economy.

Eleven Round Surveys

Our analysis of East Laguna Village is based mainly on household surveys conducted eleven times during the three decades between 1966 and 1997. The first eight surveys and the eleventh survey covered all the households in the village, while the ninth and tenth surveys (in 1996 and 1997) covered only the households of farmers (farm operators) and excluded those of non-farmers. The surveys were undertaken for different purposes and therefore questionnaires were designed differently. The degree of intensity of the data collection varied across subject matter among different surveys.

The major characteristics of the surveys are summarized in Table 1.1. The first survey, carried out in 1966 by Hiromitsu Umehara, was intended

Table 1.1 Surveys conducted in East Laguna Village

Year	Principal investigator	Major information collected[a]							Remarks
		Population & households	Land tenure & labour relations	Rice farming		Non-rice farming	Non-farm activities	Income level & distribution	
				Yield	Inputs & factor income				
1966 (December)	H. Umehara	l	l	l	n	n	n	n	Reconnaissance on agrarian structure and rural life
1974 (November)	Y. Hayami	c	l	c	l	l	l	l	Baseline survey for a record-keeping project
1976 (December)	Y. Hayami & M. Kikuchi	c	c	c	c	l	l	c	With major focus on land tenure and community institutions
1980 (June)	M. Kikuchi	c	l	c	c	l	l	c	With major focus on labour migration, mainly for the dry season
1983 (February)	M. Kikuchi	c	l	c	c	l	l	c	Follow-up of the 1980 survey for the wet season
1987 (November)	Y. Hayami	c	l	c	c	l	l	c	With major focus on effects of land reform
1992 (March)	M. Hossain	c	l	c	c	l	l	c	Baseline survey for a rural poverty project
1995 (July)	Y. Hayami & M. Kikuchi	c	c	c	c	l	c	c	With major additional focus on non-farm activities
1996 (July)	Y. Hayami & M. Kikuchi	n	l	c	c	n	n	n	Follow-up of the 1995 survey for rice farming, with the focus on irrigation
1997 (July)	Y. Hayami & M. Kikuchi	n	l	c	l	n	n	n	With the focus on marketing of output/inputs in rice farming
1997 (October)	Y. Hayami & M. Kikuchi	l	n	n	n	n	n	n	Exclusive focus on demographic variables

Notes: a, ... late data collected; l, limited data collected; n, data not available

to provide quantitative support for his geographical and sociological accounts of the Philippine rural sector. As a reconnaissance survey its coverage was limited mainly to the static data of population and households in relation to landholdings. Yet the limited quantitative data from the survey, together with many insightful qualitative descriptions in his report (Umehara, 1967), provides invaluable information about the traditional village situation before the advent of MV. Although IR8 was released in 1966, it was not planted in this village in the Umehara survey period except in an experimental trial by one farmer.

The other ten surveys were organized by the IRRI Social Sciences Division (formerly the Agricultural Economics Department). The 1974 survey was a baseline survey for a household record-keeping project (Hayami and associates, 1978). It was intended to produce a simple village-wide socioeconomic map on which the positions of sample households chosen for daily record-keeping on both household consumption and production activities could be ascertained. Through twice-weekly visits to this village, often involving an overnight stay, during the fourteen months of record keeping (from April 1975 to June 1976), we developed intimate relationships not only with record-keeping families but also with other villagers. Informal chats with them have been an invaluable source of information.

During this record-keeping project, several intriguing phenomena were observed on land tenure and labour employment relations in accordance with traditional community norms. The 1976 survey aimed at producing data for the analysis of those relations (Hayami and Kikuchi, 1981, ch. 5). The 1980 survey and 1983 surveys aimed at extending the analysis of labour relations involving labour migrations from within to outside East Laguna Village (Kikuchi and Opena, 1983). The 1980 survey was especially detailed on demographic variables so that population data could be extended to 1918 by means of family reconstitution.

The 1987 survey was initiated as part of a study aimed at identifying the impact of land reform in the Philippines (Hayami, Quisumbing and Adriano, 1990). However, by comparing this year's survey results with those of the previous five surveys, we were convinced of the effectiveness of analyzing the historical dynamics of agrarian change by means of our village survey data (Hayami *et al.*, 1990). This conviction prepared the eighth-round survey for 1995, with the widest data coverage, for the explicit purpose of making its results the benchmark for the thirty-year historical account. The 1995 survey was supplemented by a partial survey in 1996 on farmers' households, focusing on the relationship between rice farming and the deterioration in the service of national irrigation system to this village, which has become serious in recent years. Another partial survey limited to farmers' households was conducted in July 1997 to collect data pertinent to rice marketing. Finally, the October 1997 survey covered all the households for collecting exclusively demographic variables for family reconstitution for the period 1980–97.

The 1992 survey organized by Mahabub Hossain used significantly different questionnaires from those of Hayami and Kikuchi for the purpose of an analysis of rural poverty. Yet it produced useful information to bridge our 1987 and 1995 survey results.

Throughout this book, unless otherwise stated, all the data and statistics referred to in this book (tables and figures as well as text) are collected by the authors mainly based on these eleven-round surveys. In addition to those within-village surveys, we have conducted several other surveys extending beyond the border of East Laguna Village, such as about rice harvesting (Chapter 7), rice marketing (Chapter 8), and rural manufacturing (Chapter 9), which shall be specified where their outcomes will be analysed.

Data Limitations

The surveys collected data mainly from one-shot interviews with household members, although the interview was often repeated several times in a household because some working members of the family were critically absent during the first interview, or a data check showed obvious inconsistencies. Such a survey procedure is bound to entail errors to the extent that respondents' memories are inaccurate. This problem is, of course, much more serious for flow data, such as rice outputs and inputs recalled for a previous crop season, than for stock data, such as number and characteristics of household members.

Besides the possibility of large observational error, our data are subject to large fluctuations in environmental as well as market conditions. To judge the productivity trend in rice farming in terms of average yield per hectare, for example, observed data for particular survey years must be adjusted for crop fluctuations caused by the weather and other natural conditions.

It must also be recognized that our surveys are not comprehensive. Except for July 1996 and July 1997, our surveys covered all the village households as well as a wide range of information, from demographic and household characteristics to farm and non-farm economic activities, including community and market institutions controlling these activities. However, a major gap in our data collection pertains to the area of consumption and savings to which one-shot interviews used in our surveys are inherently incapable of being applied. This aspect was covered in great detail by the record-keeping project for 1975–6 based on a small sample (Hayami and associates, 1978) but no comparable data were obtained over time. Thus our data are weak in estimating changes in the standard of living and the structure of consumption, although the estimates of changes in the level's and distribution of income are reasonably accurate. Another weakness relates to the relationship between the village and the outside economy. The 1980 and 1983 surveys generated a considerable amount of information on the labour market linkage between the village and the outside world. Additionally, a major focus of the 1995, 1996 and 1997 surveys was on the linkage of industrial and commercial activities in the village with those of the urban sector. However, these data are much less detailed and comparable over time than the data for in-village economic activities.

Recognizing these limitations, the analysis must proceed with maximum care to adjust and correct possible biases, errors and gaps in our survey data by means of supplementary information from official statistics for the region as well as from informed villagers.

PLAN OF THE BOOK

After this introductory chapter, Chapter 2 advances a chronological summary of our major findings on economic and social changes in East Laguna Village. We chose to place the summary at the beginning of the book rather than at the end to reduce the danger of general readers being drowned in a pool of detailed data and explanations. The historical overview developed in this chapter will help readers to understand how the individual issues analyzed in subsequent chapters are related to the total complex of economic and social changes in the village.

Chapter 3 traces demographic changes in East Laguna Village and parallel changes in the characteristics of population and households, such as occupation, education and family size. A special focus is placed on the process by which strong population pressure on limited land has interacted with new rice technology and land reform to result in a major change in the village's class structure in terms of relative shares of farmers' and landless agricultural labourers' households.

Chapter 4 documents major changes in land tenure systems in East Laguna Village corresponding to the implementation of land reform programmes. It shows that, although the reform programmes resulted in a major income transfer from landlords living in towns to sharecroppers in the village, they contributed to widening income disparity within the village between farmers and agricultural labourers, as well as to narrowing the ladder that enabled agricultural labourers to ascend to the status of farm operators.

Chapter 5 analyzes changes in agricultural productivity and production structure corresponding to development and diffusion of MV technology. The nature and consequences of new rice technology were investigated by means of input–output, cost–return, and factor-share analyses upon which the growth of total factor productivity (TFP) in rice farming are estimated. The TFP analysis shows how quickly the potential of new rice technology was exploited within about a decade and half of the release of IR8, and was exhausted thereafter.

Chapter 6 focuses on a deterioration in the service of a national irrigation system supplying water to East Laguna Village in the 1990s. Previously, the development of this system was the key to the successful diffusion of new rice technology. It was found that a hasty hand-over of irrigation management from a state agency to local communities can produce a disastrous result in the case of a large system beyond the organizational capacity of local communities, especially in the study area, where the communities have had little experience in organizing themselves for the maintenance of local infrastructure.

Chapter 7, on the other hand, shows that traditional community norms and relationships are instrumental in making the necessary adjustments to reduce the major disequilibrium in the labour market created by the diffusion of new rice technology. The analysis of labour contracts in rice harvesting illustrates the case of complementarity between community and market in achieving efficient resource allocations.

Chapter 8 derives the same conclusion from the analysis of product marketing. An important finding from the study of rice marketing in East Laguna Village is that small farmers are not necessarily passive agents to be exploited by traders. Many are active entrepreneurs involved in trading, and their participation makes the rice market highly competitive and efficient.

Penetration of urban economic activities into the village economy operates ubiquitously through the product, labour and other input markets. Chapter 9 attempts to illustrate its impact on small cottage industries recently developed in East Laguna Village and its surroundings under subcontracting arrangements with large manufacturers and traders in Metro Manila. The high potential of rural-based industries to generate employment and income relative to that of rice farming is clearly demonstrated.

Chapter 10 aims to show how much the average household income increased and how income distribution among households changed over the three decades of our study. A detailed breakdown of household incomes across economic activities and social classes will show influences of various modernizing forces on the level and distribution of income in East Laguna Village. The development of new rice technology in the period from the late 1960s to the early 1980s, and the increase in non-farm employment opportunities in the more recent period, especially the 1990s, are identified as major factors that prevented per capita income from declining, and income disparity from worsening.

2 Chronology of the Village

This chapter aims to develop a historical overview on economic and social changes in East Laguna Village. Subsequent chapters will present detailed accounts of the influences of major modernizing forces, such as population growth, technological change and urbanization. In this chapter a chronological summary of those major events in East Laguna Village is advanced. It intends to facilitate readers' understanding of the interrelationships in a historical sequence of factors that will be analyzed separately later. It must be cautioned that readers will find several descriptions in this chapter to be reiterated in the subsequent chapters; such repetition is inevitable because of the nature of this chapter serving as a summary of the whole volume.

For expository convenience, the history of East Laguna Village is demarcated into the following five periods: (i) 1880s to mid-1950s; (ii) late 1950s to mid-1960s; (iii) late 1960s to late 1970s; (iv) 1980s; and (v) 1990s. The first period covers the initial settlement and subsequent growth based mainly on opening new land for rainfed rice farming. In the second period, the land frontier was closed, while public infrastructures such as irrigation systems, roads and schools were built, which created conditions for shifting the momentum of economic growth from expansions in cultivated areas to increases in land productivity. The third period covers the heyday of the Green Revolution, with rapid increases in rice yields per hectare resulting from the diffusion of modern varieties and increased fertilizer application. Concurrently, land reform programmes were extended to this village, converting the majority of villagers from sharecroppers to leasehold tenants with rents fixed at low rates. While East Laguna Village remained as a predominantly agrarian community until towards the end of the third period, it began to be exposed to greater influence of urbanindustrial activities following improvements in the highways in the late 1970s. However, the initial boost in villagers' earnings from non-farm sources in the early 1980s was interrupted by a serious recession of the Philippine economy caused by political instability following the downfall of President Ferdinand Marcos. Meanwhile, the Green Revolution also ran out of steam. As the economy recovered from the 'lost decade', the urbanindustrial impacts on East Laguna Village were resumed, and villagers' income from non-farm sources grew rapidly to surpass that from farm sources in the 1990s.

It must be noted that there is a major gap in our knowledge about East Laguna Village between before and after 1966, the year when Hiromitsu

Umehara's survey was conducted. Before 1966, the only quantitative data available, of rather questionable quality, were about population, from national censuses and our family reconstitution exercises (Chapter 3). All the other information, both quantitative and qualitative, is based on the recollections of knowledgeable older people in this village and in the surrounding area. Our knowledge is limited by the sheer paucity of written historical documents (this appears to be more pronounced in the Philippines than in many other countries in South-east Asia). Thus our descriptions for the first two periods are much thinner and less factual than for the later periods.

The understanding of historical developments documented below may be facilitated by a chronological table of major events in East Laguna Village (see Table 2.1).

INITIAL SETTLEMENT AND LAND OPENING
(1880s TO MID-1950s)

According to the legends of old-settled families in East Laguna Village, their grandparents or great-grandparents began to settle here around the 1880s. Before then, not only East Laguna Village but also much of the paddy fields on the Laguna de Bay side of the highway passing through the *poblacion* (town) of Pila was uncultivated, marshy, jungle.

Pila *poblacion* is an old town which has been established since the early Spanish period. Most towns in the Laguna rice belt were originally developed as trading posts connected by lake lanes, and are equipped with ports even to the present day. Pila *poblacion* is now located about three kilometres away from the lake shore, but it would not be an unreasonable guess that, when established, it was on the shore of Laguna de Bay, so most rice fields in the lake side of Pila Municipality including East Laguna Village were under water. Nor would it be unreasonable to guess that, as the lake coast receded, people in surrounding elevated areas that had been settled earlier began to open the newly-emerged marshes for rice cultivation where possible, under the pressure of population increases in their native areas. As East Laguna Village is located closest to the lake within the municipality, it would have been one of the later settlements in this area. The fact that this village is popularly called 'Tanza' (grazing land) seems to indicate that it had been left uncultivated and used for grazing *carabaos* by farmers in surrounding villages until some time near the end of land opening up in this area.

The initial settlers in East Laguna Village migrated not only from elevated locations within Laguna Province but also from highlands in neighbouring

Table 2.1   Major events in rice farming and village life in East Laguna Village
since its settlement

Year	Events [a]
1880s	○ Settlement began, with extensive rainfed rice farming
1950s	○ Land frontier closed
1958	● Irrigation system constructed; complete rice double cropping established
Early 1960s	● Hand tractor introduced
	● Improved cultural practices introduced (fertilizers, chemicals, avenue planting, rotary weeders, dry seed-bed)
	● *Gama* system introduced
1962	○ Elementary school opened (up to 2nd grade)
1965	○ Country road to the *poblacion* opened
1967	○ Elementary school extended to 4th grade
Late 1960s	● MV introduction, with further improvements in cultural practices (intensified use of fertilizers and chemicals, hand weeding, check-row planting)
	● *Gama* system diffused rapidly
1968	● Operation Leasehold in land reform started
1972	● Operation Leasehold intensified
1973	● The *Masagana 99* programme launched
	○ Electricity line extended
1978	○ Manila South Super Highway extended to Calamba; Masapang Highway opened
Late 1970s	● Herbicide use intensified
	● Portable mechanical thresher introduced
	○ Overseas employment in Middle East became available
	○ Job opportunities in Metro Manila increased
1978–84	● Major rehabilitation project in the irrigation system
Early 1980s	● Operation Land Transfer of land reform started
Mid 1980s	○ Non-farm employment declined because of economic depression
Early 1990s	● Deterioration of the irrigation system; irrigation pump introduced
Mid 1990s	○ Village-based metal manufacturing boomed
	○ Non-farm income exceeded farm income
1994	○ Country road to the *poblacion* paved
1995	○ Elementary school extended to 6th grade
1996	○ *Barrio* chapel began to offer regular Sunday mass

Note: [a] ○ Events general to village life; ● Events specifically related to rice farming.

Batangas and Cavite Provinces, where people settled early because of the
areas' lesser incidence of malaria and other infectious diseases. The lands
they began to open, however, were not no-man's-lands but were the possessions of landlords mainly living in the *poblacion*. Many landlords in
this area were the descendants of the Spanish conquerors who established

legal claims on large tracts of uncultivated land outside the communal possessions of native tribes. Over time their estates were subdivided progressively through inheritance. Meanwhile, the Spaniards intermarried with local chiefs who established private property rights on communal lands as well as with Chinese traders who accumulated land through land-pawning arrangements. Over time these groups fused to form a landowning elite class. For example, a big landlord family that has dominated local business and politics in Pila for generations is said to be the offspring of an illegitimate connection between a Spanish priest and the daughter of a Chinese merchant. In this process of class formation, our study area is no exception in rural Philippines.

For the landed elites with strong political power and sufficient resources to file legal procedures, it should have not been difficult to register the new lands reclaimed from the lake as parts of their estates. First, they planted coconuts in elevated spots amid the marsh, within which the houses in villages are now clustered. Later, they invited migrants from old-settled areas to open lowlands for rice cultivation. A common arrangement was that landlords allowed settlers to use land parcels gratis for the first several years of land opening, while advancing them credits for subsistence, with the understanding that they would enter a sharecropping arrangement after the gratis period. The settlers were allowed to build bamboo-nipa huts in the elevated coconut lands, with no rent payable.

As one such case, East Laguna Village was established as a village composed of share tenants who had no legal claim on either the land they cultivated or the land where they lived. Yet the tenure of their tenancy on this land was relatively secure and stable. Although no formal contract was exchanged, the rights of tenants to continue cultivating the lands they themselves or their parents had opened up were socially recognized, so that tenants were seldom evicted except for major misconduct. In the settlement stage in particular, labour was scarce and landlords would have had little incentive to evict tenants. Usually, tenants living in the village and landlords in the nearby town were tied by paternalistic or patron–client relationships. Landlords tried (or, at least, gestured) to aid tenants' subsistence crisis by advancing credits and giving gifts, and tenants tried to reciprocate by conscientious farm work and rent submission as well as through personal services.

In the settlement stage, characterized by scarce labour and abundant land for new opening, rice farming typically was extensive. It relied purely on rainfall stored in paddy fields, which were divided by mud banks. As the soil was submerged by water with the coming of monsoon rain sometime between May and July, the fields were puddled with *carabaos*, and rice seedlings were transplanted. After that, virtually no crop care, such as weeding, was applied before harvest. Mature rice plants were cut either by hand-held knives at the neck of the panicles (this practice had largely disappeared by the 1920s) or by sikles at the bottom of the stems, and threshed by hand-beating on wooden plates or bamboo stands. Harvesting was a kind of community work. Anyone in the village could participate in others' harvesting and receive the one-sixth of paddy he or she harvested .

Traditional rice varieties were characterized by photosensitivity: that is, flowering was triggered by shortened day length, so that crops ripened in late November to December when the rainy season was over, irrespective of the planting time. Harvested paddy was hauled across dried-up fields to the village for home consumption, or to the *poblacion* for rent payments in kind to landlords and for market sales. In those days there was no road built for carts, so movement of both people and cargoes in the rainy season had to rely on the narrow, slippery banks of the rice fields. Under such conditions photosensitivity in traditional varieties was a real blessing to farmers. Although rice yields were low, less than two tons per hectare in paddy terms, since labour input was also low, output per hour of labour would not have been low.

We have no clue to gauge how population and rice production grew in the first three to four decades after the initial settlement. According to our family reconstitution, fifty-two inhabitants in East Laguna Village, as enumerated by the 1918 National Census, was a fairly reliable estimate. The family reconstitution also gives an estimate of 36 hectares for the paddy area cultivated by the rice farmers in the village in 1918. Since the cultivated paddy area at that time was only about a third of cultivatable area, land frontiers were wide open and attracted a large number of migrants. Our family reconstitution estimates indicate that between 1918 and 1940 the population in East Laguna Village grew at a rate of about 5 per cent per year, of which 2.8 per cent was accounted for by a net migration, and 2.2 per cent by natural growth. Although data are not available, it should not be unreasonable to imagine that the expansion of the cultivated area largely paralleled the population growth in this period.

The economy of the Philippines including Laguna Province was greatly disrupted by the Japanese military invasion in the 1940s. However, it appears that the influence of the war was relatively modest in East Laguna Village. In fact, the village, protected by the coconut grove and separated by marshy paddy fields with no access road from outside, represented a safe hiding place. According to the memory of older villagers, a number of town dwellers were evacuated to this village at the height of the war.

The *Hukbalahap* (or *Huk*) rebellion that began as a resistance to the Japanese army and later became a peasants' liberation movement against landlords could have had a significant impact. However, few villagers commented on their relationships with the *Huks*.

The population continued to grow rapidly at about 4 per cent per year throughout the 1940s and 1950s. However, unlike in the previous two decades, this growth resulted mainly from natural growth. The rate of social increase or net migration decreased sharply, from 2.8 per cent per year during the period 1918–40, to 0.6 per cent during the period 1940–60. The decline in migration into East Laguna Village seems to reflect the fact that the process of land opening reached its limit during this period. Indeed, it is estimated that the paddy area cultivated by villagers reached 94 hectares in 1960, which was close to the cultivable area of about 100 hectares within the territory of East Laguna Village, although the exact area is difficult to measure because villages' territorial boundaries are not clearly defined in the Philippines. Population density, as measured by the number of villagers per hectare of cultivated paddy area, increased from 1.3 people in 1918 to 3.2 people in 1960. Though the data are not available for 1940, it seems reasonable to assume that much of the reduction in the land–person ratio occurred between 1940 and 1960.

TRANSITION TO INTENSIVE PRODUCTION (LATE 1950s TO MID-1960s)

Continued population growth after the closure of land frontiers should have impoverished people in East Laguna Village, unless the momentum of economic growth would have not shifted from the expansion in land under cultivation to the increase in land productivity. An epochal change in this regard was the extension of a national irrigation system to the village in 1958. This system was based on the surface flow of water diverted from the Sta. Cruz River, which originates in Mount Banahaw. River water diverted by a dam was designed to flow by gravity along a network of canals and laterals ending in Laguna de Bay after irrigating about 4000 hectares of paddy fields in thirty-seven villages.

The beginning of this system's service resulted in an almost complete conversion of rice farming in East Laguna Village from rainfed single cropping to irrigated double cropping for both wet and dry seasons. Furthermore, irrigation prepared the ground for the introduction of better cultural practices and increased input application. Assured water supply reduced the risk of crop failure, thereby making the application of cash inputs such as commercial fertilizers and chemicals less hazardous. Improved water control in irrigated fields enabled farmers to plant younger seedlings grown in dry seed-beds in home yards instead of the traditional wet beds in the fields. This so-called *dapog* method saved labour for both seed-bed preparation and transplanting while also improving the care of seedlings. Both the use of young seedlings and the application of fertilizers increased the hazard of weed growth, and hence increased the profitability of weeding, which had rarely been practised under the rainfed condition. Correspondingly, the straight-row (or 'avenue') planting of seedlings was introduced, and farmers pushed rotary weeders along the straight avenues between seedlings. These practices, long used in Northeast Asia including Japan, Korea and Taiwan, had been recommended by government extension services, but their adoption was limited until the arrival of the irrigation service.

Thus rice farming in East Laguna Village began to shift its growth momentum from area expansion to yield increase based on the development of the irrigation infrastructure in the 1950s. The growth of yield per hectare planted under rice should have been rather modest before the diffusion of modern high-yielding varieties a decade later. However, the shift from rainfed single-cropping to irrigated double-cropping resulted in more than double the total rice output per year, because rice yields are usually higher in the dry season than the wet season. For this great output-increasing effect of irrigation, rice output per capita in East Laguna Village nearly doubled from about 0.5 tonnes to 1 tonnes, during the 1956–66 period, despite rapid population increases. The output increase should have largely been paralleled by the increase in rice farmers' income under the traditional sharecropping tenancy, in which both output and cost were shared 50:50 between tenants and landlords.

Two other major events of this decade, which were just as important as the development of irrigation, were the opening within the village of an elementary school up to the second grade in 1962 (extended to the fourth grade in 1967), and the construction of a country road connecting Pila *poblacion* and the village in 1965. Until then, children had had to walk on the narrow mud banks of paddy fields to reach a school in the *poblacion*; this had been especially hard during the wet season. This problem, aggravated by the burden of farm and household chores on children, such as caring for the *carabaos* and the collection of firewood, resulted in a high rate of school drop-out. Rapid improvements in children's school attendance after the establishment of the village school were reflected in the fact that the percentage of adult population (21 to 64 years old) with no schooling decreased from about 20 per cent in 1966 to only 2 per cent in 1997.

Over the same period, the percentage of adults with schooling of more than four years rose from less than 30 per cent to nearly 80 per cent. It was on the basis of this improvement in education that villagers were able to take advantage of major expansions in non-farm employment and income-earning opportunities that became available to them in later years.

The construction of the country road had an equally far-reaching impact. The road cuts straight across the paddy fields from Pila *poblacion* to East Laguna Village. It looks like a long bridge hanging over the sea to an island covered by coconut trees. The road was originally made of mud and gravel, only just wide enough for two *jeepneys* (informal minibuses) to pass each other. It was elevated by about a half metre above the paddy fields, so that the road surface would not be submerged by the occasional floods.

Needless to say, the integration of East Laguna Village with the markets was greatly promoted by this road. Prior to its construction, housewives seldom went shopping in the town of Pila as it took nearly half a day for the return trip. With the road, they could ride on pony-drawn wagons (*kalesa*) and, later, on motor tricycles, reaching the town in less than thirty minutes. Thus not only the town market of Pila but also a bigger market in Sta Cruz became accessible shopping places for villagers.

Similarly, the hauling of farm products, such as paddy (unhusked rough rice) and coconuts from the village to market places, which had previously been dependent on men's shoulders or mud sleighs drawn by *carabaos*, began to be handled by *jeepneys* and pick-up trucks. The prices farmers received for their product were raised, and those they paid for input purchases were reduced by the extent of reduced transportation costs. Without this road infrastructure, the diffusion of modern rice varieties with the intensive use of purchased fertilizers and chemicals that occurred in the following decade would have been severely curtailed.

It was rather surprising to find that, in none of these three basic infrastructures, did villagers make any substantial contribution to construction, operation or maintenance. The irrigation system was constructed by the National Irrigation Administration (NIA), a public corporation owned and controlled by the central government. Farmers who received water from the NIA were obliged to pay irrigation fees proportional to their operational holdings, but the system's operation and maintenance were handled by the NIA's field staff, with almost no participation by local beneficiaries. Very recently NIA has been trying to hand over some of its operation and maintenance activities to local communities, but with little success (Chapter 6).

Both the village school and the country road were built and maintained using the finances of the municipal office of Pila, which was largely based on the reallocation of the central government budget via the provincial office. Older villagers emphasized how strongly they lobbied both the municipal and the provincial governments regarding the budget appropriations using several political connections. Yet they seldom contributed either money or labour to the enhancement of this infrastructure. Indeed, Umehara (1967) expressed surprise at observing that few villagers showed up to help repair the country road, despite the call of the *barangay captain*. This was a real puzzle for a scholar who had been accustomed to seeing tight collaboration among villagers for the construction and maintenance of local infrastructure in Japanese rural communities. According to our observations, however, such behaviour in villagers is somewhat typical of many villages in the Philippines as well as of traditionally resource-rich areas in South-east Asia.

Another significant development in this decade was the spread of the use of hand tractors for land preparation. We are not sure when 'tractorization' began. According to Randolph Barker *et al.* (1972), tractorization in the Philippines as well as in other Asian economies was promoted in the late 1950s by tariff exemption and subsidized credits towards tractor purchase by farmers via a World Bank loan, based on the popular misconception that the use of modern machinery was the basis of 'agricultural modernization'. However, there were several advantages in the use of tractors in East Laguna Village. Those with floating wheels designed for moving on slippery soft mud in wet paddy fields could operate in deeply-flooded fields adjacent to Laguna de Bay, where even *carabaos* often got stuck. Some farmers felt it was necessary to replace *carabaos* by tractors because of the increasing scarcity of grazing land as a result of the expansion of the cultivated area, and others pointed out the advantage being able to store tractors under cover because of incidents of animal theft.

In any case, by 1966 nearly 40 per cent of farmers were using tractors and as many as fourteen tractors (as compared with twenty-one *carabaos*) were owned by villagers. At this time probably half or more of the paddy fields would have been ploughed and harrowed by tractors because the general tendency was that earlier tractor adopters were larger farmers. An important point to be remembered is that tractorization began before the diffusion of modern, high-yielding rice varieties that marked the Green Revolution of the next decade, so the Green Revolution was obviously not the cause of tractorization.

Continued population growth after the closure of cultivation frontiers began to change the social structure of East Laguna Village. In the earlier settlement and land-opening stages, farmland was easily available for the young to rent, if they wished to start farming. As the land opening approached its limit, it became progressively more difficult for the sons of farmers in this village, and more so for migrants from other villages, to acquire lands to establish themselves as farmers. They had to subsist on wages from hired work on neighbours' farms.

In earlier days too, a few agricultural labourers had lived by hired employment, but they were mainly young boys living in their parents' houses, or newly-married couples in bamboo-nipa huts built in their parents' yards. Sooner or later they rented land to become farmers under a sharecropping contract as they gained experience in farm work, and some savings to buy farm equipment and draft animals – the process of ascending the 'agricultural ladder' in the classic definition by Spillman (1919). However, after the frontiers were closed, they had to continue living as agricultural labourers, except for a few fortunate ones who were able to inherit land cultivation rights from their parents, so the hitherto homogeneous village community consisting mainly of sharecroppers began to be segmented into farmers and agricultural labourers.

GREEN REVOLUTION AND LAND REFORM (LATE 1960s TO LATE 1970s)

The decade beginning in 1966 was the heyday of the 'Green Revolution'. It was marked by the diffusion of semi-dwarf modern varieties (MV) of rice with high-yielding capacities (see Chapter 5).

For chronologists, it was fortunate that the Umehara survey was conducted in 1966, at the point when IR8, the first modern, high-yielding variety from the International Rice Research Institute (IRRI) was officially released. On 28 November 1966, the day that IR8 was released, the IRRI announced that any farmer who came to the IRRI could pick up two kilograms of the new seed free of charge. Umehara recorded that one farmer in East Laguna Village tried IR8 on an experimental scale in the 1966/67 dry season – the season when this variety was released. This farmer could have been one who had picked up seed from the IRRI, or been given some by a friend in a nearby village. In any case, East Laguna Village was one of the villages in the tropics where MV was first planted.

The following year, Governor San Luis of Laguna Province distributed one kilogram of the new seed to each of the officers in the *barangays* under his jurisdiction. The seed received by the captain and council members in the villages were sown, and subsequently grew into plants with sharply-pointed leaves that were almost half the height of traditional varieties. At harvest, the villagers were struck by their high yield – nearly twice that of traditional plants. Harvested paddy of the new variety was given to other villagers in exchange for the ordinary rice they grew.

A more permanent channel of diffusion was on-farm demonstration experiments conducted by a Pila branch of the Bureau of Agricultural Extension. According to their programme, the production of IR8 and subsequent MVs was demonstrated on farms in rotation among various villages within Pila Municipality. Paddy produced from those demonstration plots was sold to farmers in cash or exchanged for paddy from old varieties. In addition, some IRRI researchers who tried to conduct on-farm experiments found that giving them small packs of the new seeds was instrumental in obtaining the farmers' co-operation. There were cases also in which the IRRI's local staff members from farming backgrounds grew the new seed on their parents' farms to distribute to relatives and neighbours.

These anecdotes illustrate the advantage to farmers in East Laguna Village and its surroundings in the adoption of the new MV technology because they were close to Los Baños, where the IRRI as well as the University of the Philippines' College of Agriculture are located, as well as having the advantage of the development of the irrigation infrastructure in the previous decade.

Indeed, the diffusion of MV was fast and complete in East Laguna Village. According to our 1976 survey, in which the data on farmers' choice of varieties were first collected, 97 per cent of farmers in the village were already using MV. The speed of diffusion was not uniform between 1966 and 1976, however. According to the recollections of several veteran farmers there was a significant setback because of an outbreak of brown planthoppers and tungro virus disease in 1972. Some identified the poor eating quality and high grain breakage in the milling process of MV as a brake on its diffusion. Nevertheless, the rate of MV adoption by farmers in East Laguna Village reached almost 100 per cent within only about ten years, indicating that MV's merit of high yield more than compensated for the high pest risk, and the low prices caused by poor grain quality. Moreover, the successive development of MVs with increased pest resistance, such as IR 36, and of better-quality grain, such as IR 64, increased the advantage of using MV. Thus the rate of MV adoption in East Laguna Village continued to be almost 100 per cent thereafter, involving major shifts in varieties within MV.

The diffusion of MV was accompanied by the increased application of fertilizers and chemicals. Although exact data are not available, we can make a reasonable guess that the input of fertilizer, as measured by the aggregate weight of nitrogen, phosphate and potash, increased more than four times from less than 20 kg to about 80 kg per hectare during the decade of the Green Revolution. Correspondingly, the average paddy yield per hectare per crop season doubled from a little less than two tons to nearly four tons. However, this yield increase was barely sufficient to maintain rice output per capita in East Laguna Village because of its high population growth, augmented by migration from outside the village.

Rapid yield increases in the decade of the Green Revolution, particularly in the early 1970s, were a real benefit to farmers, because high rice prices were also maintained under the influence of the 'world food crisis' in 1973–4. In addition to the labour-intensive nature of the new rice technology, especially for weeding and fertilizer–chemical applications, farmers whose incomes increased tended to employ hired labour for the tasks that had previously been undertaken by family labour. The increased demand for hired labour attracted migrants from coconut villages in the hills and mountain, where no major technological advance had occurred comparable to MV.

The rice farmers' bonanza was further enhanced by a government programme called 'Masagana 99' that was initiated in 1973 under President Marcos. *Masagana* is a Tagalog word meaning 'bountiful', and 99 specifies the yield target of 99 *cavans* – that is, about 4.5 tons of rice per hectare, as against the prevailing national average of about 35 *cavans*. It was an extension–credit–input package programme intended to promote diffusion of the new rice technology. The main element was a system of supplying credit without collateral to farmers for the purchase of modern inputs under the supervision of government agricultural extension workers. First, a farmer received a certificate from an extension worker detailing the standard recommended package of inputs for his/her farm. The farmer took the signed certificate to a bank (either a rural bank or a branch of the Philippine National Bank) for a loan disbursement. The farmer was allowed to borrow up to 700 pesos (about US$100) per hectare at an interest rate 1 per cent per month (where informal moneylenders often charged 10 per cent per month or more). The loan was partly in cash and partly in kind. The cash portion was given to cover hired labour and machine rental, and the other was for the purchase of fertilizers and chemicals, issued in the form of a voucher that the farmer could exchange for specified products at the agricultural supply store. The storekeeper received payment by submitting the voucher to the bank.

The Masagana 99 programme should have eased farmers' credit constraint significantly for the purchase of modern inputs associated with MV, particularly because the traditional credit line from landlords was cut off as a result of concurrent progress in land reform programmes. It also acted as a mechanism of major income transfer to rice farmers. In addition to heavy credit subsidy, repayments on the loans were low. In principle, it was intended that bank managers and extension workers would co-operate in supervising farmers, both in production and in loan repayments. However, no strong incentive existed on the banks' side to enforce repayments because the Masagana loans were recovered through rediscounting by the central bank. Also, because the Masagana loans were so easily restructured, farmers tended to consider the loans as being a gift from the government instead of a credit to be repaid. In fact, in the initial stage of this programme, the government made banks take cash to villages to distribute credits to farmers – the so-called 'mobile banks'. After seeing bank officers handing out cash so freely, it was natural that farmers felt that they were distributing gifts rather than credits, and anticipated no obligation of repayment.

So the default rate was high, and these accumulated bad debts plus the high subsidy cost resulted in the scaling-down of this programme after a few years, and an eventual fading out by 1980. The programme gave a significant windfall gain to farmers, particularly to those who defaulted, at great cost to the government. The experience of farmers in East Laguna Village was no exception in that respect. Masagana 99 was typical of the crash programmes that are by their nature un-sustainable.

Another government programme which had a far more basic and long-lasting impact on East Laguna Village was land reform (see Chapter 4). The present structure of land reform in the Philippines was moulded by the Agricultural Land Reform Code enacted in 1963 under President Diosdado Macapagal. The code specified two steps in land reform. First, the conversion of share tenancy to leasehold tenancy with rent fixed at a low rate (25 per cent of average harvest for three normal years prior to the start of the conversion); and second, the transfer of land ownership for land in excess of a landlords' retention limit to tenants. This land reform was largely limited to pilot areas in Central Luzon, where large *haciendas* prevailed, and had had little impact in Laguna, which was characterized by small and medium landowners, until the issuance of Presidential Decrees No. 2 and No. 27 under Martial Law proclaimed by President Marcos in 1972.

In East Laguna Village, the first step (called Operation Leasehold after the Presidential Decrees) was started on a pilot scale in 1968, and in 1972 the operation was intensified to cover all the paddy fields cultivated by villagers. (The second step of transferring the ownership did not start in this village until the 1980s.) As a result, the percentage of sharecroppers among rice farmers decreased sharply, from 80 per cent in 1966 to 40 per cent in 1976, while that of leasehold tenants increased from 20 per cent to

70 per cent. Share tenancy continued to be practised, but within the narrow circle of relatives and close friends despite the law denouncing this contract. Land tenure relationships in this village were thus drastically altered.

Operation Leasehold resulted in a major income transfer from landlords to tenants. Land rent in traditional sharecropping arrangements was about 40 per cent of total rice output after deducting input costs shared by landlords from the 50 per cent share of gross output. Because the rent that new leaseholders had to pay to landlords was fixed at 25 per cent of output at the time of the programme's implementation, their rent reduction amounted to about 15 per cent of output; this represented an income transfer from landlords to tenants resulting from Operation Leasehold. More important, under the fixed land rent, the income transfer to new lease holders increased automatically by the amounts that rice yields increased. In effect, Operation Leasehold established a right of tenants to receive a part of the economic return from the land. With the progress of the new rice technology, the part of the income from land that accrued to tenants progressively increased relative to that accrued to landlords.

Correspondingly, the income position of leasehold tenants improved significantly relative to agricultural labourers who did not receive any claim on the income from the land through the reform. Thus Operation Leasehold contributed to a reduction in income disparity between landlords in towns and tenants in villages but, ironically, it widened the disparity between tenant farmers and agricultural labourers living in the same village.

Moreover, the land reform programme had a strong effect in consolidating class segmentation between farmers and labourers. A tenant's claim against the income from the land was based on his/her holding of the leasehold title or the right to continue cultivation with the payment of a controlled rent. This right was, however, conditional on his/her own cultivation being in accord with land reform laws. If the tenant sublet the land to someone else, and if this incidence was reported to the Agrarian Reform Office, the tenant's title would be forfeited and transferred to the sub-tenant, who was recognized as the tiller of the land. Given this risk, not many farmers dared to sublet their lands even if they were willing to do so for such reasons as being sick or finding better-paid off-farm jobs. Instead, many preferred to continue cultivation based on hired labour under their own management. Thus, the route for agricultural labourers to rise to become farm operators, which had been narrowed in the process of closing land frontiers, was almost completely closed by the land reform laws. Thereafter, under continued population pressure, the number of agricultural labourers continued to increase rapidly, whereas the number of farmers remained almost constant. Indeed, the share of agricultural labourers in the total number of households in East Laguna Village increased from about 30 per cent in 1966 to 50 per cent 1976, and to 60 per cent in 1980.

Despite the sharp increase in the number of agricultural labourers, East Laguna Village was able to provide subsistence for them with no expansion in cultivation frontiers. This was made possible partly because of increased labour demand because of the new rice technology, and partly because of the substitution of hired labour for family labour in the farms of well-to-do land-reform beneficiaries. The tendency for better-off villagers to leave farm work and employ poor neighbours seems to be much more pronounced in the Philippines and other economies in South-east Asia than in North-east Asia, especially Japan. The sharing of income through the sharing of work might accord to the norm of Philippine village communities including East Laguna Village. Substitution of hired labour for family labour by well-to-do farmers became progressively greater as their children received a high education and took up urban occupations. Through this process, the benefit of land reform that was initially gained exclusively by farmers spilled over to agricultural labourers in the form of increased wage employment.

An interesting institutional development that facilitated substitution of hired labour for family labour was the diffusion of *gama* contract in rice harvesting. The traditional rice harvesting contract was the one called *hunusan* (a Tagalog word for 'sharing') in which, when a farmer announces the day he/she plans to harvest his/her rice crop, any villager can participate in the work and he/she is renumerated by a certain share (usually one-sixth) of the paddies he or she harvested and threshed. It represented a community mode of work and income-sharing among villagers. However, as rice yield increased while labour wage rates remained fairly stable under strong population pressure, the output share of one-sixth became an extraordinary compensation for labour input relative to the prevailing market wage rates. Subsequently, it was replaced by *gama* (a Tagalog word for 'weeding') in which a labourer who did weeding in a farmer's field without pay is given the exclusive right to harvest the crop in that field and to receive a share of one-sixth. In this way, the wage rate per hour of labour was reduced: weeding labour was added to harvesting labour for the same share. Yet this contract was acceptable to villagers as it was consonant with the form of traditional *hunusan* contract and appeared to be consistent with the community norm of work and income-sharing. Because of this, the *gama* contract diffused very rapidly and replaced *hunusan* almost completely by the mid-1970s.

An important event we must mention was the extension of electricity to this village in 1973, the year Masagana 99 was launched.

Immediately, kerosene lamps were replaced by electric bulbs; televisions became the focus of entertainment in place of transistor radios; and refrigerators and hi-fi sets became symbols of affluence. While the influence of electrification on consumption was obvious, its impact on production within the village was not very clear. Until the 1990s, when metal manufacturing workshops were introduced, a small rice mill (*kiskisan*) was the only machinery in the village operated by an electric motor. However, electricity provided longer hours to read and write as well as access to the images of urban life via the broadcasting media, which increased villagers' educational aspirations and attainment, and thereby prepared them to adapt to urban market activities in future decades. An older villager mischievously said to us that electric light reduced the population growth rate as it cut down young couples' time in bed. His remark might contain a germ of truth, since the birth rate in the village began to decline rather sharply from the mid-1970s.

THE LOST DECADE (1980s)

At the end of the 1970s it looked as though economic prosperity was a reality for East Laguna Village during the next decade. Major improvements in highways were expected to increase non-farm employment and incomes to villagers, and a major rehabilitation of the national irrigation system servicing paddy fields in this village was undertaken under the support of the Asian Development Bank (ADB); which was intended to improve the water supply significantly. It was believed that the new rice technology would continue to increase productivity in rice farming. Those expectations, however, failed to materialize.

The extension of the Manila South Super Highway up to Calamba and the opening of Masapang Highway in 1978 did open a new era to the economy of East Laguna Village. The South Super Highway was the major blood line connecting Laguna Province with Manila, and the Masapang Highway was a short cut from Los Baños to Pila. In total, the construction of these two highways cut down the travel time from Pila *poblacion* to Metro Manila from more than three hours to about two hours. Improvement in transportation infrastructure was associated with the rapid expansion of urban-industrial activities from Manila to the west coast of Laguna de Bay along the South Super Highway. It was less than one hour for villagers to reach Calamba, the southern edge of this newly industrializing zone. Urban-industrial activities on the industrializing west coast spilled over to local towns on the east coast, encouraging their commerce, transportation and small-scale manufacturing.

Correspondingly, non-farm employment opportunities were expanded for people in East Laguna Village. Before the improvement of the highways, it was not uncommon for villagers to join a crew of workers for a construction project in Metro Manila, staying there for a extended period of time (for example, staying at the construction site on weekdays and returning home at weekends). While such semi-migratory employment continued to expand, more employment opportunities became available to villagers within daily reach of their homes. Increased labour demand for non-farm jobs resulted in an increase in the real wage rate (deflated by the price of rice) from the late 1970s to the early 1980s in East Laguna Village, whereas it had been nearly constant during the decade of the Green Revolution.

A new development was that not only casual employment, such as that for construction and transportation (tricycle and *jeepney* driving), but also permanent salaried employment became accessible to residents in the village. Thus a new class of 'non-farm workers' began to emerge in the 1980s who lived within East Laguna Village, did not engage in any farm work, and commuted to salaried jobs in towns.

However, the growth of non-farm employment and income for villagers was interrupted by the prolonged economic recession of the Philippine economy caused by political instability before and after the downfall of President Marcos in February 1986. Non-farm employment shrank, and the real wage rate measured in rice stopped rising and, in fact, dropped during the period 1983–7. In effect, East Laguna Village shared the damage of the 'lost decade' alongside the economy of the Philippines.

Another setback to East Laguna Village was the failure of the ADB-assisted project in rehabilitating the national irrigation system (see Chapter 6). It was a highly ambitious project, designed not only to renovate the facilities of the existing system, such as water gates and irrigation roads, but also aimed at doubling the irrigation service area by means of pumping up water from Laguna de Bay. For the latter purpose, ten big pumps were installed in a station near the lake and a new canal system was dug for the distribution of pumped water. It was a big project extending over 1977–84 and costing nearly US$10m.

East Laguna Village was affected adversely by this project through occasional interruptions and shortages in water supply caused by the construction work. In the dry seasons in 1981–3, for example, no water was supplied, so farmers were forced to leave their paddy fields idle or to plant other crops such as water melon. The sad fact was that, despite such a sacrifice, this project ended in a complete failure. The big pumps did not operate beyond several test runs, and all related structures were also unused. All that was left were the ruins of the pump station, and a large number of electricity poles fallen in the paddy fields. The whole new construction was *walang silbi* (useless), as villagers called it.

After the rehabilitation project, the supply of irrigation water was slightly improved. But it soon deteriorated as a financial crisis forced the National Irrigation Administration to cut down expenditure on the operation and maintenance of the irrigation system. Insufficient operation and maintenance later culminated in a crisis situation in the 1990s.

Relative to the previous decade, the lost decade was also characterized by a deceleration in the increase in productivity in rice farming. The growth trend of average rice yield per hectare in East Laguna Village decreased significantly, with a kink at around 1980. This deceleration resulted partly from deterioration in the service of irrigation. However, the fact that a similar kink in the yield growth trend was observed in Laguna Province as well as in many well-irrigated rice areas in tropical Asia seems to show that the yield-increasing potential of the new rice technology was about to be exhausted within a decade of the advent of MV.

It was not that no significant innovation occurred in rice production during this decade; in fact, several important advances took place. For example, MVs with better eating quality, such as IR64, were developed and replaced older MVs; and corresponding to the increase in the real wage rate measured in rice, the application of herbicides increased with the significant effect of saving weeding labour. Another major labour-saving innovation was the introduction of portable threshing machines. Within only about five years of the late 1970s and early 1980s, threshing via hand-beating of harvested rice plants on wood and bamboo plates was almost completely replaced by machine threshing. However, despite these innovations, the growth of total factor productivity – rice output per unit of aggregated inputs – showed a significant deceleration in the 1980s, suggesting that the new rice technology ran out of steam after the decade of the Green Revolution.

However, a more serious effect on rice farmers was the sharp decline in rice prices. From the mid-1970s to the mid-1980s, the domestic price of rice in the Philippines declined by more than half relative to the consumer price index (CPI). A similar price decline also occurred in the international rice market. The major underlying factor was the rapid increase in the supply of rice through the diffusion of MV technology in tropical Asia that outpaced the increase in rice demand. In this way, innovators' profit that first accrued to the early adopters of new rice technology was reduced as followers continued to adopt the technology, and all the surplus created by the new technology was transferred to the consumers, who were able to enjoy increased supplies at reduced prices. The effects of the price decline were felt not only by rice farmers but also by agricultural labourers, whose wages were often paid in kind. Indeed, although the wage rate deflated by the price of rice rose in the late 1970s to the early 1980s, it declined if deflated by CPI.

Thus East Laguna Village faced contraction in income-earning opportunities from both farm and non-farm sources in the 1980s. The only opportunity that continued to expand was overseas employment. Demand for foreign workers from the Middle East began with the first oil boom in 1973–4, which spilled over to East Laguna Village in the late 1970s. The first villagers who went to Saudi Arabia as overseas contract workers brought home huge sums of money (in the eyes of villagers). Typically, they built splendid, urban-style houses that had never previously been seen in the village. This conspicuous consumption motivated other villagers to go abroad, and while the labour demand from Middle East was somewhat reduced after the collapse of the second oil boom in 1981, the number of villagers who went for overseas contract work continued to increase in such destinations as Singapore, Hong Kong and Malaysia. Although there were several tragedies, many workers were successful, and there were steady increases in the numbers of large, luxurious houses.

The overseas employment opportunities were, however, limited to relatively well-to-do villagers, because some education and skill were required. Even in those who were employed in low-skilled jobs, such as drivers and maids, a decent command of English was needed; this limited application largely to high school graduates (with ten years of schooling). Moreover, a significant sum was needed as a payment to the overseas employment agent. To raise this money, several farmers sold their land. Thus earnings from overseas employment tended to be concentrated in the upper- to middle-income classes in the village. Also, as successful overseas workers returned home, they bought not only houses but also land cultivation rights from tenant farmers in the village, and sometimes ownership of land from original landlords. Under the land reform laws, they preferred cultivating the land based on hired labour under their own management rather than renting it out to someone else. In this way, overseas employment tended to widen the disparity in income and asset distribution within the village.

AWAY FROM THE AGRARIAN COMMUNITY (1990s)

With the succession of President Fidel Ramos after President Corazon Aquino in 1992, political instability and economic stagnation in the

Philippines began to subside. Economic recovery in the next half decade was speedy, largely because the great reservoir of low-cost but relatively high-quality labour in the Philippines attracted foreign direct investment in labour-intensive manufacturing on the basis that the wage rates had risen significantly in the Philippines' ASEAN neighbours, such as Thailand and Indonesia, because of their exceptionally high economic growth in the previous decade – so-called 'East Asian Miracle'.

Increased labour demand from urban industries and services spilled over to rural areas, including East Laguna Village. Non-farm employment opportunities for villagers expanded faster than they had in the late 1970s and early 1980s. The wage rate began to rise, not only relative to the price of rice but also relative to the CPI. Increased non-farm wage earnings from outside stimulated self-employed service activities within the village, such as tricycle driving and petty trading by small village stores (*sari-sari*) and peddlers.

A remarkable change in recent years has been the introduction of manufacturing activities into this village, where non-farm economic activities, apart from a small rice mill (*kiskisan*), had been limited to providing services. By the late 1980s the agents of export contractors in Manila had begun a putting-out contract operation in towns and villages around East Laguna Village, under which housewives were mobilized to make garments from cloth and other materials supplied by the agents and were paid at a piece rate for finished products. In East Laguna Village too a few wives who owned sewing machines entered into putting-out contracts. However, garment manufacturing under a subcontract with export contractors was soon concentrated in relatively large workshops in towns based on hired-in workers, because the operation had the advantage of using high-speed electric sewing machines, which the village wives could not afford.

A significant development of manufacturing activities in the village began in 1993, with the introduction of a metalcraft industry under a sub-contract arrangement with export contractors in Manila (see Chapter 9). The products of this industry were mainly Christmas ornaments such as candle-sticks and Santa Claus dolls. The manufacturing process was simple – cutting and twisting tin plates and wires, and assembling them into the finished product using soldering irons. It was highly labour-intensive, requiring little capital except soldering irons, hammers and cutters. The operators of this industry were farmers and non-farmers who had accumulated some small capital through non-farm business. They built small, open workshops with no solid walls next to their own houses, where labourers, who were employed not only from within the village but also from outside, engaged in the craft work. Some of tasks, such as cutting tin plates into prescribed forms, were contracted out to neighbouring households at piece rates. Within a few years of 1993 this industry had become a significant component of the economy of East Laguna Village, generating nearly 10 per cent of village income.

Non-farm employment opportunities for villagers increased rapidly, not only in unskilled casual jobs but also in permanent salaried jobs requiring high education and skill. Indeed, the share of non-farm workers commuting to such occupations in towns in the total number of village households increased from 4 per cent in 1987 to 23 per cent in 1997. The population of non-farm workers was augmented by migration from towns to the village. A number of salaried employees working in urban offices and factories migrated into East Laguna Village to build their houses because housing lots in urban areas became excessively expensive to them.

Their migration to the village was promoted by the paving of the country road connecting Pila *poblacion* and East Laguna Village, as well as the main roads within the village in 1994, again financed by the municipal government with no tangible contribution from villagers except for political lobbying. Transportation was greatly speeded up on the paved roads, especially in the wet season, when tricycles and *jeepneys* had often got stuck in potholes caused by flooding. It is now possible to reach the town hall of Pila from the centre of East Laguna Village in about 10 minutes on a tricycle, whereas it used to take 20 minutes or longer on the mud gravel road in the rain. A year after the road improvement, the elementary school, which had previously accommodated pupils up to the fourth grade, was upgraded to cover the curriculum of a full six years.

An interesting cultural change resulting from increased urban influence and education was a surge in Catholic beliefs among villagers. In the past, villagers' contact with Catholic priests was largely limited to occasions of social ceremony, such as weddings and funerals. The chapel in the village used to open for mass only on the *barrio fiesta* day, on which babies born in the preceding year were baptized. Few villagers attended regular mass on Sundays in the town church. In recent years, however, the number of village women joining religious groups for prayers increased. Many of their active members had a high level of education and belonged to the non-farm worker households. In response to their request, a regular mass began to be offered on Sundays in the village chapel in 1996, and it now attracts more villagers than the chapel can accommodate.

According to Akira Takahashi (1972), Catholic beliefs have traditionally been strong among the urban middle and upper classes but weak among rural villagers in the Philippines. If Takahashi is correct, the recent upsurge in Catholic activities in East Laguna Village represents an acculturation of rural people to an urban value system.

While non-farm employment and income increased rapidly in the 1990s, rice farming suffered from a deterioration in the service of the national irrigation system (see Chapter 6). The deterioration was the result of a budget cut by the National Irrigation Administration (NIA) for the operation and maintenance of irrigation systems under its auspices. NIA's financial position worsened in the 1980s, partly because of declines in rice prices where irrigation fees collected by the NIA were paid in paddy (100 kg for the wet season and 150 kg for the dry season per hectare), and partly because of a decrease in foreign aid for irrigation in developing economies, including the Philippines, because of the depressed international rice market.

Accumulating effects of insufficient maintenance showed up in the form of a reduced area served with irrigation water from the NIA system. Deterioration in the water supply was concentrated in the areas along the lower streams of five main laterals which flow down from a canal on the hillside to Laguna de Bay. East Laguna Village was most severely affected because it is located at the tail end of one of the laterals. A significant reduction in water supply began in 1987 and the situation worsened precipitously to the point that paddy fields receiving no water from the NIA amounted to almost 80 per cent in the dry season of 1994. It was shocking to observe during our 1995 survey that paddy fields which previously used to be well irrigated were dried up, the water distribution canals were buried under weeds, and the head gate was completely broken.

Farm leaders in East Laguna Village repeatedly made complaints to NIA's branch office in Pila, but with no positive result. They also tried to prevent farmers in the upstream portion of the same lateral from abusing water. In fact, they padlocked water gates upstream to prevent farmers there from taking out water illegally during the turn of water rotation downstream. However, the chains and locks were destroyed during the night. Dismayed by such incidents, many farmers in East Laguna Village bought pumps to cope with the deteriorating water supply from the NIA, rather than wasting time on protesting to the NIA and the upstream farmers. In the paddy fields adjacent to Laguna de Bay, the underground water table is high and the ground water is easily replenished as it is pumped up, yet water pumping is more costly than paying irrigation fees for NIA water. Therefore, although rice yields were somewhat higher with pumps, the cost of rice production was raised, resulting in reductions in income from rice farming compared to the time when farmers relied on NIA water.

Overall, the share of non-farm income increased sharply relative to the income produced from farming during the 1990s. The share of income from non-farm origin, defined as the sum of wage earnings from non-farm employment and incomes from self-employed non-farm activities, which was only about 10 per cent in the 1970s and about 40 per cent in the 1980s, rose to more than 60 per cent in the mid-1990s. It is not clear whether East Laguna Village can still be classified as an agrarian community.

3 Population Growth and the Evolution of Households

East Laguna Village has been characterized, above all, by very high rates of population growth for nearly a century. Rapid population increases have put pressure on fixed land resources, especially since the 1950s, when the opening of new land for cultivation was stopped. This strong population pressure has been counteracted to some extent by developments in irrigation infrastructure and new rice technology. These forces have interacted with each other under land reform programmes and ever-increasing urban influences to create a unique class structure in this village. This chapter traces this process from the perspective of demographic changes.

POPULATION STATISTICS

During the period 1966–97 our surveys enumerated, at eight points in time, numbers and characteristics (such as age, sex, occupation and educational level) of people living in all the households in East Laguna Village. Before 1966, the population statistics in this village were recorded in the national censuses conducted in 1903, 1918 and 1960 (they were not recorded in the 1939 and 1948 censuses), and these census data provide invaluable information on earlier situations. However, the first census population of 94 people in 1903 was almost twice as large as the 52 people in the 1918 census. Such a decline in population was highly unlikely to occur in a settlement process involving large population inflows. It is likely that the first census figure represents an overestimation which arose from counting as the village population those who cultivated paddy fields within the territory of East Laguna Village while living in the town of Pila (which was a common practice, especially in the early settlement phase). The hypothesis that the second census population of 52 people was a relatively reliable figure is consistent with the finding that this census result matches well with an estimate for the same year of 47 people based on our family reconstitution study extending back to the early years from the 1980 survey data. The family reconstitution has been extended to the years between 1980 and 1997 from the 1997 survey data.

Estimates of village population obtained from the family reconstitution study, together with survey data for later years, are shown in Table 3.1.

Table 3.1   Changes in population and paddy area, East Laguna Village, 1918–97

Year	Population (no.)[a] Total (1)	Population (no.)[a] Economically active[b] (2)	Labour force ratio (%) (2)/(1)	Paddy area[c] (ha) (3)	Population/land ratio (person/ha) (1)/(3)	Population/land ratio (person/ha) (2)/(3)
1918	47 (52)[d]	32	68	36	1.3	0.9
1940	131	79	60	n/a	n/a	n/a
1960	305 (349)[d]	154	50	94	3.2	1.6
1966	399 (393)[e]	211	53	104	3.8	2.0
1974	548 (549)[e]	303	55	105	5.2	2.9
1976	639 (644)[e]	330	52	108	5.9	3.1
1980	707 (698)[e]	363	51	85	8.3	4.3
1983	739 (747)[e]	405[f]	55	80	9.2	5.1
1987	871 (821)[e]	542[f]	62	89	9.8	6.1
1995	1185 (1141)[e]	772[f]	65	97	12.2	8.0
1997	1214[g] (1209)[e]	772	64	82[h]	14.8	9.4
Growth rate (%/year)						
1918–40	4.8	4.2	−0.6	n/a	n/a	n/a
1940–60	4.3	3.4	−0.9	n/a	n/a	n/a
1960–66	4.6	5.4	0.8	1.7	2.8	3.6
1966–76	4.8	4.6	−0.2	0.4	4.4	4.2
1976–83	2.1	2.4	−0.1	−5.8	8.9	8.7
1983–87	4.2	7.6	3.3	2.7	1.5	4.8
1987–97	3.4	3.6	0.2	−0.8	4.2	4.5

Notes: [a] Estimated by the family reconstitution; the end-of-year population unless other-wise noted.
  [b] Population 13–64 years old.
  [c] Area cultivated by village residents.
  [d] National census data.
  [e] Village household survey data.
  [f] Estimated by applying the labour force ratio at the time of the survey each year.
  [g] The year-end population extrapolated using the growth rate between January–October, 1997.
  [h] Estimated by assuming 2 ha of average cultivating size per farmer.

Note that some discrepancies necessarily arise from the differences in the point of time to which statistics pertain: that is, the survey data stand for the number of people living in village households at the points of survey interview, while the family reconstitution estimates stand for the ends of years. For an unknown reason, there is also a relatively large discrepancy between the census and the family reconstitution data for 1960.

For the sake of consistency with the data of demographic dynamics such as birth and death rates to be discussed later, we shall base our analysis in this section mainly on the population estimates from the family reconstitution study. Conclusions remain largely the same as if the national census and the survey data were to be used instead for the earlier years.

The family reconstitution, in the tradition of historical demography (see, for example, Wrigley and Schofield, 1981; A. Hayami, 1973) was attempted partly to obtain information dating from before 1966, but more importantly to generate dynamic statistics, such as birth, death and migration rates, which cannot be produced from single-point interview surveys. For this purpose, our 1980 survey collected detailed data on family history over the previous three generations, from which family reconstitution forms, one for each family, were prepared. Answers obtained from one family were checked with those of their relatives, as well as the memories of older knowledgeable people in the village. We also adjusted data extended by family reconstitution from the 1980 benchmark in comparison with previous survey results.[1] Similar exercises were performed for the years between the 1980 and 1997 surveys, in which data collection was concentrated on demographic variables. For annual data obtained, see Appendix A.

DYNAMICS OF POPULATION GROWTH

The two basic conditions that determined the pattern of population growth in East Laguna Village were: (a) it is located in the lowland rice belt surrounded by hills and mountains planted with coconut trees and other upland crops; and (b) it is a relatively new village settled since around the 1880s, initially with poor infrastructure but with open land frontiers until the 1950s. The former underlies the high rate of population growth since the 1950s/1960s, whereas the latter underlies the high rate for the earlier period.

Population growth in this village during the three decades covered by our surveys was indeed very fast, amounting to an average rate of 3.7 per cent between 1966 and 1997 (see Table 3.1). This rate was significantly higher than the Philippine national average of 2.7 per cent in the 1960–90 inter-census period. Such rapid population growth was typical of lowland areas, in which successful intensification of rice production because of better irrigation and new rice technology significantly increased farm employment and, at the same time, relatively easy access to urban economic activities expanded non-farm employment opportunities. In this respect, upland farming areas in the hills and mountains were left

behind, with no major technological breakthrough occurring comparable
to the introduction of modern varieties (MV) of rice, and the transportation/
communication infrastructure remained inferior.

These differences are reflected in the differential growth rates of population across municipalities in Laguna Province as shown in Figure 3.1.
By comparing this figure with Figure 1.1, it should be evident that municipalities with lowland areas along Laguna de Bay recorded much higher

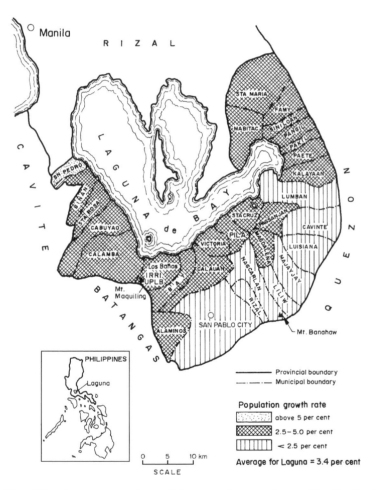

Figure 3.1   Average annual population growth rates by municipality in the
                Province of Laguna, 1970–90
Source: Population Census 1970 and 1990.

population growth rates than upland municipalities for the period 1970–1990. The population growth rates were especially high on the rapidly urbanizing west coast of the lake, but even on the east coast, which is still essentially a rural area, the population growth rates were as high as between 2.5 per cent and 5 per cent per year. In this respect, our study village was not exceptional.

Although the population growth of East Laguna Village has thus been very rapid over the past three decades, it was even faster before the 1960s. The average annual growth rate for 1918–66 is calculated at 4.6 per cent from the family reconstitution data (and 4.3 per cent from the national census and the village survey data). Such a high rate reflected a large inflow of population together with fast natural growth in the settlement process, especially before the 1940s, when new lands were brought rapidly into cultivation.

Indeed, the data of demographic dynamics estimated from family reconstitution show that more than half the population growth in 1918–40 was a social increase or net immigration (see Table 3.2 and Figure 3.2). It is very probable that the social increase was more dominant in the settlement process before 1918. Although the rate of immigration declined after the closure of the cultivation frontiers, the village continued to record high rates of population growth, together with significant net inflows over the following two decades. Underlying the continued high population growth in this period was the doubling of the rice-crop area because of the extension of the national irrigation system to this village in 1958, which resulted in a complete shift from single cropping in the wet season to cropping in both wet and dry seasons.

ble 3.2 Birth, death and migration rates in East Laguna Village, 1918–97 (%/year)[a]

	Natural increase			Social increase			Total population growth
	Birth	Death	Net	In	Out	Net	
918–40	4.6	2.4	2.2 (44)	3.2	0.4	2.8 (56)	5.0 (100)
940–60	5.2	1.4	3.8 (86)	1.9	1.3	0.6 (14)	4.4 (100)
960–70	4.7	1.4	3.3 (79)	2.0	1.1	0.9 (21)	4.2 (100)
970–80	4.6	0.8	3.8 (83)	3.5	2.8	0.7 (17)	4.5 (100)
980–90	3.1	0.7	2.4 (74)	4.2	3.4	0.8 (26)	3.2 (100)
990–97	2.6	0.6	2.0 (60)	5.2	3.8	1.4 (40)	3.4 (100)
918–97	4.4	1.5	2.9 (68)	3.1	1.7	1.4 (32)	4.3 (100)

ote: [a] Percentages to totals are in parentheses.
urce: This volume, Appendix A.

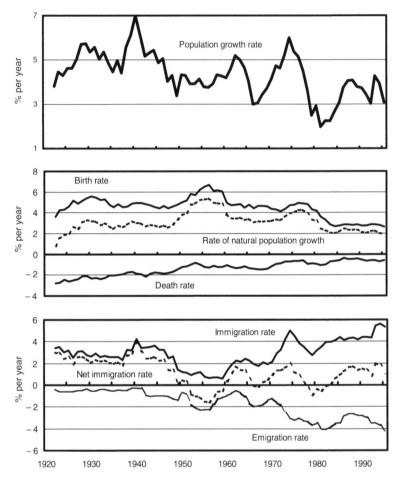

Figure 3.2   Dynamics of population growth in East Laguna Village, nine-year moving averages for 1922–40 and five-year moving averages for 1940–95
Source: This volume, Appendix A.

It is reasonable to expect that among people newly migrated into this village in the land-opening process, the greater number were single youths and young couples with a relatively small number of children. This conclusion is consistent with the high level of economically active people in the total population in 1918 and 1940 ('Labour force ratio' in col. 3, Table 3.1). It is also expected that the high ratio of young couples would have later been translated into a high birth rate and a high ratio of children below working age. Also, the environment of easy access to land for farming (though under tenancy) as well as agricultural employment opportunities would have encouraged the earlier marriage of young people, contributing to the high birth rate.[2] Indeed, the labour force ratio dropped successively from 68 per cent in 1918 to 60 per cent in 1940, and 50 per cent in 1960.

Through this process, while immigration began to decelerate in the 1940s/1950s, the birth rate began to increase in the 1950s and was maintained at a high level until the 1970s (see Figure 3.2). It appears that the continued high fertility rate was a common characteristic of rural areas in the Philippines.[3] Meanwhile, the death rate decreased, which compensated for the decreases in net immigration to maintain total population growth at a high level. The decline in the death rate was particularly rapid in the decade following the Second World War, presumably because of the eradication of malaria through the use of DDT.[4] Continued high population growth with high birth rates was also reflected in the continued widening of the base of the population pyramid from 1966 to 1976, as shown in Figure 3.3. However, the labour force ratio did not decline after 1966 because of a large inflow of labour force into the village, mainly from the surrounding hills and mountains, which corresponded to the increased labour demand for irrigated rice farming in the heyday of the Green Revolution.

Subsequently, the population growth rate dropped significantly to 2.1 per cent per year for 1976–83, as compared with 4.8 per cent for 1966–76 (see Table 3.1). This drop was resulted from a sharp increase in the rate of emigration from the village for construction and other work in urban areas, especially Metro Manila, corresponding to improvements in the highway systems in the late 1970s. Although the emigration of villagers subsided in the mid- to late 1980s caused by the economic depression resulting from the political crisis, it began to increase again in the 1990s with the recovery of the national economy. The outflow of villagers to urban areas, however, was more than compensated for by the inflow of residents from nearby towns seeking inexpensive residential plots. Their immigration is now the major source of rapid expansion in the number of 'non-farm workers' in the village.

Meanwhile, the birth rate decreased from 4.6 per cent in the 1970s to 3.1 per cent in the 1980s, and 2.6 per cent in the 1990s (see Table 3.2). The decline in the birth rate is reflected in a relative shrinkage of the base of the population pyramid between 1976 and 1987, and in 1997 (see Figure 3.3). It is clear that from the 1980s this village entered the final phase of demographic transition characterized by decreases in the birth rate in the face of a low, stable death rate.

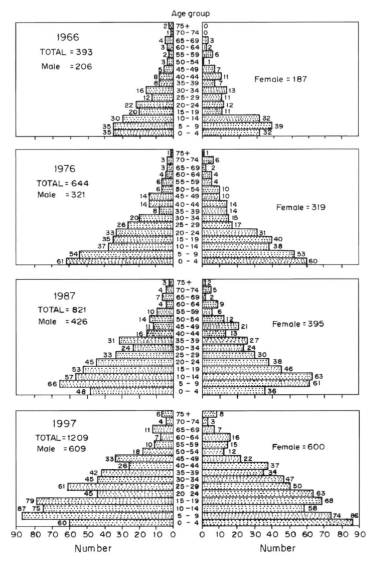

Figure 3.3   Age distribution of population in East Laguna Village, 1966–97

POPULATION PRESSURE AND LANDLESSNESS

High population growth in East Laguna Village, especially upto the mid-1970s, has caused heavy pressure on limited land resources. We measured the land resource available for agricultural production by villagers in terms of paddy field area cultivated by farmers living in the village. This measure is used instead of the area within the boundary of the village territory, because borders with neighbouring villages are not clearly defined (as is common in Philippine villages),[5] and the coconut area in the village is mostly owned and used for agricultural production by non-villagers. It appears that the land resource in this village thus defined increased through land opening to reach a level of about 100 hectares at some time in the 1950s. Since then, it has fluctuated mainly through the transfer of cultivation rights between farmers in this village and others in surrounding villages and towns.

Under continued population growth the population–land ratio deteriorated rapidly (see Table 3.1). The average population per hectare of the paddy field area in the village increased from 1.3 people in 1918 to 3.8 people in 1966, and to 14.8 people in 1997; this was paralleled by increases in economically active population per hectare from 0.9 people in 1918 to 2.0 people in 1966, and to 9.4 people in 1997.

This strong population pressure underpinned the formation of a unique class structure in this village. In an agrarian community such as East Laguna Village, based mainly on rice farming, income levels and social status of villagers were traditionally dependent on their control of paddy land. Since most paddy land are owned by absentee landlords, it is not the land ownership but the right to cultivate land or the tenancy right that has been the major factor differentiating villagers in economic and social status. Since the early 1970s the tenancy rights have been strongly protected and land rents controlled at lower-than-market rates under land reform programmes. Even before then, most tenants had relatively secure tenure on lands they cultivated, as they were either the original settlers who opened the lands, or their heirs. Their rights to continue farming the lands were respected, though not guaranteed by written documents. In fact, tenants' rights on lands were such that it was customary for them to receive payments when their tenancy rights were transferred to someone else, though this charge was not very large before the implementation of the land reform programmes.

In terms of the right to cultivate paddy land, two major classes in this village were 'farmers', who operated their own farms either as tenants or as owners; and 'agricultural labourers', who have no farm to operate but stake out a living by means of wage earnings from casual farm employment. More recently, however, a new class, which may be called 'non-farm workers' has emerged since the 1980s. Their income source is either employment in non-farm work (such as teachers, clerks and factory workers, mainly outside the village) or self-employed non-farm activities such as commerce and transportation.

One consequence of the growing scarcity in the availability of land for cultivation was a sharp increase in the number of agricultural labourers' households relative to that of farmers'. The increase in the total number of households from 1966 to 1997 largely paralleled the growth of the population (see Table 3.3); it increased from 66 in 1966 to 126 in 1980, and to 266 in 1997. The number of landless labourer households increased noticeably faster than the number of farmer households. As a result, the number of agricultural labourers in the total number of households increased from 30 per cent in 1966 to 60 per cent in 1980, and to 62 per cent in 1987.

Table 3.3   Number of households by type, East Laguna Village, 1966–97 survey years

Year	Farmer[a]	Agricultural labourer[b]	Non-farm worker[c]	Total
1966	46	20	0	66
	(70)[d]	(30)	(0)	(100)
1974	54	41	0	95
	(57)	(43)	(0)	(100)
1976	54	55	0	109
	(50)	(50)	(0)	(100)
1980	46	76	4	126
	(37)	(60)	(3)	(100)
1983	44	76	5	125
	(35)	(61)	(4)	(100)
1987	53	98	7	158
	(34)	(62)	(4)	(100)
1995	51	150	41	242
	(21)	(62)	(17)	(100)
1997	41	163	62	266
	(16)	(61)	(23)	(100)
Growth rate (%/year)				
1966–74	2.0	9.4	—[e]	4.7
1974–80	−2.6	10.8	—	4.1
1980–3	−1.5	0.0	7.7	−0.3
1983–7	4.8	6.6	8.8	6.0
1987–97	−2.5	5.2	24.4	5.3

Notes: [a] Households cultivating paddy fields.

[b] Households having no land to cultivate and engaging in hired farm work.

[c] Households having no land to cultivate and engaging only in non-farm activities.

[d] Percentages to totals are shown in parentheses.

[e] — stands for data undefined.

Since 1980 the share of non-farm workers' households has become significant. Correspondingly, the share of farmer households decreased from 70 per cent in 1966 to 16 per cent in 1997.

The increase in the number of agricultural labourers can be seen from the family reconstitution data on the formation of households given in Table 3.4. New households were created either through the independence of children from parents who lived within the village, or through migration from outside. In both cases the farmers' shares declined and those of agricultural labourers increased. After the land frontiers were closed, the opportunity for children to become farmers by opening new lands disappeared and they had to make a living as wage labourers while waiting to inherit parents' farms. Similarly, in earlier years migrants were attracted to this village to become farmers on new lands, but in later years more people immigrated only because employment was available for landless agricultural labourers.

The sharp increase in the number of agricultural labourers, however, was due not only to population pressure but also to land reform regulations regarding land tenancy contracts, and to the expansion in labour demand for rice farming because of the diffusion of new rice technology, which will be discussed in Chapters 4 and 5, respectively.

Strong population pressure affected family structure, too. As is common in rural villages in the Philippines, most families in East Laguna Village are of the nuclear type, consisting of a married couple (or a widow) and their (her) children. When the children marry, they usually move to a hut near their parents' house and make their living as casual workers, labouring on their parents' and neighbours' farms, until they inherit the parents' farms. As a step towards inheritance, it is common for children to have a sharecropping arrangement with their parents. When retiring from farming, parents sometimes keep one child (often the youngest) living in their house after marriage.

A change in the life-cycle pattern seems to be reflected in changes in the distributions of households by family type across four household categories: that is, large farmers with operational farm sizes of two hectares and above; small farmers with operational farm sizes below two hectares; agricultural labourers; and non-farm workers (see Tables 3.5 and 3.6). In 1966, as many as 85 per cent of households were of the nuclear type, while the share of extended families was higher among farmers, especially large farmers, than among landless workers. Correspondingly, average family size was significantly larger for large farmers than for small farmers and agricultural labourers. However, while nuclear families continue to be predominant, the difference in the distribution in average family size

Table 3.4 Formation of households by period, East Laguna Village,[a] by number of households; percentages in parentheses

Date of formation	Farmer			Agricultural labourer			Non-farm worker			Total
	Independence	Migration	Total	Independence	Migration	Total	Independence	Migration	Total	
Before 1920	0	9	9	0	0	0	0	0	0	9
	(0)	(100)	(100)	(0)	(0)	(0)	(0)	(0)	(0)	(100)
1920–39	9	11	20	0	2	2	0	0	0	22
	(41)	(50)	(91)	(0)	(9)	(9)	(0)	(0)	(0)	(100)
1940–9	9	7	16	0	4	4	0	0	0	20
	(45)	(35)	(80)	(0)	(20)	(20)	(0)	(0)	(0)	(100)
1950–9	12	3	15	2	1	3	0	0	0	18
	(67)	(17)	(83)	(11)	(6)	(17)	(0)	(0)	(0)	(100)
1960–9	13	10	23	8	3	11	0	0	0	34
	(38)	(29)	(68)	(24)	(9)	(32)	(0)	(0)	(0)	(100)
1970–9	3	8	11	20	25	45	2	1	3	59
	(5)	(14)	(19)	(34)	(42)	(76)	(3)	(2)	(5)	(100)
1980–9	2	7	9	27	34	61	4	8	12	82
	(2)	(9)	(11)	(33)	(41)	(74)	(5)	(10)	(15)	(100)
1990–7	2	3	5	26	53	79	7	28	35	119
	(2)	(3)	(5)	(22)	(45)	(66)	(6)	(24)	(29)	(100)
Total	50	58	108	83	122	205	13	37	50	363
	(14)	(16)	(30)	(23)	(34)	(57)	(4)	(10)	(14)	(100)

Note: [a] For the periods before 1980, based on the family reconstitution, including households that once existed but had disappeared because of the deaths of household members or through emigration; for the remaining periods, the data have been obtained only for the households that existed in the village in the survey years of 1983, 1987, 1995 and 1997. Throughout the years, changes of household category after its establishment in the village are not taken into account. Independence = both the couple or the husband are/is from the village; migration = family migration (including return migration) or a newly-formed household where the husband is from outside the village.

Table 3.5   Distribution of households by type of family, East Laguna Village, 1966, 1976, 1987 and 1997

	Large farmer (2 ha and above)	Small farmer (below 2 ha)	Agricultural labourer	Non-farm worker	Total
1966 Households (no.)	25	21	20	...[a]	66
Percentage of nuclear families	(77)	(95)	(86)		(85)
1976 Households (no.)	21	33	55	...	109
Percentage of nuclear families	(57)	(82)	(93)		(88)
1987 Households (no.)	18	35	92	11	156
Percentage of nuclear families	(83)	(71)	(89)	(91)	(85)
1997 Households (no.)	16	25	163	61[b]	265
Percentage of nuclear families	(63)	(76)	(85)	(74)	(80)

Note: [a] ... stands for 'not applicable'.
[b] Excludes one special case (convent).

between farmers and agricultural labourers has disappeared over time. Most importantly, almost double the number of males above 13 years old in the large farmer households than in the small farmer and landless labourer households in 1966 was reduced to the same level as the latter by 1997.

This change seems to reflect the closure of the so-called 'agricultural ladder' (Spillman, 1919). In the days when land was relatively abundant and its rental market was not regulated by land reform laws, a young boy who began as an agricultural labourer could move up to become a share-cropper, and sometimes to a leasehold tenant, as he accumulated farming experience and savings to buy farm equipment and water buffalo (*carabao*); as his family size increased and children grew to working age, he was able to expand his cultivated area by renting more land. As population pressure on the limited land area increased, however, the opportunities for a landless labourer to ascend this agricultural ladder and become a tenant farmer, or for a small farmer to expand his operational farm size in response to growth in his family size, became progressively smaller. The ladder was further narrowed as the land reform regulations made the land rental market inactive. People who started as casual agricultural labourers were forced to remain at the same level;[6] this was particularly the case for the landless labourers who migrated from outside the village.

Table 3.6   Average family size, East Laguna Village, 1966, 1976, 1987 and 1997, by number of persons

Year		Large farmer (2 ha and above)	Small farmer (below 2 ha)	Agricultural labourer	Non-farm worker	Total
1966	Male	3.4	3.0	2.9	…[a]	3.1
	(13 and above)	(2.6)	(1.4)	(1.5)		(1.9
	Female	3.6	2.3	2.4	…	2.8
	(13 and above)	(1.8)	(0.8)	(1.3)		(1.3
	Total	7.0	5.3	5.3	…	5.9
	(13 and above)	(4.4)	(2.2)	(2.8)		(3.2
1976	Male	4.1	3.2	2.4	…	3.0
	(13 and above)	(2.4)	(1.9)	(1.3)		(1.7
	Female	4.0	2.4	2.5	…	2.9
	(13 and above)	(2.8)	(1.6)	(1.3)		(1.7
	Total	8.1	6.2	4.9	…	5.9
	(13 and above)	(5.2)	(3.5)	(2.6)		(3.4
1987	Male	3.1	2.9	2.6	2.8	2.7
	(13 and above)	(2.4)	(2.1)	(1.5)	(1.9)	(1.8
	Female	2.2	3.3	2.3	2.2	2.5
	(13 and above)	(1.7)	(2.3)	(1.4)	(1.4)	(1.6
	Total	5.3	6.3	4.9	5.0	5.3
	(13 and above)	(4.1)	(4.4)	(2.9)	(3.3)	(3.4
1997	Male	2.7	1.7	2.5	1.7	2.3
	(13 and above)	(1.9)	(1.9)	(1.7)	(1.0)	(1.5
	Female	2.0	2.0	2.2	2.5	2.3
	(13 and above)	(1.6)	(1.5)	(1.4)	(1.8)	(1.5
	Total	4.7	4.4	4.7	4.1	4.5
	(13 and above)	(3.5)	(3.4)	(3.1)	(2.8)	(3.1

Note: [a] … stands for 'not applicable'.

This inter-class immobility also seems to have underlain the disappearance of the positive association between farm and family sizes.

OCCUPATION, EDUCATION AND MIGRATION

The impact of the strong population pressure are also reflected in changes in the occupational structure of the village labour force as measured by the economically active population of 13–64 year olds (see Table 3.7). In 1974, 47 per cent of the male labour force engaged in rice farming on their own farms as their major occupation, while only 19 per cent engaged

Table 3.7   Percentage distribution of economically active population (13–64 years), East Laguna Village, 1974–97, by major occupation

		1974	1980	1987	1997
MALES					
Self-employed					
Farm:	Rice	47	26	21	9
	Duck-raising	15	2	1	0
	Fishing	0	1	2	0
Non-farm:	Commerce/trade	2	1	1	1
	Driver (tricycle/*jeepney*)	0	1	2	9
	Rural industry	0	0	0	1
Hired work					
Farm hired work		19	46	48	44
Carpentry/construction		1	2	1	5
Other casual work					6
Salaried worker		3	6	6	7
Education		12	13	16	15
None		1	2	2	3
Total		100	100	100	100
Farm total		81	75	72	53
Non-farm total		6	10	10	29
FEMALES					
Self-employed					
Farm:	Rice	12	3	1	1
	Duck/pig-raising	1	11	3	1
Non-farm:	Commerce/trade	4	6	10	9
	Rural industry	0	0	0	1
Hired work					
Farm hired work		8	16	13	13
Sewing		1	3	3	1
Maid		0	2	4	2
Other casual work		0	1	0	4
Salaried worker		3	3	6	6
Education		11	18	12	15
House-keeping/none		60	37	48	47
Total		100	100	100	100
Farm total		21	30	17	15
Non-farm total		8	15	23	23

in hired work in rice farming. As population pressure continued to mount, however, self-employment and hired work reversed their shares by 1980: the share of self-employed rice farming decreased to 26 per cent, and that of hired rice work increased to 46 per cent. As a result, the share of economically active males dependent on rice farming, both self-employed and hired, remained as high as more than 70 per cent during 1974–87, reflecting the traditional nature of East Laguna Village as a 'rice-based economy'. This predominance of rice farming as an economic activity declined after 1987. In 1997 the share of self-employed rice farming decreased to 9 per cent, and that of hired rice work to 44 per cent, totalling only 53 per cent. Meanwhile, the share of non-farm work, including both self-employed and hired work, increased from 10 per cent in 1987 to 29 per cent in 1997, reflecting the rapid intrusion of urban economic activities into the village economy. In fact, relative expansion of non-farm economic activities was going on before 1987. Although rice farming had continued to be dominant until 1987, other agricultural activities such as duck raising had shrunk, and non-farm activities such as tricycle driving and carpentry expanded progressively from 1974.

It is important to note that the share of rice work itself dropped significantly in the early 1980s but recovered in 1987, corresponding to a sharp increase in the share of non-farm work and its subsequent reduction. Such irregular movements in the village occupational structure in the 1980s reflect a major slump in the Philippine economy because of political and social instability arising from the downfall of the Marcos regime. The major drop in GDP was particularly severe in the industrial and service sectors (see Figure 3.4). It was natural that the access of villagers to non-farm employment was reduced sharply in the mid-1980s. If the

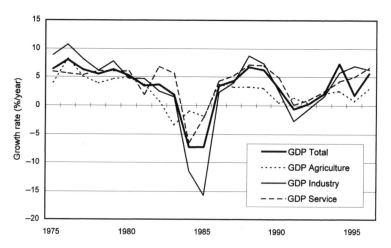

Figure 3.4   GDP growth rates, Philippines, 1975–96
Source: National Statistical Coordination Board (various issues).

economic growth of the Philippines had not been interrupted by the 'lost decade', a shift of East Laguna Village away from a rice-based economy, which has been increasingly visible in the 1990s, should have been in progression a decade earlier.[7]

Similar trends are observed for the female labour force, though with lower labour participation rates. One difference found is that commerce/trade, such as running a *sari-sari* store, rice trading and food vending, is the major non-farm self-employed opportunity for female. Another difference for females is that the share of non-farm employment became higher than that of farm employment in 1987, and by 1997 the difference had further increased. It is interesting to note that changes over time in the labour participation rate as measured by the share of the labour force with a major occupation (farm total plus non-farm total) differ between males and females. While this share stayed nearly constant at around 85 per cent for males, it increased from 29 per cent in 1974 to 45 per cent in 1980, and remained at that level or declined slightly thereafter for females.

It is obvious that the expansion of non-farm employment opportunities underlay the emergence of 'non-farm worker households' since 1980, as was observed in Table 3.3. An especially rapid increase in the number of households in this category since the mid-1980s indicates that East Laguna Village is changing from a purely rural community to a more complex one.

The shift of occupational pattern away from agriculture was accompanied by improvements in the educational level of the village labour force (see Table 3.8). In 1966, about a half of the total village labour force had had education in elementary school up to only grade 4 or below, and about 20 per cent had had no formal education. In 1997, the share of the labour force with these lower educational levels declined to a minority comprising only a fifth, with a third having reached elementary grade 5–6 level, and another third with a high school education, while those with no formal education represented only 2 per cent of the labour force. The number of college graduates also increased, relatively and absolutely from 1974 to 1987, and absolutely from 1987 to 1997. Particularly impressive is the increase in the labour force with a high school education. As pointed out by Kikuchi and Opena (1983), the segmented labour markets in the urban/industrial sectors in the Philippines require high educational attainments of new entrants. College degrees are necessary to gain stable professional jobs, such as government employees, teachers, clerks and nurses. A high school background, or more frequently a high school diploma, is required even for manual jobs in the urban formal sector, such as construction worker and factory labourer. Rapid increases in the number of villagers who find jobs in non-farm labour markets have been supported

Table 3.8 Percentage distribution of adult population (21–64 years), East Laguna Village, 1966, 1976, 1987 and 1997, by educational level

Educational attainment	Male				Female				Total			
	1966 (N=77)	1976 (N=121)	1987 (N=174)	1997 (N=281)	1966 (N=68)	1976 (N=112)	1987 (N=172)	1997 (N=279)	1966 (N=145)	1976 (N=233)	1987 (N=346)	1997 (N=560)
No Schooling	18	8	3	2	25	8	4	2	21	8	3	2
Primary												
Grades 1–4	54	41	31	21	48	41	29	18	51	41	30	20
Grades 5–6	20	28	31	33	17	37	36	33	19	32	34	33
Secondary												
Grades 7–10	8	16	20	31	8	10	15	34	8	13	18	32
College												
Grades 11–12	0	2	6	8	0	1	5	4	0	1	6	6
Grades 13–	0	5	9	5	2	4	10	9	1	4	9	7
Total	100	100	100	100	100	100	100	100	100	100	100	100

by the improvements in their educational level. In other words, for those who want to find stable, non-farm employment, the only way is to invest in education.

Significant differences in levels of education can be observed across different social classes in the village. For both sexes and over the years, except for males in 1966, the average number of school years per adult family member was the highest in the large farmer and the non-farm worker households, and lowest in the agricultural labourer households (see Table 3.9). This is a pattern we expected to observe, considering the differences in the financial capacity to be able to send children to school across the categories of household. Also, in the case of non-farm workers, a high level of education was the key to accessing high-income, non-farm jobs.

It may appear reasonable to expect that the increased level of education under strong population pressure and rapid expansion in the urban labour market would have induced a large labour outflow from East Laguna Village to the urban sector. However, as has already been shown in Table 3.2, this village continued to record major net population inflows. Underlying this apparent anomaly was a process by which the outflow of highly

Table 3.9   Average number of school years per adult (21–64 years), East Laguna Village, 1966, 1976, 1987 and 1997, by household category

	Large farmer (2 ha and above)	*Small farmer* (below 2 ha)	*Agricultural labourer*	*Non-farm worker*	*Total*
Male					
1966	3.3	3.5	3.2	...[a]	3.4
1976	6.8	5.1	4.2	...	5.2
1987	8.1	7.0	5.6	9.6	6.6
1997	10.7	9.5	5.9	8.8	7.1
Female					
1966	4.1	3.1	2.3	...	3.3
1976	5.8	4.8	4.3	...	4.8
1987	9.0	6.9	5.6	6.3	6.5
1997	10.3	7.9	6.6	8.5	7.4
Total					
1966	3.7	3.3	2.8	...	3.3
1976	6.3	4.9	4.2	...	5.0
1987	8.6	7.0	5.6	8.0	6.5
1997	10.5	8.8	6.2	8.6	7.3

Note: [a] ... stands for 'not applicable'.

educated people to urban activities was more than compensated for by the large inflow of uneducated labourers from other rural areas. The process can be demonstrated in the records of net migratory flows in East Laguna Village by household category (Table 3.10). Before the 1960s, the linkage of this village with the urban labour market was rather weak, as reflected in the negligibly small net outflows to the urban sector (and negative net inflows), while both outflows and inflows were small (Appendix B). Meanwhile, a large number of people migrated from unfavourable upland areas to settle in this village as large farmers by opening new lands before the cultivation frontiers were closed in the 1950s. These immigrants had little formal education, but had sufficient ability in practising traditional rice farming in rainfed paddy fields on a relatively large scale. After 1940, the immigration of those aiming to become farmers stopped and the village became more neutral in terms of net migratory flows to both the rural and urban sectors during 1940–59.[8]

In the 1960s, East Laguna Village experienced another burst of immigration from upland areas. Unlike the period before 1940, the majority of the new immigrants settled in this village as small farmers. They acquired small pieces of rice land through marriage or the purchase of tenancy rights; this corresponded to reductions in average farm size as well as in the share of large-scale farms, to be shown in the next chapter. Underlying this process was increased land productivity resulting from developments in irrigation systems and new rice technology on the one hand, and the unregulated land-rental market before the implementation of land reform programmes. While farm labour thus migrated in, a significant emigration was recorded in this period from large farmers' households to the urban formal sector. It appears that increased investment in education by large farmers whose incomes rose because of increased land productivity began to bear fruit in their children's access to respectable jobs in urban areas.

This trend of the children of large farmers to migrate out of East Laguna Village was further accelerated in the 1970s. Not only did an increased number move to the urban sector, but an even larger number migrated to other rural areas to start up knowledge-intensive agribusiness such as specialized in-house production of broilers and eggs, fish culture and fruit orchards, together with the processing and marketing of farm products and inputs. On the other hand, a large inflow of agricultural labourers was recorded for this period, especially from unfavourable upland areas. They were attracted by increased employment opportunities in the irrigated village with the successful diffusion of Green Revolution technology. Migratory flows to this village were thus characterized by a dualistic structure. On the one hand, a large number of intra-rural migrants

Table 3.10 Net migration inflows to East Laguna Village, 1918–97[a]

	Rural		Urban		Total
	Lowland rice area	Upland area[b]	Formal	Informal	
1918–39					
Large farmer	0	27	−1	...	26
Small farmer	5	8			13
Ag. labourer	...[c]	...	...	...	
Total	5	35	−1	...	39
1940–59					
Large farmer	8	8	−2	1	15
Small farmer	−7	−4	...	...	−11
Ag. labourer	6	2	...	...	8
Total	7	6	−2	1	12
1960–9					
Large farmer	−6	7	−8	...	−7
Small farmer	5	17	−1	1	22
Ag. labourer	5	3	...	3	11
Total	4	27	−9	4	26
1970–9					
Large farmer	−14	−18	−9	0	−41
Small farmer	−9	7	−8	−5	−15
Ag. labourer	11	64	−4	14	85
Non-farm	...	...	1	...	1
Total	−12	53	−20	9	30
1980–9					
Large farmer	−3	5	−2	7	7
Small farmer	10	7	−20	−2	−5
Ag. labourer	15	23	−17	−14	7
Non-farm	...	...	16	−5	11
Total	22	35	−23	−14	20
1990–7					
Large farmer	0	-6	−9	...	−15
Small farmer	−15	0	−18	1	−32
Ag. labourer	54	65	−41	17	95
Non-farm	2	5	2	33	42
Total	41	64	−66	51	90

Notes: [a] Number of immigrants minus number of emigrants.

[b] Include fishing villages.

[c] ... stands for 'not applicable'.

Source: This volume, Appendix B.

flowed to the village from the upland areas and accumulated at the bottom of the social strata as landless agricultural labourers with a low education. On the other, a stream of rural–urban migration was flowing from the upper strata of the village society with its higher education to the urban formal sector.

Hidden behind the data of net migratory flows presented in Table 3.10 were very frequent incidences of in- and out-migrations of the labour force with a low education. For example, a net inflow of nine people to this village from the urban informal sector was recorded in 1970–9, based on 38 immigrants and 29 emigrants. In 1990–7 the net inflow of seventeen people from the urban informal sector to the agricultural labour class in the village resulted from the inflow of 79 people and the outflow of 62 people (Appendix B). As these data suggest, the rural sector and the urban informal sector were well integrated in a single labour market in which manual labourers with a low education move around very frequently. In fact, there are many immigrants who changed their place of living several times after they left their birthplace and before they arrived at this village. This type of step or chain migration is fairly common, especially among those coming from remote regions. Also, there are villagers who repeat piston-like movements between the village and outside.

Although people are generally very mobile, their decision to migrate is usually made to a sure prospect for better employment opportunities. There is rarely a case in which a migrant moves to a place where he or she is not sure whether he/she can establish a better livelihood than before. In other words, information on economic opportunities in the place where a migrant chooses to move plays a critical role in the migration decision. For example, an important channel of such information is the seasonal migration of harvesters across the rice-growing areas with different harvesting periods, and between rice-growing areas and the surrounding upland areas. Many villagers go to other rice villages in Laguna and its neighbouring provinces for harvesting work, and people from these other villages come to this village during its harvesting season. The circle within which people move around seeking work opportunities as well as marriage across rural areas overlaps with the circle within which people move around for harvesting. Once this channel results in marriage across villages, kinship and friendship ties further strengthen the channel.

Another important information channel is migrants who go out to urban centres for temporary jobs such as construction work. On a construction site, they meet co-workers from other places, whom they may inform about the availability of work opportunities in the home village in the harvesting season. Many of those who migrated to this village from remote areas, in fact, came through this channel. Once the migrants from remote areas establish their livelihoods in the village as agricultural labourers, they may bring their relatives and friends from their original homes to the village. There are many other information channels through which people obtain information about migration. Under ordinary circumstances in rural areas, people rarely move just for the reason that they have difficulty in making a living in their original place. And they seldom move as a result of a casual calculation of probability of their finding lucrative jobs in the urban formal sector, as assumed in the model of Harris and Todaro (1970).

One may puzzle as to why the net inflow of 11 people occurred in the category of non-farm workers in 1980–9 and as many as 42 people in 1990–7. Those are the people who came to the village just to live there while earning incomes from urban jobs outside the village. Such cases have been increasing especially rapidly since the recovery of the philippine economy from the slump of the mid-1980s, and as the cost of housing rose sharply in the town and transportation to the village improved with the paving of the access road in 1994. They either commute every day to their workplaces in nearby local towns, or go to work in the Metro Manila area, and return to the village to spend the weekends with their families. The close linkage of people in this category with the urban labour market is demonstrated by the fact that as many as 108 people moved into this village from the urban sector, with a reverse flow of 66 people moving out during 1990–7 (see Appendix B).

ANECDOTES OF FOUR SOCIAL CLASSES

For the purpose of identifying the demographic and occupational characteristics of East Laguna Village, we have so far used the classification of village households into large farmers, small farmers, agricultural labourers and non-farm workers. In order to give a more concrete image on life and work in the village, we shall present four short case histories (upto 1995) of families representing each of the four social classes.

Ilyo Balagtas – A Large Farmer

Basilio (Ilyo), 44 years old in 1995, belongs to one of the oldest families in the village. His great-grandfather migrated to the village from the Province of Morong (now Rizal) around 1880 to open new land. His mother was born in an upland area of Batangas, but came to a nearby village in the

1930s with her parents who opened paddy fields there. Ilyo's father was also a large farmer known for his good knowledge and high skill in farming. He twice held the office of *barangay captain*. Ilyo is the third son, with four brothers and three sisters (one brother died in infancy). His father and mother were both eager to give their children a good education, and all except him graduated from college. Now his brothers and sisters are all living outside the village, holding down stable employment in government offices, hospitals and private companies.

Ilyo also attended a college, but he did not like schooling much and dropped out in the second year when he decided to become a farmer. He was also rather exceptional among the youth of the village, because he did not see much attraction in urban life. His parents were disappointed at his dropping out, but at the same time were relieved to see that at least one of their children would continue to live close by and succeed them in farming.

In 1970 his father gave Ilyo a two-hectare leasehold parcel he had cultivated under a sub-tenancy arrangement with 50 : 50 crop-sharing; this is a relatively common step in the intergenerational transfer of land cultivation rights within a family. Eight years later, Ilyo inherited formally from his father the cultivation rights of this parcel that was protected by land reform laws, establishing himself as the permanent lessee of this land, which is owned by a small landlord living in Pila. In addition, Ilyo inherited in 1992 one hectare of paddy field owned by his father. This was part of three hectare of leasehold land cultivated by his father, but when the landowner sold the ownership title of this land in 1988, one hectare was given to the father as compensation for the loss of the cultivation rights on the other two hectares. In the late 1980s, Ilyo also cultivated 2.5 hectares on behalf of his brother-in-law, who purchased the cultivation rights of this land with money from his savings earned in the Middle East. This land, however, is at the time of writing being cultivated by the brother-in-law himself, who lives in Pila town after returning from the Middle East at the time of the Gulf War.

So Ilyo Balagtas is a large farmer cultivating three hectares of paddy field, the tenth largest operational holding in the village. His wife, Paulina (Lina), is from a coconut village where her father still operates a coconut farm of nine hectares, partly owned and partly tenanted. Ilyo and Lina were classmates in the high school in Pila *poblacion*. They got married when Ilyo gave up attending college. His desire to marry her as soon as possible was one reason for his decision to leave college for farming. However, Lina continued her course and completed her college education. Since graduation, she has been working in a government office in Pila.

Now two of their daughters are working, one as a teacher and the other as a midwife; one lives outside the village with her family and the other at home with them. They have another daughter who is now attending a college and two sons attending the high school in the town. Ilyo, now busy as an important member of the Barangay Council while managing his own rice farm, wonders whether one of his five children will succeed to his farm in the future, as he did a quarter of a century before.

Crispin (Ipin) Magtibay – A Small Farmer

Crispin (Ipin) was born in 1947 in a fishing village in Bay, two municipalities away from Pila. When he came to this village in 1950 with his mother, who had been widowed and had subsequently married a farmer sharecropping 2.7 hectares in this village. Ipin helped his stepfather with rice farming until 1968, when he married his wife, Jacinta (Cinta), one of the daughters of a small farmer in the village. After staying with his parents for one year, he and Cinta built their own house. His godfather, who lived in the town, gave him 0.7 of a hectare under a share tenancy, and a year later, he inherited one hectare under a share tenancy from his stepfather. He also purchased the cultivation rights of 0.8 of a hectare under lease from a village farmer in 1971. Thus he became a large farmer, cultivating 2.5 hectares. To cultivate his farm, he bought a hand tractor on credit. In 1972, all his lands were converted to a leasehold tenancy under the land reform programme.

Unfortunately, however, his farm suffered serious crop failures in 1973 and 1974, which took him heavily into debt. In his case, the conversion from share to leasehold tenancy worked against him. Under the traditional sharecropping arrangement, the risk of crop failure was shared between tenant and landowner, and some production costs, such as those for fertilizers, were also shared. After becoming a leaseholder, he had to shoulder the whole risk of crop failure. Unpaid leasehold rents accumulated, and loan payments with a high interest rate for his hand tractor aggravated his financial position. In 1975, Ipin sold a tenancy right of one hectare to two farmers – one in the village and one outside, in order to clear a part of his debt, leaving one and half hectares for him and his family to cultivate.

Seven children – three sons and four daughters – were born between 1969 and 1986. Ipin and Cinta were eager to give their children as high an education as possible, and this aggravated the family's financial crisis. The first son and first daughter went to college but had to drop out because of Ipin's financial difficulties. After engaging occasionally in casual work in the village, however, the first daughter obtained a job in an electronics factory in Metro Manila. The second daughter, after graduating from high school, married the son of a small farmer in a neighbouring village and works as an agricultural labourer there. In 1988, in order to obtain cash to send his eldest son to Saudi Arabia as an overseas contract worker, Ipin mortgaged 0.5 of a hectare of the remaining land to a town resident. With the son's remittances from abroad, however, Ipin was able to get the mortgaged land back two years later. Even after the Gulf War, this son continued to work abroad, with remittances from him paying for the education of the remaining four children.

Pablo (Ambo) Casimiro – An Agricultural Labourer

Pablo (Ambo) and his wife, Andrea (Andeng) were born in a sugar cane village in Calauan, Laguna in the 1930s. After finishing school at Grade 4 and Grade 5, respectively, they both worked as sugar cane labourers. Alongsides his hired labour work on the sugar cane farms, Ambo learned carpentry skills from his uncle through an apprenticeship. After his marriage to Andeng, Ambo occasionally went to Manila and other places for carpentry jobs, while living in the sugar cane village. However, life was hard for Ambo and Andeng, since the income from hired work on the sugar cane farms and from sporadic carpentry employment was rarely sufficient to support their growing family. Andeng bore fifteen children, of whom four died in infancy and three others in childhood.

When their fifteenth child died during infancy, Ambo's uncle, who had migrated to East Laguna Village as a small farmer before the Second World War invited them to become rice harvesters under a '*gama*' contract and Ambo and Andeng migrated to the village with their eight surviving children. Both of them are industrious, contracting with several farmers for rice harvesting work and received nearly five tons of paddy per year as wages.

Meanwhile, carpentry job opportunities increased in Metro Manila with the Philippine economic recovery from the late 1980s. Ambo's brother in the sugar cane village, who was a foreman of a group of construction workers for contractors in Manila, asked him to undertake carpentry jobs in the urban centre, so Ambo started to work again as a carpenter. He even recruited some fellow agricultural labourers and small farmers in the village to his brother's working group. His brother found him one contract after another, so Ambo stayed almost continuously on construction sites in Manila, thus becoming a typical 'circular migrant'. Every Friday evening he goes home with one week's wages, and every Monday morning goes to Manila with enough rice for one week's consumption. During the harvesting season in the village, he stays at home and works with his wife and children to finish harvesting the rice on their contracted paddy fields.

Of the eight living children, four daughters are already married and living in neighbouring villages, their husbands being either agricultural labourers or carpenters. The eldest son has joined his father in construction work, and the other children are all working as agricultural labourers and living in the village.

Benita (Nita) Balagtas – A Non-Farm Worker

Benita (Nita), born in1960, is a teacher at an elementary school in Pila town. She was born in Quezon Province, but grew up in San Pablo City with her grandparents, who owned a five-hectare coconut farm. Her husband, Mario Balagtas, was her classmate in college. He is a member of the Balagtas family in East Laguna Village; Mario's father, operating a farm of four hectares, is a great uncle of Ilyo Balagtas.

On graduating from college in 1980, Nita and her husband took up teaching posts, Nita in Calamba, Laguna, and Mario in Tanauan, Batangas. Therefore, after they married in 1983, they lived separately and only spent weekends together in Mario's parents' house in the village. Mario changed his job in 1984 to work in a government office in Manila, and then joined the army in 1985. In the meantime, Nita was able to get a teaching position at an elementary school in Pila *poblacion*, to which she could commute from the village. They built their own house in the village in 1987.

At the time of writing, Captain Mario Balagtas is stationed with his battalion in Samar, coming home only occasionally. When Nita is teaching, their four children are taken care of at home by a thirteen-year-old maid, the daughter of an agricultural labourer in the village. The life style of the Balagtas thus represents the arrival of a non-farming elite in the village.

4 Agrarian Structure and Land Reform

It goes without saying that land tenure systems are the critical determinant of production and income distribution in agrarian communities. As with other irrigated rice areas in the Philippines, the land tenure system in East Laguna Village has seen major changes since the 1960s, resulting mainly from land reform programmes. Yet the size distribution of operational landholdings among farmers has changed relatively little, while the numbers of landless agricultural labourers have increased sharply relative to the number of farmers. In this chapter we look at how such a pattern of agrarian change has emerged through the interaction of land reform with strong population pressure and the development of new technology.

EVOLUTION OF AGRARIAN SYSTEMS IN THE PHILIPPINE RICE BOWL[1]

By their nature, agrarian institutions are heavily dependent on their historical path. The process of agrarian change in East Laguna Village cannot properly be understood without examining its regional characteristics in a broader historical context. Before proceeding to the case of East Laguna Village, a historical overview will be advanced here of the evolution of two distinct agrarian structures within a major rice-producing area in the Philippines since the Spanish regime.

Regional Classification

Two provinces in the Southern Tagalog Region (Laguna and Rizal) and five provinces in the Central Luzon Region (Bulacan, Nueva Ecija, Pangasinan, Pampanga and Tarlac) constitute the largest contiguous rice-producing area in the Philippines, commonly referred to as the 'rice bowl' (see Figure 4.1). Despite their contiguity, the agrarian structures of the seven provinces are not homogeneous. We divide the region into two sub-regions: the Coastal Region; and Inner Central Luzon. The Coastal Region includes Laguna, Rizal, the southern parts of Bulacan and Pampanga, and the northern part of Pangasinan. Inner Central Luzon encompasses the remaining landlocked area.

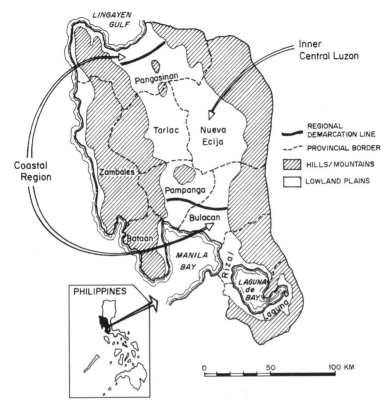

Figure 4.1   Two regions with different agrarian structures in the Central Plain of
Luzon, Philippines

Most areas in the Coastal Region are easily accessible by sea or lake,
and have a long history of settlement. Laguna, southern Bulacan and
Pampanga were major suppliers of rice to Manila before Inner Central
Luzon developed as a rice-producing region in the late nineteenth and
early twentieth centuries.

Corresponding to the difference in settlement age, there is a major
difference in the pattern of land ownership. Both regions are characterized
by pervasive landlordism; however, land holdings in the Coastal Region
are relatively small and scattered. Land accumulation here proceeded piece
by piece, mainly through money-lending–mortgaging operations. In general,
the landlord–tenant relationship is a paternalistic one. The landlord patron-
izes the tenant by advancing credit and by using his/her connections

and influence, in return for the loyalty of the tenant (Anderson, 1964; Larkin, 1972).

In contrast, Inner Central Luzon saw the development of huge estates (*hacienda*) of several hundred to thousands of hectares that originated from royal grants and purchases of undeveloped royal domain. The land-lord–tenant relationship in the large *haciendas* with their hundreds or thousands of tenants was inevitably less paternalistic than in the Coastal Region. Typically, the *hacienda* owners lived in Manila, and management was carried out by a farm manager (*encargado*) and a number of overseers (*katiwala*) (Umehara, 1974). The tenure contract was geared to economic considerations and was enforced more rigorously by legal means than through a sense of obligation based on the patron–client relationship. As a result, the *haciendas* became a hotbed of tenant uprisings (Dalisay, 1937; Pelzer, 1945; Rivera and McMillan, 1954). The agrarian unrest spotlighted the need for the land reform programmes that have resulted in the demise of the *hacienda* system.

It is critically important to recognize that the agrarian structure of East Laguna Village before the land reforms was typical of the Coastal Region.

The Origins of Philippine Agrarian Structure

Philippine society before the Spanish conquest in the sixteenth century consisted of small communities called *barangay* – the term referred to the 'boat' in which Malayan migrants travelled to the Philippines. The migrants settled along the sea coasts and on riverbanks, and depended for their subsistence mainly on rice farming. Although no consensus has yet been established on the social structure of the *barangay*, it appears that class differentiation already existed before the Spanish conquest. Typically, the *barangay* consisted of chiefs (*datu*), freemen (*maharlica* or *timagua*), serfs or peons (*aliping namamahay*) and slaves (*aliping saguiguilid* or *saguiguilir*).[2] The slaves usually lived in quarters provided by their masters and worked under their direct supervision, but the serfs, whose status was based mainly on debt peonage, lived in their own houses and turned over to the master the output of half the land they cultivated (Pelzer, 1945, p. 88; Corpuz, 1997, p. 18).

Land ownership was communal in the sense that the *barangay* had rights to a certain territory, and individual families had usufruct rights to specific parcels of land as long as they occupied it (Phelan, 1959, pp. 17–24). Because land was abundant and population scarce, usufruct rights could be obtained by a community member on the amount of land he/she could cultivate with the labour of his/her family and dependents.

The source of wealth and power was the control of labour, not land. The economy was at an earlier stage than that where stipulation of private property rights in land was required for efficient resource allocation.

At the Spanish conquest, the Philippines became the Spanish Crown's estate (*real hacienda*) (Corpuz, 1997, pp. 40–44). Legally all the lands belonged to the Crown and, *de facto*, other than those on which native tillers' usufruct rights were approved were disposable by the Crown. Thus the Crown's private property rights were established over vast areas of uncultivated land, including much of the commons used by the natives; that provided a basis later for the establishment of large private estates through grant and purchase of the royal domain (*realenga*). Monastic orders such as the Augustinian and Franciscan friars acquired large land-holdings in the early period of the Spanish regime.

Introduction of the notion of private property rights in land brought the opportunity for the indigenous elites to encroach on communal land. The Spaniards were careful not to disturb the traditional organization of *barangay* communities and utilized them for ruling the native people. *Datu* and other leading families, or *casiques*, as they were called by the Spanish, were assigned the tasks of collecting taxes, organizing compul-sory labour services and administering justice at a local level. Often the *casique* advanced credit to the freemen for tax payments and, if they defaulted, established claims to both the land and labour of the indebted. In this process, debt peonage, conceived as an arrangement between *datu* and *namamahay*, shifted to a sharecropping arrangement between landlords and tenants called *kasamahan*, a Tagalog word meaning 'partnership'.

This social transformation progressed slowly during the first 200 years of the Spanish regime. Originally, the Spaniards were concerned mainly with the re-export of Chinese goods from Manila to Mexico by ship. Immense profits from the monopoly of the re-export trade resulted in a long neglect of the need to develop Philippine products for the export market (Larkin, 1972, p. 42). As both domestic and foreign demand for agricultural products was limited, land continued to be a relatively abun-dant resource. In such a situation the economic incentive to accumulate land was also limited, even though the legal notion of private property rights in land had been introduced.

Two Types of Landlordism

Incentives to private landholding increased sharply with the expansion in the external demand for Philippine products through trade liberalization in the late eighteenth and early nineteenth centuries. The British occupation of Manila (1762–64) during the Seven Years' War, and the subsequent opening of Manila and other ports to foreign commerce and shipping resulted in a sharp increase in the demand for commercial crops such as sugar, indigo and tobacco. Farmland became scarce, which stimulated local elites to establish their exclusive rights to the use of land.

The development of landlordism was facilitated by the commercial operations of Chinese *mestizos* (who were of mixed Chinese and native Filipino stock) in the anciently-settled Coastal Region. Since before the time of trade liberalization, and in response to the expanding needs of Manila, the Chinese and Chinese *mestizos* had developed internal trade and gained control of trading posts along the littorals of Manila Bay, the Laguna de Bay and major rivers. With the commercial wealth they accumulated, the *mestizos* began to acquire land by lending money to native landholders. In a money-lending arrangement called *pacto de retroventa*, the lender secured control of the land as a mortgage for his/her loan. During the loan period, the borrower continued to cultivate the land as a sharecropper of his/her creditor. If the borrower was unable to repay the loan at the termination of the loan period, he/she relinquished claim to the land to cover the debt (McLennan, 1969, pp. 659–60).

Land acquisitions by means of the *pacto de retroventa* arrangement increased in number in the late eighteenth century with the growth of commercial agriculture, despite Spanish attempts to prohibit the use of this device by the Chinese and Chinese mestizos. In the process, not only the usufruct rights of small peasants' but also many of the holdings of traditional elites (*datu-casique*), characterized by those who fell into debt because of their weakness for conspicuous consumption, were transferred to the hands of Chinese *mestizos*. Over time, the *mestizos* and the *casiques* intermarried and fused into a land-owning elite class called the *principalia* (Larkin, 1972, pp. 48–56). *The pacto de retroventa* arrangement vastly expanded landlordism in the form of the sharecropping system rooted in *barangay* communities. Because the land acquired by this device was in small parcels, the pattern of land ownership defined in the eighteenth and early nineteenth centuries for the anciently settled areas of the Coastal Region was 'scattered holdings', as characterized by McLennan (1969, p. 661).

In the sharecropping system, typically both output and production costs were shared equally by landlord and tenant. As mentioned previously, the landlord–tenant relationship was generally paternalistic in the Coastal Region. The majority of small- and medium-sized landlords lived in local towns (*poblacion*) and had close contacts with their tenants. The landlord patronized his tenants by advancing credit and utilizing his connections and social influence, in return for the tenants' loyalty: 'In a society built on patronage, having such a patron is highly valued' (Murray, 1972, p. 161). To behave like a benevolent patron was an efficient way for a landlord to establish his/her status as a legitimate member of the elite, and the least costly way to protect his/her property and to enforce his/her contract with the tenants in the local community.

In contrast to the scattered holdings in the Coastal Region, huge estates (*hacienda*) of several hundreds or thousands of hectares were developed in Inner Central Luzon. According to McLennan (1969, pp. 665–7) the *hacienda* system originated in the *inquilino* or *inquilinato* system in the friar estates located in the environs of the coastal area along Manila Bay. Stimulated by expanding trade in rice and sugar, many of the monastic orders began to lease pasture and idle land to agricultural entrepreneurs. These lessees (*inquilino*) turned the task of cultivation over to sharecroppers, paid a fixed rent to the landowners, and reaped the middlemen's profits.

Private *haciendas* were established through royal grants and purchases of royal domain. This process of land acquisition by the Spaniards began in the eighteenth century after the removal of restrictions on Spanish residence in the provinces. The royal grants and large-scale purchases were concentrated at the frontiers of settlement – Inner Central Luzon – 'which accounts for the distribution of today's large haciendas' (McLennan, 1969, p. 668).

Until the late nineteenth century, most areas in Inner Central Luzon were covered by jungle, and the large *haciendas* were primarily engaged in cattle ranching. The cattle raising ended during the 1880s when a series of rinderpest and foot-and-mouth disease epidemics decimated cattle herds. Subsequently, the *haciendas* located in the lowland areas developed a system of rice monoculture run by the tenants who had migrated from Ilocos and Southern Tagalog, while those located in upland areas were converted to sugar plantations.

In the early stage of the development of rice *haciendas*, the common tenure arrangement was the fixed-rent leasehold (*canon*). The *hacienderos* gave parcels gratis to settlers for the period of land opening, and requested only nominal rents even after the gratis period ended. However, as the population and the labour force grew, the *canon* was raised gradually, and finally it shifted into the sharecropping system (Hester and Mabbun, 1924).

Attempts to increase land rent and to expand the holdings of *haciendas* through land-grabbing during the period of land title registration aroused peasants' indignation. The Spanish government issued royal decrees in 1880 and 1894, in an attempt to encourage landholders to secure formal titles, with the intention of promoting commercial agricultural production. Later, the American government initiated cadastral surveys and land registration under the Torrens system. These government policy attempts to modernize land registry opened up rare opportunities for land-grabbing by a powerful elite. Where the majority of illiterate peasants, accustomed to unwritten rules of land tenure, were ignorant about the new laws, unscrupulous elites registered their land to claim extensive areas occupied by smallholders (McLennan, 1969, p. 673; Pelzer, 1945, pp. 89–90 and 108–10). This process occurred in the Coastal Region too, but it was more pervasive in the frontier areas of Inner Central Luzon, where the power structure was more unevenly distributed and where indigenous property-rights relations were less clearly established in local communities. Agrarian unrest in Inner Central Luzon was thus deeply rooted in the historical process of land accumulation.

The landlord–tenant relationship in large *haciendas* was inevitably less paternalistic and based on more strict contracts.[3] The *hacienda* owner living in Manila generally had no personal contact with his/her tenants and little concern for the tenants' personal problems. Unlike the small- and the medium-sized landlords in the Coastal Region, they were powerful enough to protect their property through the police and a private army, and to enforce contracts by legal means. In general, *kasamas* were bound to the *hacienda* by perpetual debt, which often forced them to surrender most of their produce to the *hacienda* manager at harvest time. It was natural that the class confrontation between landlords and tenants was sharpest in the *hacienda* areas of Inner Central Luzon, as represented by the *Hukbalahap* (or *Huk*) revolt as a continuation of the resistance movement against the Japanese army during the Second World War (Kerkvliet, 1977).

Land Reform in the Philippines

Land reform programmes have long been envisioned as a means of coping with mounting agrarian unrest.

Land reform was first envisaged by the independent Filipino government at Malolos during the 1896–99 revolution against Spain. As the first step, the friar estates were confiscated and distributed among the peasants. But the Treaty of Paris (1898), which concluded the Spanish–American War, bound the USA to protect the property rights of the monastic orders in the new territory ceded from Spain. In order to avoid agrarian conflicts, the American occupation administration decided to buy these estates, while crushing the Filipino Republic (Corpuz, 1997, pp. 216, 266–70). Government purchase of private estates for redistribution among smallholders was also undertaken during the Commonwealth period for an intended transition to independence from 1935 to 1946, but it was never implemented on a large scale (Murray, 1972, p. 154).

Another measure was government regulation of landlord–tenant relations. In 1933, under the Administration of Governor General Theodore Roosevelt, the Philippine legislature passed the Rice Share Tenancy Act (Public Act No. 4054) aimed at protecting share tenants against abuses by landlords. However, the law could come into effect 'only in provinces where the majority of the municipal councils shall, by resolutions, petition for its application to the Governor General'. With this provision the law was ineffective, because the *principalia* controlled the municipalities. Subsequent amendments designed to make the law effective were invalidated by the resistance of the *principalia* class (Kerkvliet, 1971; Pelzer, 1945, pp. 98–101).

The need for land reform was more keenly felt with the *Huk* revolt in the period immediately following the Second World War. The US government, seriously involved by then in the Cold War, obliged the Philippine government to undertake social reforms as a condition for receiving aid. In this connection, Robert Hardie, a land reform specialist, was sent to the Philippines by the American Mutual Security Agency. The Hardie Report (1952) recommended (a) the abolition of tenancy; (b) the establishment of owner-operated family-sized farms; and (c) fair tenancy practices. This report paved the way for a reform programme under President Ramon Magsaysay. Magsaysay, who had led the battle to subdue the *Huk* rebellion, was well aware of the social unrest that supported the *Huk* movement. The Magsaysay reform was based on the Agricultural Tenancy Act (Republic Act No. 1199) in 1954 and the Land Reform Act (Republic Act No. 1400) in 1955; the former was intended to enforce fair tenancy practices and the latter was designed to expropriate and redistribute large estates. Because of resistance from the landed interests, in the process of passage by the Congress both Acts were so watered down as to leave little of the original proposal intact (Wurfel, 1958). The Land Tenure Administration was set up for the expropriation and redistribution of large estates. However, the estates to which the programme was applicable were limited to those larger than 300 hectares and petitioned by a majority of tenants. Because of landlord resistance, inefficient administration and inadequate financial backing, the total area expropriated by the Land Tenancy Administration during the first six years after its establishment was less than 20 000 hectares (Takigawa, 1976, p. 23).

The Agricultural Land Reform Code, enacted in 1963 under President Diosdado Macapagal, represented a major advance in agrarian reform legislation, in line with the liberal reform tradition aimed at achieving social stability and economic progress by emancipating peasants from 'feudal' bondage. The stated goal was 'to establish owner-cultivatorship and the economic family-sized farm...to make the small farmers more independent, self-reliant and responsible citizens, and a source of genuine strength in our democracy' (Section 2, Republic Act No. 3844). Macapagal, the son of a peasant in Pampanga, saw land reform as a critical counter-measure against the latent danger of Communist infiltration into the rural sector, a danger compounded by the growing tension in South-east Asia with the spread of the Vietnam War. His idea was supported by the urban industrialist class fostered by the import-substitution industrialization policy that began in the 1950s (Takigawa, 1976, pp. 31–7). The interests of urban commerce and industry were reflected in a stipulation of the Code that one of the reform goals were to 'divert landlord capital to industrial development' (Section 2).

A new aspect of the Agricultural Land Reform Code distinct from earlier legislation was that land reform was considered to be a major means of increasing agricultural productivity. As stated in the Code, 'to create a truly viable social and economic structure in agriculture conducive to greater productivity and higher farm incomes'. As Vernon Ruttan (1964) pointed out, the emphasis on the role of land-tenure reform in raising agricultural productivity was based on young economist-technocrats' assumptions of inefficient resource allocation under the sharecropping arrangement according to traditional neoclassical theory (so-called 'Marshallian inefficiency'). But more basically it reflected the demands of urban commerce and industry for rapid gains in agricultural productivity to ensure the supply of cheap food for urban workers in order to keep their living costs and wages low. To achieve the goal of high productivity, the Code made provision for the creation of the Agricultural Credit Administration and the Agricultural Productivity Commission to advance credit and technical extension services to small landholders.

The major thrust of the Code was the creation of owner-cultivatorship in rice and corn lands by means of confiscation of lands from landlords above landlords' retention limit of 75 hectares and distributing them to tenants on the lands. The reform procedures, as modified by Presidential Decrees No. 2 and No. 27 under the Martial Law proclaimed in 1972 by Ferdinand Marcos, involved two steps: first, 'Operation Leasehold', which converted share tenancy to leasehold tenancy with a rent fixed at a rate of 25 per cent of average harvest for the three normal years preceding the Operation; and, second, 'Operation Land Transfer', which transferred land ownership to tenants. In the latter operation, the government expropriated land in excess of the landlords' retention limit, with compensation to land-lords being 10 per cent of the land value in cash and the rest in interest-free redeemable Land Bank bonds. The land was resold to the tenants for annual mortgage payments over twenty-five years, while they were granted 'Certificates of Land Transfer' (CLT). Upon completion of the mortgage payments, the CLT holders are given 'Emancipation Patents' (EP) on the lands: that is, a land ownership title with the restricted right of land sale. Relative to Operation Leasehold, Operation Land Transfer takes a much longer time to complete as it involves costly and time-consuming exercises such as cadastral surveying/mapping, land valuation and mortgage payments.

Land reform operations based on the 1963 Agricultural Land Reform Code were limited mainly to pilot areas in Central Luzon, and its imple-mentation at any level of intensity was confined to the pilot project in Nueva Ecija Province (de los Reyes, 1972). President Marcos extended land reform to the whole nation in 1972, with automatic conversion of all share tenants to leaseholders with his Presidential Decrees. The landlord's retention limit was reduced successively from 75 to 7 hectares, and the mortgage period was shortened to fifteen years.

It is easy to enumerate the shortcomings of the Marcos reform pro-grammes. The retention limit was still too high compared with average farm size, and it was often evaded by registering excess holdings in the names of relatives and friends. The land reform applied only to tenanted land planted with rice and corn and did not apply to land under the direct administration of landlords. Nor did it apply to land used for cash crops such as sugar. Therefore it was a widespread practice for landlords to expand the area under their direct management by evicting tenants under the guise of voluntary submission of land from tenants to landlords, or to plant sugar in paddy land. Collusion between the landed elite and local officials often invalidated the effects of the land reform programmes. Operation Land Transfer was particularly tedious, and its effects have been limited (Putzel, 1992; Riedinger, 1995; Takigawa, 1994).

Despite such apparent failures, it was the fact that large *haciendas* were broken up, and that most tenants established their status as leaseholders or mortgaged owners during the 1970s, though sizeable areas remained under the landlords' direct administration (Hayami, Quisumbing and Adriano, 1990, ch. 4; Umehara, 1992, 1997).[4] After the reform, its beneficiaries were able to gain a large economic surplus because rice yields increased significantly because of irrigation development and the application of new varieties and fertilizers, while both rent and mortgage payments remained fixed. Thus the land reform was successful in transferring much of the economic return to land from absentee landlords to ex-sharecroppers. On the other hand, it produced inefficiency in land use, as the reform regulations made land market inactive. It also created serious income inequality within village communities because no direct gain accrued to landless labourers, whose income did not rise or even declined because the strong population pressure on land prevented their wages from rising despite agricultural productivity increases.

These are the aspects that will be scrutinized in relation to East Laguna Village.

REFORMS OF LAND TENURE RELATIONS

Both the environmental and socioeconomic conditions surrounding East Laguna Village are typical of the Coastal Region as defined in the previous section. Detailed historical accounts of the changes of land tenure relations in East Laguna Village since the 1960s will develop a clear image of the nature of agrarian change in the Coastal Region under the land reform programmes.

Among our village surveys, the one conducted in 1976 was especially focused and detailed on land tenure relations. Therefore, in historical comparisons in this chapter, the 1976 data are commonly used as a benchmark.

Transfers of Land Ownership

As in other rice-producing areas in the Philippines, including both the Coastal Region and Inner Central Luzon, East Laguna Village is characterized by pervasive absentee landlordism.

The coconut grove under which the villagers' houses are located covered 15.7 hectares (see Table 4.1). In 1976, the area owned by the villagers was only 13 per cent of the total coconut land, but had increased to 42 per cent by 1995. The coconut land has not been subjected to the land reform programmes, though expansion of the programmes beyond the subsistence crop to the cash crop sector was prescribed in the Comprehensive Agrarian Law of 1988. Yet transfer of the coconut land from absentee landlords to villagers has progressed rapidly, because the fear of possible future confiscation prompted landlords to sell the land. A strong incentive has also operated among villagers, especially among relatively well-to-do large farmers and non-farm workers, to establish ownership of their residential plots, because sharp increases in the price of residential land in the town of Pila and along the highways are expected to be transmitted to East Laguna Village.

Table 4.1   Land area and use, East Laguna Village, 1976, 1987, and 1995

		Area (ha)			Percentage of area owned by villagers
		Owned[c] by		Total	
		Villagers	Absentees		
1976	Paddy fields[a]	2.4 (0)	105.8	108.2	2 (0)
	Coconut land[b]	2.1	13.6	15.7	13
	Total	4.5	119.4	123.9	4
1987	Paddy fields[a]	16.4 (8.1)	72.2	88.6	19 (9)
	Coconut land[b]	6.5	9.2	15.7	41
	Total	22.9	81.4	104.3	22
1995	Paddy fields[a]	33.3 (9.3)	63.7	97.0	34 (10)
	Coconut land[b]	6.6	9.1	15.7	42
	Total	39.9	72.8	112.7	35

Notes: [a]Area cultivated by villagers.
[b]Residences located under coconut trees.
[c]CLT holders are considered as owners. CLT areas, including those rented out to other village farmers, are shown in parentheses.

As explained in the previous chapter, it is difficult to measure paddy area belonging to this village unambiguously, because the village border is not clearly defined. In terms of area cultivated by villagers, this was 108.2 hectares in 1976, of which only about 2 per cent was owned by villagers (see Table 4.1). If we define 'area owned by villagers' as including the area cultivated by the holders of Certificates of Land Transfer (CLT) who have not yet paid up mortgages to the Land Bank (which is the legal owner), owner-cultivated land is increased rapidly from 2.4 hectares in 1976 to 16.4 hectares in 1987, and further to 33.3 hectares, or a third of total paddy area, in 1995, reflecting the slow but steady progress of Operation Land Transfer. If we exclude the area under CLT, however, owner-cultivated land was 24 hectares, or a quarter of total paddy area in the village, in 1995. The area on which CLT has been conferred so far is about 15 hectares, of which 9.3 hectares are still mortgaged.

This rather limited coverage of Operation Land Transfer was based on the structure of landlordism in this village as being typical of the Coastal Region: that is, characterized by small, scattered holdings by small- to medium-sized landlords. According to our 1976 survey, only 1 out of 61 landlords owning paddy fields in East Laguna Village owned more than

7 hectares (see Table 4.2). Fifty-seven out of 61 landlords were resident outside the village, 32 of whom lived in the municipality of Pila, 19 in local towns in Laguna and neighbouring provinces, and 6 in Manila. This pattern represents a sharp contrast to that of Inner Central Luzon, where large contiguous estates or haciendas – often one *hacienda* covered one whole village or even more – used to prevail and most *hacienda* owners used to live in Manila.

A major change occurring between 1976 and 1995 was the large increase in the number of resident landowners in the village and their holdings at the expense of absentee landlords. In particular, those living in Manila decreased from six to one, and their holdings from 17.4 to 1.5 hectares. Yet, as of 1995, rice land owned by villagers was only a third of

Table 4.2   Distribution of landlords owning paddy fields in East Laguna Village, 1976, 1987 and 1995[a]

Distribution	1976		1987		1995	
	Landlords (no.)	Area owned (ha)	Landlords (no.)	Area owned (ha)	Landlords (no.)	Area owned (ha)
By residence						
East Laguna Village[b]	4	2.4	14	16.4	32	33.3
Towns or other villages in the same municipality	32	60.0	22	43.9	28	37.8
Other municipalities in Laguna	7	8.8	8	9.9	3	5.5
Neighbouring provinces[c]	12	19.6	13	14.0	12	18.9
Manila	6	17.4	4	4.4	1	1.5
Total	61	108.2	61	88.6	76	97.0
By ownership size						
<1 ha	15	7.5	21	9.5	27	9.9
1–2.9 ha	36	53.6	34	50.8	42	65.8
3–6.9 ha	9	33.5	5	17.1	3	11.2
>6.9 ha	1	13.6	1	11.2	1	10.1
Total	61	108.2	61	88.6	73	97.0

Notes: [a]Paddy fields cultivated by villagers, not including areas owned outside East Laguna Village.
[b]Include non-cultivating owners and mortgaged CLT holders.
[c]Include Batangas, Rizal and Cavite.

that they cultivated. Because not so many landlords holding lands in East Laguna Village owned more than the limit of 7 hectares they were allowed to retain under land reform laws, relatively little of their land was subjected to Operation Land Transfer. Thus, ex-tenants who were given CLT from the Department of Agrarian Reform remained in a minority among farmers in this village. Although the effect of Operation Land Transfer was not insignificant, a much larger transfer in land ownership to villagers occurred through purchases of the ownership titles by well-to-do leasehold tenants on the lands they cultivated, whose incomes increased because of low fixed rents under Operation Leasehold. A more important source of money for villagers' land purchases were remittances from well-educated family members with lucrative urban jobs, including overseas employment in such places as Saudi Arabia. The same applies also to the purchase of residential plots in the coconut area.

Tenancy Reform

In East Laguna Village, a much greater impact from land reform was produced by tenancy reform under Operation Leasehold than by Operation Land Transfer, at least during the 1970s and early 1980s.

Traditionally, the commonest form of land tenure contract in East Laguna Village was the sharecrop tenancy, with output and cost shared 50:50. The most common arrangement was 100 per cent of the cost of land preparation was borne by tenants, 100 per cent of the irrigation fee was borne by landlords, and other costs, including seeds, fertilizers and chemicals, planting, weeding, harvesting and threshing, were shared equally. There were variations: for example, where the whole cost of fertilizers and chemicals in addition to the irrigation fee was shouldered by landlords. Leasehold tenancy was limited to a small number of large farmers settled before the land reform began.

The landlord–tenant relationship was usually a paternalistic one, and no written contracts were exchanged before the land reform. Contract enforcement was mainly based on a sense of reciprocity under a patron–client relationship. Although the tenants had no legal claim to land, their tenure position was fairly secure and they were seldom evicted except for significant misconduct. The security of tenure might partly be explained by the history of the settlement of this area. In the process of settlement, landlords gave settlers land parcels gratis and advanced credits for subsistence during the period of land opening, with the understanding that they would enter into a sharecropping arrangement after the gratis period. Therefore, the *de facto* right of tenants to till the land that they or their

A Rice Village Saga

ancestors opened has been assumed in the local community. The eviction of a tenant involved in no major misconduct will bring social opprobrium upon the landlord.

In 1966, before the land reform programmes were extended to this area, 80 per cent of farms and 63 per cent of paddy areas were under share contracts (see Tables 4.3 and 4.4). As Operation Leasehold began in this village from 1968, and was strengthened by the proclamation of Martial Laws in 1972, the incidence of sharecropping declined sharply, to 40 per cent of farms and 27 per cent of area in 1976. The incidence of share tenancy declined further over time to only 12 per cent of farms and 15 per cent of area in 1995. Correspondingly, the share of farms under leasehold arrangement increased from only 19 per cent in 1966 to 68 per cent in 1976. The share of leasehold farmers decreased between 1976 and 1995, but this was more than compensated for by increases in

Table 4.3   Distribution of farms by tenure status, East Laguna Village, 1966–95[a]

	Tenure status	*Farms*		*Average size per farm (ha)*
		(No.)	*(%)*	
1966	Owner/part owner	2	4	5.2
	Leasehold	7	15	2.6
	Share	35	76	1.9
	Leasehold/share	2	4	5.0
	Total	46	100	2.3
1976	Owner/part owner	3	6	3.7
	Leasehold	29	54	1.7
	Share	14	26	1.8
	Leasehold/share	8	14	3.0
	Total	54	100	2.0
1987	Owner/part owner	12	23	1.9
	Leasehold	27	51	1.5
	Share	10	19	1.8
	Leasehold/share	4	7	1.9
	Total	53	100	1.7
1995	Owner/part owner	22	43	1.8
	Leasehold	23	45	1.6
	Share	2	4	3.9
	Leasehold/share	4	8	3.0
	Total	51	100	1.9

Note: [a]Sublet areas are grouped according to the mode of rent paid to the first tenant.

Table 4.4   Distribution of plots by tenure status, East Laguna Village, 1966–95

	Tenure status	Plots		Area	
		(No.)	*(%)*	*(ha)*	*(%)*
1966	Owned	2	3	1.3	1
	Leasehold	12	19	29.9	29
	Sharecrop	44	70	66.1	63
	Sublet	5	8	6.9	7
	Pawning arrangement	1		0.5	
	Sharecrop arrangement	4		6.4	
	Total	63	100	104.2	100
1976	Owned	3	3	1.7	2
	Leasehold	44	48	67.7	63
	Sharecrop	30	32	29.7	27
	Sublet	16	17	9.1	8
	Pawning arrangement	5		1.5	
	Leasehold arrangement	2		0.8	
	Sharecrop arrangement	9		6.8	
	Total	93	100	108.2	100
1987	Owned[a]	14	17	11.6	13
	Leasehold	39	46	46.1	52
	Sharecrop	21	25	21.9	25
	Sublet	10	12	9.0	10
	Pawning arrangement	3		1.4	
	Leasehold arrangement	3		1.8	
	Sharecrop arrangement	4		5.8	
	Total	84	100	88.6	100
1995	Owned[a]	25	31	28.0	29
	Pawning of ownership	2	2	0.8	1
	Leasehold	37	46	47.7	49
	Sharecrop	13	16	14.6	15
	Sublet	4	5	5.9	6
	Pawning arrangement	2		3.5	
	Sharecrop arrangement	2		2.4	
	Total	81	100	97.0	100

Note: [a]Includes CLT land.

owner/part-owner farmers as a result of progress in Operation Land Transfer. In 1995, the combined share of leasehold tenants and owner farmers was 96 per cent, cultivating nearly 80 per cent of the paddy area.

However, despite a law denouncing share tenancy (Republic Act 3844, Section 2), nearly 30 per cent of the rice area was still under the sharecrop contract in 1976, and 15 per cent remained so in 1995. Share tenants could obtain leasehold titles if they applied to the Municipal Office of

Agrarian Reform. So why did they not try to change their status? The answer was that their landlords were either relatives or friends who had been good to them. Such attitudes reflect the social norm of reciprocity involving '*utang na loob*' (debt of gratitude).

Operation Leasehold resulted in a significant income transfer from landlord to tenant, because leasehold rent was fixed at 25 per cent of average rice yield for three normal years preceding the year of programme implementation. Land rent in the traditional sharecropping arrangements is considered to be about 40 per cent of total rice output after subtracting production costs shared by landlords from the 50 per cent share of gross output. Therefore an income transfer from landlords to tenants through Operation Leasehold was about 15 per cent of rice output (40 per cent minus 25 per cent) at the time of programme's implementation. A similar income gain should have accrued to holders of CLT under Operation Land Transfer, because the annual mortgage payment was usually set at about the same level as the controlled leasehold rent.

Under the fixed rent and mortgage payment, income gains to the land reform beneficiaries continued to increase automatically when rice yields increased because of the development and diffusion of new rice technology. In 1966, rent paid by traditional leaseholders was about 19 per cent. From 1966 to 1976, rice yield per hectare increased by more than 35 per cent, but leasehold rent also increased at about the same rate, so that the share of rent in output remained at 19 per cent (Table 4.5). Average leasehold rent per hectare increased during this period because the rents determined on lands converted from share to leasehold tenancy by Operation Leasehold were generally set higher than the rents on traditional leasehold lands.[5] The share of leasehold rent decreased to about 16 per cent in 1987, and to about 14 per cent in 1995, corresponding to yield increases, while the absolute magnitude of leasehold rent in kind remained largely the same.

Income Redistribution

As the result of the reform programmes, the share of income (in terms of gross value added) from rice farming that accrued to farmers in the village increased at the expense of land owners who lived in towns (see Table 4.6). The income share of landlords decreased precipitously from the pre-reform level of more than 40 per cent in the mid-1960s to about 30 per cent in the late 1970s, and further down to only about 10 per cent in 1995. Meanwhile, major gains in the income share accrued to farmers, while hired labourers' gains were relatively modest; this reflects the differential impacts of land reform between farmers and agricultural labourers.

Table 4.5   Changes in average rent and yield per hectare of land under leasehold tenancy (in paddy), East Laguna Village, 1966–95

Year	Season	Leasehold rent (kg/ha) (1)	Yield (kg/ha) (2)	Share of rent (%) (1)/(2)
1966[a]	Wet	414	2 448	16.9
	Dry	581	2 723	21.3
	Total	995	5 171	19.2
1976[b]	Wet	556	3 244	17.1
	Dry	751	3 549	21.2
	Total	1 307	6 793	19.2
1979	Wet	551	3 418	16.1
	Dry	744	3 900	19.1
	Total	1 295	7 318	17.7
1987	Wet	603	3 944	15.3
	Dry	745	4 233	17.6
	Total	1 348	8 177	16.5
1995[c]	Wet	591	4 015	14.7
	Dry	684	5 417	12.6
	Total	1 275	9 432	13.5

Notes: [a]Based on farmers' recollections in 1976 survey.
[b]1974–6 averages.
[c]1995–6 averages.

However, the possibility must be recognized that agricultural labourers' income share increased faster than the income share of 'hired labourers', as shown in Table 4.6, because the earlier the period, the higher the percentage of hired labour provided in the form of mutual employment among farmers. It is likely that farmers' labour employed by neighbouring farmers has been replaced progressively by the work of agricultural labourers.

In any case, the experience in East Laguna Village shows unambiguously that land reform in the Philippines, despite its many shortcomings, resulted in a major income transfer from rich landlords living in towns to poorer people in villages, thereby contributing much to a reduction in income inequality in the rural sector, including local towns.

EMERGENCE OF ALTERNATIVE MARKETS

Land reform programmes are characterized by strong regulations on land markets, such as the protection of tenancy rights and control of land rents

Table 4.6   Shares of income from rice production per hectare among farmers, hired labourers and land owners, East Laguna Village, 1966–95[a]

Season	Gross value added		Farmer[a]	Hired labourer	Land owner[b]
	Rough rice equivalent (kg/ha)	Percentage	(%)	(%)	(%)
Wet season					
1966[c]	1750	100	33	23	44
1976	2490[d]	100	42	29	29
1982	2910[e]	100	50	26	24
1987	3530	100	50	26	24
1995	3230[f]	100	53	35	12
Dry season					
1965	1860	100	29	24	47
1979	3320[g]	100	50	24	26
1987	3830	100	49	25	26
1995	4580[f]	100	61	28	11

Notes: [a]Includes all factor payments for capital, in addition to those for family labour and operator's surplus.
  [b]Include mortgage payments of CLT holders to the Land Bank.
  [c]Obtained from yields given in Table 5.2 (see page 110) and factor shares in Table 5.12 (see page 126), whiile estimating wage paid to hired labourers and land rent paid to landlords by the method used in Table 5.4 (see page 114).
  [d]Average for 1974–7.
  [e]Average for 1979–82.
  [f]Average for 1995–6.
  [g]Average for 1978–82.

below the market-clearing rates. These regulations were effective in transferring the incomes from land from landlord to tenant but, at the same time, the reform made the land-rental market inactive. 'Alternative markets' were developed to evade the reform regulations.

Sub-Tenancy Arrangements

One form of alternative market is a sub-tenancy by which a leasehold tenant rents out part (or the whole) of his/her operational holding to other farmers or agricultural labourers, and extracts from the sub-lessee a rent revenue over the payment to his landlord that is fixed at lower-than-market rates by land reform laws.

It must be noted, however, that sub-tenancy was practised in this village even before land reform. As has already been explained, tenants' security of tenure was traditionally strong, especially for some of the large farmers descended from the initial settlers who opened the new lands. Among these large farmers the incidence of leasehold tenancy was not exceptional, particularly with landlords who lived far away from the village and therefore found it difficult to ascertain rice yields and collect share rents. In such cases, land rents were rather sticky relative to changes in rice yields, partly because of imperfect information and partly because of the time lag involved in contract renegotiation. For example, a large farmer, the son of an initial settler, was under a leasehold contract with a landlord living in a remote town, paying rent of 40 *cavans* of paddy (about 1700 kg) for 2.5 hectares of land. The landlord had not realized that double-cropping had been practised since the extension of the national irrigation system in 1958, and when he found this out in 1968, he demanded an additional rental payment of 23 *cavans* for the dry season crop. However, he was successful in raising the rent only by 9 *cavans,* but in 1975, when a written contract was exchanged as a part of the land reform programme, the farmer agreed to increase the rent by another 14 *cavans* in order to secure the landlord's signature. Sometimes traditional leasehold tenants, as this example, entered into sub-tenancy contracts with other villagers and pocketed the difference between the rent received from sub-tenants and the rent paid to the original landlord.

Indeed, the average share of leasehold rent in rice output in East Laguna Village was below 20 per cent in 1966, less than half the rent accrued to landlords under the traditional sharecropping contract involving 50:50 sharing of both output and cost (see Table 4.5). This gap between leasehold rent and share rent was the force underlying the practice of sub-tenancy even before the land reform.

Sub-tenancy can be classified into three types. In the first, the sub-lessor and the sub-lessee share output and costs on a 50:50 basis; this is the most common type. In the second type, the sub-lessor receives a fixed rent from the sub-lessee. This is a rather special type limited to the cases in which parents sub-lease their tenanted land to their children. In the third type, the sub-lessor puts his/her land in pawn to the sub-lessee; in other words, the sub-lessee advances credit to the sub-lessor in order to establish a right to cultivate the land until the loan is repaid.

As expected, the incidence of sub-tenancy began to increase as the Leasehold Operation converted many sharecroppers into leaseholders. The number of land plots under sub-tenancy contracts increased from five in 1966 to sixteen in 1976 (see Table 4.4). Thereafter, however, the number of sub-tenancy plots decreased, returning to only four in 1995, despite continued wide difference between economic rent and controlled leasehold rent. The reason was the high risk for land-reform beneficiaries involved in sub-tenancy arrangements. Sub-tenancy is illegal in terms of the land reform laws (Republic Act No. 3844, Section 27). If a sub-lessee reports to the Municipal Office of Agrarian Reform and proves that he or she is the cultivator of the land, he or she can obtain a formal title of lease-hold tenancy, and his/her lessor's title is forfeited. In fact, in 1980 one sub-lessor dared to take such a legal action and succeeded in establishing himself as a formal tenant. Naturally, this incident strongly discouraged leaseholders from using sub-tenancy contracts thereafter, except within a narrow circle of relatives and close friends.

Transactions of Land Cultivation Rights

The sub-tenancy arrangements were developed as a device to bypass land reform regulations adjusting operational farm size to an operator's entre-preneurial ability or family labour endowment. The land-pawning type of sub-tenancy was also used as a means of easing the credit constraint under the condition that neither the CLT nor the leasehold title was allowed to be used as collateral for institutional loans. However, transaction costs for sub-lessors were high because of the possible penalties involved if the transaction was discovered by officials.

An alternative to the land-pawning arrangement for land reform benefi-ciaries to mobilize finance from the usufruct rights on land is to sell their cultivation rights. Unlike the pawning arrangement, the sale of leasehold titles can be made legally (although the sale of the CLT is illegal) if a seller is able to obtain the signature of his/her landlord to the effect that the landlord accepts voluntary surrender of the land from the selling tenant and agrees to designate the buyer as a new tenant. The landlord may well agree if he or she is offered a reasonable compensation. It must be noted that the transfer of leasehold cultivation rights with compensation (*kara-patan*) was also practised before the land reform.[6]

The sales of tenancy rights increased between the 1960s and 1970s, par-allel to the increase in the incidence of sub-tenancy, and corresponding to the implementation of Operation Leasehold (see Table 4.7). During this period, the deflated price of tenancy rights increased, while that of land ownership titles decreased. This apparent anomaly arose from the fact that the values of land ownership titles recorded in Table 4.7 were for those with tenants on the land. The buyer of the land had to pay for the eviction of tenants in order to recover his right to use the 'top of the soil'. It seems

Table 4.7   Transactions and price of paddy land ownership and tenancy rights, East Laguna Village, 1959–96

r	Ownership title				Tenancy right				Percentage of tenancy right price to ownership title price
	No.	*Area (ha)*	*Current price (P000/ha)*	*1995 price[a] (P000/ha)*	*No.*	*Area (ha)*	*Current price (P000/ha)*	*1995 price[a] (P000/ha)*	
59–65	3	7.8	6	135	4	8.4	1	12	9
66–70	4	5.3	13	211	11	14.3	1	16	8
71–5	5	5.3	13	114	12	16.7	3	22	19
76–80	n/a	n/a	n/a	n/a	12	20.6	9	52	n/a
81–5	2	3.3	56	260	19	22.3	13	54	21
86–90	4	3.1	98	213	7	6.8	41	85	40
91–6	4	5.9	353	390	14	14.6	82	93	24

te: [a]Deflated by the rough rice price index for Southern Tagalog area (1995 = 100).

reasonable to assume that this compensation for the eviction of tenants became more expensive as land reform programmes were consolidated. The real price of leasehold titles continued to rise, corresponding to increases in rice yield per hectare, until the late 1970s, when the yield began to stagnate.

Both the price of leasehold titles and the price of ownership titles began to rise sharply in the 1990s because of the increased expectation of the conversion of farmland for urban use following rapid increases in the price of industrial and residential land in places close to East Laguna Village.

After the mid-1970s, while the incidence of sub-tenancy declined, as observed in Table 4.4, the sale of tenancy rights continued at a high level. During the 1970s, sales to non-villagers increased. Tenanted land area sold by farmers in the village exceeded the area bought by farmers in the village by a wide margin (see Table 4.8); this implies a large net outflow of land cultivation rights from villagers. Buyers of the cultivation rights were either the original landlords or other relatively wealthy people in local towns engaging in urban occupations, such as teachers, government workers, local traders and manufacturers. In the main, they operated the farms with hired labour, either under their direct management or under the supervision of overseers. When they rented out land, tenants were selected from among close relatives and friends who would not create conflicts by resorting land reform laws.

The increased sales of cultivation rights do not necessarily reflect impoverishment of small leaseholders and CLT holders. Of course, there

Table 4.8   Transfer of paddy fields through purchase/sale, East Laguna Village, 1960–95 (ha)

| From \ To | Buy-in | | | | Total |
| | Small farmer | Large farmer | Non-villager | | |
			Landlord	Other	
Sell-out					
1960–9					
Small farmer	1.0	…	…	4.0	5.0
Large farmer	…[a]	…	…	…	
Non-villager	2.9	6.9	…	…	9.8
Total	3.9	6.9	…	4.0	14.8
1970–9					
Small farmer	0.8	2.3	9.2	4.8	17.1
Large farmer	…	2.0	5.0	8.9	15.9
Non-villager	0.5	…	…	…	0.5
Total	1.3	4.3	14.2	13.7	33.5
1980–7					
Small farmer	1.5	0.8	1.6	1.7	5.6
Large farmer	…	…	5.2	3.4	8.6
Non-villager	5.1	5.3	…	…	10.4
Total	6.6	6.1	6.8	5.1	24.6
1988–95					
Small farmer	1.0	1.1	0.4	0.3	2.8
Large farmer	…	…	4.4	2.0	6.4
Non-villager	3.2	4.3	…	…	7.5
Total	4.2	5.4	4.8	2.3	16.7

Note: [a] … stands for 'no case reported'.

were cases in which sellers lost their titles and slipped down to the rank of landless labourers as a result of excess consumption or misfortunes such as crop damage and sickness. But there were also cases in which they tried to mobilize funds for starting non-farm businesses, going abroad to work, or giving a higher education to children; these represented a process in which land reform beneficiaries transformed themselves from tillers of the land to the non-farm middle class. Growing incomes from non-farm activities by villagers, including remittances from children working outside the village, were later used in a significant part for the purchase of cultivation rights, or even of ownership title. As a result, villagers' purchases from non-villagers began to exceed villagers' sales to non-villagers in the 1980s.[7] Thus, investments in children's education, which had initially been financed from the sales of land cultivation rights by villagers, bore fruit with a time lag in the form of the children's increased earning capacity, and became a financial source for villagers to buy back the cultivation rights.

Closing of the Agricultural Ladder

Despite the development of alternative land markets, the agricultural ladder by which labourers ascend to farm operators seems to have significantly narrowed under land reform laws. The number of 'new farmers' defined as villagers who were newly established as farm operators (mainly from being agricultural labourers) decreased from twenty-five in the 1960s to seventeen in the 1970s (see Table 4.9). Meanwhile, the creation of new farmers through inheritance did not decline, while that from other routes decreased sharply, from twelve to four, reflecting the tendency of the agricultural ladder to be limited to the children of farmers. Understandably, the incidence of landlords' new land renting disappeared with Operation Leasehold in the 1970s, although it revived in the 1980s because some villagers who became land owners from non-farm incomes rented out their lands to relatives or close friends.

It may seem anomalous to observe decreases in the number of new farmers created by the use of sub-tenancy and the purchase of tenancy titles from the 1960s to the 1970s, despite the activation of these alternative land market transactions. This apparent anomaly reflects the fact

Table 4.9   Number of new farmers created within East Laguna Village by type of land acquisition, 1960–95[a]

Years	Inherited	Rented from landlords	Sublet from tenants	Purchase of tenancy right	Total
1960–9	13	3	8	1	25
	(52)	(12)	(32)	(4)	(100)
1970–9	13	0	4	0	17
	(76)	(0)	(24)	(0)	(100)
1980–6	7	4	4	1	16
	(44)	(25)	(25)	(6)	(100)
1987–95	7	1	1	0	9
	(78)	(11)	(11)	(0)	(100)

Note: [a]Percentages to totals are shown in parentheses.

that these transactions were more commonly practised among farmers than between farmers and agricultural labourers.

It is important to note that the limited incidence of sub-tenancy in the 1970s and thereafter was limited to transactions within the narrow circle of relatives and close friends because of its illegality, and therefore did not apply to the poorest segment of agricultural labourers who had no effective connection with well-to-do farmers. An alternative route to rise to become farm operators through the purchase of land cultivation rights was generally too narrow for agricultural labourers, because of their weak financial capacity in mobilizing funds for the purchase of land assets. Thus the agricultural ladder was virtually closed for 'pure' agricultural labourers, other than the children and relatives of farmers.

CHANGES IN THE DISTRIBUTION OF OPERATIONAL LANDHOLDINGS

As a typical case of 'land-to-tillers' programmes in Asia, the Philippine land reform aimed exclusively at reforming the land-tenure relationship between landlords and tenants. As such, the reform included no programme to change operational farm-size distribution. Yet some significant changes in the distribution of operational landholdings did occur in East Laguna Village in the process of land reform.

Relative to the major changes in land-tenure relations, the size distribution of operational holdings of paddy fields among farmers changed rather more modestly (see Table 4.10). Reflecting continued population pressure, a tendency can be observed for farm sizes to become smaller. The average operational holding per farm decreased from 2.3 hectares in 1966 to 2 hectares in 1976, and to 1.7 hectares in 1987, though it increased slightly to 1.9 hectares in 1995. Meanwhile, the percentage of farms below 2 hectares increased progressively from 46 per cent in 1966 to 64 per cent in 1995, and that of farms above 3 hectares decreased from 37 per cent to 20 per cent.

There is no significant tendency observed for lands to be concentrated in the hands of large farmers. The share of paddy land held by farmers above 3 hectares decreased from 62 per cent in 1966 to 50 per cent in 1995, while that above 4.9 hectares changed little, from 16 per cent to 18 per cent. The Gini coefficient to measure the concentration of operational land holdings among farmers increased from 0.34 in 1966 to 0.46 in 1995. This increase in inequality, however, was created not so much

Table 4.10 Size distribution of operational holdings of paddy field in East Laguna Village, 1966–95

| Years | Holding | Operational farm size[a] | | | | | | Average farm size [b] (ha) | Gini coefficient | |
		<1 ha	1–1.9 ha	2–2.9 ha	3–4.9 ha	>4.9 ha	Total		Farmer households	All households
1966	Farmers (no.)	5	16	8	14	3	46			
		(11)	(35)	(17)	(30)	(7)	(100)			
	Paddy area (ha)	2	20	17	48	17	104	2.3	0.34	0.54
		(2)	(20)	(16)	(46)	(16)	(100)			
1976	Farmers (no.)	13	20	8	11	2	54			
		(24)	(37)	(15)	(20)	(4)	(100)			
	Paddy area (ha)	6	28	19	41	14	108	2.0	0.40	0.71
		(6)	(26)	(17)	(38)	(13)	(100)			
1987	Farmers (no.)	14	23	7	7	2	53			
		(26)	(44)	(13)	(13)	(4)	(100)			
	Paddy area (ha)	7	31	16	24	11	89	1.7	0.41	0.79
		(8)	(35)	(18)	(27)	(12)	(100)			
1995	Farmers (no.)	13	20	8	8	2	51			
		(25)	(39)	(16)	(16)	(4)	(100)			
	Paddy area (ha)	5	25	18	31	18	97	1.9	0.46	0.89
		(6)	(26)	(18)	(32)	(18)	(100)			

Notes: [a]Percentages are shown in parentheses.
[b]Total paddy area divided by the number of farm households.

from increased landholdings of large farmers as from the increased share of farmers operating in the small-size bracket.

Reductions in operational farm sizes were an outcome of increased population pressure, typically through the division of farms among heirs. This process operated less strongly among large farmers' than small farmers' households, because the children of large farmers tended to receive a better education and move out of the village into urban occupations. Typically, one son (or one daughter with her husband) remains in the village to take care of the parents' farm, while other heirs might receive parts of claims on the land or compensation in cash or in kind (rice). In contrast, the children of small farmers, who had less of an education, were more likely to stay on in the village, waiting anxiously to inherit even small pieces of land for their own cultivation and meanwhile working as agricultural labourers.[8]

In addition to subdivision through inheritance, there was a high probability among small farmers of reducing operational size through the sale of their cultivation rights. Needless to say, small farmers are usually under much stronger financial stress than large farmers. Yet they were equally eager to send their children to high schools and colleges, even borrowing money to do so. Casual misfortunes, such as crop failures and rice price declines, could easily result in a debt crisis which would force them to sell out their cultivation rights. Often the cultivation rights were purchased by non-farm workers, not only within the village but also in nearby localities (see Table 4.8), partly for expected capital gains from land price appreciation, and partly for security after retirement. Typically, they bought the cultivation rights on relatively small-sized plots with their modest savings, and cultivated the land by employing agricultural labourers.

Through these processes, a tendency emerged for small farms to become even smaller in size and larger in number, while large farms remained stable in both size and number, which together resulted in measured increases in the Gini coefficient among farmers.

Yet the increases in the inequality of landholding among farmers were modest compared with those among all the households in the village including not only farmers but also agricultural labourers, who comprised the 'reserve army' of farm operators. Indeed, the Gini coefficient for all the households increased by 65 per cent, from 0.54 in 1966 to 0.89 in 1995, while the Gini coefficient for farmers alone increased by only 35 per cent, from 0.34 to 0.46.

If such movements in the Gini coefficients are compared with sharp increases in the number of agricultural labourers in the total number of village households (see Table 3.3), it is clear that the size distribution of operational landholdings in East Laguna Village has changed since the 1960s towards becoming a source of greater income inequality within the village community.

EQUITY AND EFFICIENCY IN LAND REFORM

Land reform in the Philippines aimed to achieve (a) greater social equity by transferring land assets and incomes from landlords to tenants; and (b) higher agricultural productivity by reforming land tenure relations. How were these two goals achieved in the case of East Laguna Village?

Indeed, a major achievement resulted from the first goal. Conversion of sharecroppers into leasehold tenants with strong protection for their cultivation rights at land rents controlled at lower than market-clearing rates resulted in large income transfers from landlords to tenants. Similar benefits were obtained by CLT holders, with mortgage payments fixed at equally low rates. Traditionally, society in the rice-producing areas of the Philippines was bifurcated between poor sharecroppers living in villages, and rich landlords living in towns and cities. Land reform programmes made a great contribution to reducing this urban–rural, landed–landless disparity.

However, because the benefits of the programmes to tenants were proportional to their operational farm sizes at the time of reform, a major disparity was created within the village community. Before the reform, a sharecropper might have been cultivating a large tract of land because he or she had a large family workforce. Yet his or her income from farming after paying land rents was not much different from that of small farmers, or even agricultural labourers, on a per capita basis (though the sharecropper's income position was better to the extent that he or she had more farming experience and larger capital, such as *carabao*). The reform brought about large income transfers to sharecroppers proportional to the size of their operational holding, and their benefits increased further as rice yields increased while rents were fixed. Thus incomes of farmers with large holdings increased progressively to approach the level of the urban middle class. Indeed, many of their children have joined the urban middle class through their parents' investment in their education. On the other hand, gains to small farmers were proportionally small,[9] and more seriously, no direct benefit accrued to agricultural labourers. The lot of agricultural labourers could have been worsened because the agricultural ladder was closed by the reform laws, though the benefits that first accrued to farmers later spilled over to labourers through increased wage employment, to the extent that better-off farmers and their family members gave up farm drudgery (see Chapters 5 and 7).

If the village economy had continued to be based on rice farming, grow-ing population pressure on limited land resources under the institutional rigidity of the land-rental market should have produced ever-increasing income disparity within the village. In fact, however, inequality in income distribution was prevented from rising in East Laguna Village, mainly because of rapid increases in wage earnings by agricultural labourers through increased non-farm employment opportunities in the immediate surroundings of the village, as to be shown in the final chapter of this book.

What about the contribution of land reform to agricultural productivity? The economic theory underlying the Philippine land reform argued that the levels of inputs and outputs are less than optimal under share tenancy because tenants receive a fraction of outputs or the fruit of inputs, and that this 'Marshallian inefficiency' can be removed by converting share ten-ancy to fixed-rent leasehold tenancy or owner farming. This traditional theory has recently been demolished by a new theory which incorporates landlords' efforts to monitor tenants' inputs. This monitoring is considered to be relatively easy, requiring modest costs in communities such as East Laguna Village, where personal ties are strong and enduring between land-lord and tenant. More basically, if the contract choice is free, landlords who would choose share tenancy are likely to be limited to those living near the farming sites and knowledgeable about farming practices, so they can monitor and enforce tenants' inputs to approach optimality. In this case, significant inefficiency may not be observable in share tenancy (Hayami and Otsuka, 1993).

Indeed, comparisons in rice yields per hectare both across land-tenure types and across farm size found no significant difference between share tenancy and other forms of land tenure in both wet and dry seasons over the years 1976, 1987 and 1995 (see Table 4.11). Such results support the hypothesis that the conversion of share tenants to leasehold tenants and owner farmers by land reform programmes offered no significant contribu-tion to productivity in rice production in this village.[10]

As discussed in the previous section, although land reform programmes had no direct means of influencing on farm-size distribution, it is likely that institutional rigidity in the land-rental market under the reform laws acted as a force preventing subdivision of large farms into smaller farm units. Even if land reform influenced the size distribution of opera-tional landholdings, it would have had little influence on agricultural pro-ductivity throughout the 1970s and 1980s because statistically significant yield differences were not found between large and small farms in most

| | Wet season | | | | Dry season | | | |
| | Farm size | | | | Farm size | | | |
	Large 2 ha and above	Small below 2 ha	Total	Difference[a] Large versus small	Large 2 ha and above	Small below 2 ha	Total	Difference[a] Large versus small
1976								
Owner/leasehold[b]	3.31	2.89	3.10	0.42	3.43	3.45	3.44	−0.02
Share	2.95	3.09	3.03	−0.14	3.32	2.87	3.06	0.45
Total	3.21	2.95	3.07	0.25	3.40	3.25	3.32	0.15
Difference[a]								
Owner/lease versus share	0.36	−0.20	0.07		0.11	0.58	0.39	
1987								
Owner/leasehold[b]	4.58	4.36	4.43	0.23	5.18	4.79	4.93	0.38
Share	4.94	4.21	4.62	0.73*	5.02	5.18	5.09	−0.16
Total	4.74	4.32	4.50	0.42	5.11	4.89	4.98	0.22
Difference[a]								
Owner/lease versus share	−0.36	0.15	−0.19		0.16	−0.38	−0.16	
1995								
Owner	4.42	3.83	4.17	0.59	5.11	4.68	4.91	0.43
Leasehold	4.59	3.11	3.82	1.48**	5.93	4.92	5.39	1.01**
Share	4.83	3.24	4.43	1.59	5.78	5.76	5.78	0.02
Total	4.56	3.42	4.06	1.14**	5.54	4.90	5.23	0.64*
Difference[a]								
Owner versus share	−0.41	0.59	−0.26		−0.67	−1.08	−0.87	
Lease versus share	−0.24	−0.13	−0.61		0.15	−0.85	−0.39	
Owner versus lease	−0.18	0.72	0.35		−0.82*	−0.24	−0.48	

Notes: [a] significant at 10% level; ** significant at 5% level.
[b] Owned area is combined with leasehold area, because owned area was too small for statistical testing.

comparisons for 1976 and 1989 (see Table 4.11). One may puzzle about why significant differences emerged in 1995. This was because recent degradation in the national irrigation system servicing this village induced large farmers to introduce private irrigation pumps in 1995 ahead of the small farmers. Efficiency and equity implications of development and degradation of public infrastructure for irrigation will be the main theme in Chapter 6.

5 Diffusion of New Rice Technology[1]

As a typical settlement in the lowland rice belt in Laguna Province, East Laguna Village was characterized by the early (since the late 1960s) and complete adoption of modern rice varieties. In addition to its proximity to the IRRI (about 20 kilometres away), the rapid diffusion of modern varieties (MV) was supported by the extension of a national irrigation system that began to service almost all paddy fields in this village in 1958. This chapter aims to trace the process of MV diffusion and its impacts on rice yield, inputs and productivity.

LAGUNA IN THE GREEN REVOLUTION

Before proceeding to the case of East Laguna Village, it will be useful to identify the position of Laguna Province with respect to the diffusion of modern rice technology in the Philippines.

Popularly known as 'the heartland of the Green Revolution', the lowland rice belt of Laguna recorded the earliest and most complete adoption of MV among rice-producing areas, not only in the Philippines but also in the whole of tropical Asia. Laguna's lead in MV adoption in the Philippines is shown clearly in the top chart in Figure 5.1. MV planted area already exceeded 90 per cent of the total rice growing area in Laguna by the mid-1970s, whereas that level of diffusion was reached by the Philippines as a whole only in the 1990s.

The early start of MV diffusion in Laguna was, of course, facilitated by the location within this province of the IRRI and a large agricultural education-extension-research complex of the University of the Philippines at Los Baños (UPLB). Attempts to raise rice yields from less than 2 tons per hectare in tropical Asia to a level above 4 tons in Japan and Taiwan in paddy (rough rice) terms began almost immediately after the Second World War. Some significant outcomes were produced, with the release of several improved varieties, such as AD-27 in India, Malinja and Mashuri in Malaysia, H-4 in Sri Lanka and BPI-76 in the Philippines (Barker and Herdt, 1985, ch. 5). However, it is fair to say that the rice yield potential in tropical Asia was raised to the level of North-east Asia with the development of semi-dwarf varieties at IRRI, which are clearly distinguishable

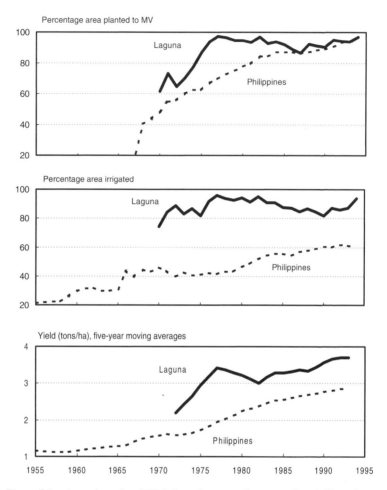

Figure 5.1   Area planted to MV, irrigated area, and average rice yield per hectare
              in the Philippines and Laguna, 1955–94
Source: Bureau of Agricultural Statistics (various issues).

from traditional varieties by their short and sturdy stems, erect, pointed
leaves, high fertilizer responsiveness, and non-photo-period sensitivity.[2]
It is therefore reasonable to set the release of IR8 (the first variety officially released from the IRRI) on 28 November 1966 as the point of
demarcation of the epoch of modern rice technology in the tropics.

   Although the Philippine government strongly promoted the propagation
of MV via its network of extension services throughout the nation, the

advantage to farmers in Laguna of their access to information regarding this technology was incomparable. From the beginning of its development, Laguna farmers were exposed to the new rice technology, either by visiting the IRRI directly or through the observation of and interaction with various on-farm research activities over the province by the staff of the IRRI and the UPLB. In fact, as explained earlier, in the year of release of IR8, the IRRI announced that any farmer who came to the IRRI could pick up 2 kg of the new seeds free of charge (Chandler, 1982, p. 112). It is reasonable to assume that the majority of the 2359 farmers who applied to this programme were from Laguna Province.

Yet easy access to a major research centre alone does not explain the almost complete adoption of MV in Laguna within only about a decade of 1966. It was the well-developed irrigation infrastructure that made MV diffusion in Laguna so rapid and so complete. It is well known that MV's high-yielding capacity can only be exploited poorly without adequate water control. Indeed, it was attested by the history of agricultural development in North-east Asia that the development of irrigation systems was a precondition to the introduction of modern rice technology (Ishikawa, 1967, ch. 1; Hayami and Ruttan, 1985, ch. 10). In this regard, Laguna Province was in an exceptionally favoured position. As shown in the middle chart in Figure 5.1, nearly 80 per cent of the rice area in the province was already irrigated in the 1960s, when the ratio was only about 40 per cent elsewhere in the Philippines. Even in Central Luzon, known as 'the rice bowl of the Philippines', the irrigation ratio in the 1960s was only about 60 per cent.

A major factor underlying the early development of irrigation systems in Laguna appears to be its unique topography. The lowland rice belt in Laguna is surrounded by hills and mountains from which relatively small rivers flow into Laguna de Bay across a narrow plain. In elevated upstream areas, communal efforts were traditionally organized even before the twentieth century to divert streams for the irrigation of small paddy fields scattered among the hills. In lower-lying areas around the lake, rainfed rice cultivation was commonly practised upto the 1950s, when large-scale irrigation systems were constructed under the auspices of the National Irrigation Administration.

The 1950s represented a transition in the momentum of agricultural growth from an expansion of the cultivated area to increases in yield per unit of cultivated area in the Philippines as well as in many areas in South-east Asia (Hayami and Ruttan, 1985, pp. 300–5). As the food supply dwindled under increased scarcity of land relative to population, major efforts of the national government and foreign aid agencies were induced to construct irrigation systems. In their endeavours, Laguna's rice belt represented a high-payoff area because it required modest investment to harness relatively small rivers for the purpose of irrigation. This contrasted with the conditions in Central Luzon, where much larger investments over longer periods were required to develop irrigation systems by controlling the large rivers flowing across wide plains.

On the basis of early irrigation development and MV adoption, Laguna experienced a major spurt of rice yield increase ahead of other areas in the Philippines in the first decade of the Green Revolution (the lower chart of Figure 5.1). However, as both the irrigation ratio and the MV adoption ratio reached almost 100 per cent, the average rice yield in Laguna began to stagnate even by the late 1970s. Meanwhile, as irrigation development and MV diffusion continued in other regions, the margin of Laguna's yield over the national average was progressively closed.

Such characteristics of Laguna Province in the adoption of MV technology should be kept in mind when the case of East Laguna Village is examined.

DIFFUSION OF MODERN VARIETIES

The process of MV diffusion in East Laguna Village is shown in Table 5.1 and the upper chart of Figure 5.2. Indeed, farmers in this village were quick and uniform in adopting MV. In 1966 all the farmers grew traditional varieties (TV), but only a decade later, in 1976, as many as 97 per cent of them had adopted MV in the wet season and 98 per cent had adopted it in the dry season. The speed of MV adoption in East Laguna Village was even faster than in Laguna Province, as can be seen from Figure 5.1.

According to Umehara (1967), who surveyed the village in the dry season of 1966/67, only one farmer had tried IR8 in a small plot. The following year, Governor San Luis of Laguna Province distributed 1 kg of the new seeds to all the officers in the *barangays* (villages) in his jurisdiction. The seeds received by the captain and seven council members in East Laguna Village were planted and yielded almost twice as much the yields of traditional varieties. Harvested paddy of the new variety was given to other villagers in exchange for the ordinary paddy they had grown.[3] Subsequently, IR8 has been remembered as the 'San Luis variety'.

Another route of diffusion was on-farm demonstration experiments conducted by the Pila branch of the Bureau of Agricultural Extension. Since before MV development, when the Bureau found new technologies worth propagating to farmers, its local offices had been directed to organize demonstration farming under a contract with farmer co-operators: a co-operator agrees to perform farm tasks on his/her fields according to

Table 5.1 Changes in rice varieties planted in East Laguna Village, 1966–96

	Wet season							Dry season					
	1966	1976	1979	1982	1987	1992	1996	1976	1979	1982	1987	1992	1996
Rate of adoption (% of farmer adopters)													
Traditional	100	3	2	…	…	…	…	2	…	…	2	…	…
MV$_1$[a]	…[d]	97	6	3	…	…	…	98	4	2	…	…	…
MV$_2$[b]	…	…	92	97	9	9	…	…	96	98	18	17	…
MV$_3$[c]	…	…	…	…	91	91	100	…	…	…	80	83	100
Top variety	n/a	IR26	IR42	IR50	IR64	IR64	RC20	IR26	IR36	IR50	IR64	IR64	RC14
Rate of adoption	n/a	75	36	68	65	26	20	67	46	79	65	28	57
Yield (tons/ha)													
Traditional	1.9	1.1	3.3	…	…	…	…	2.0	…	…	4.6	…	…
MV$_1$[a]	…	2.8	3.0	3.7	…	…	…	3.2	3.8	2.8	…	…	…
MV$_2$[b]	…	…	3.2	3.9	3.7	2.8	…	…	4.0	3.6	5.2	3.1	…
MV$_3$[c]	…	…	…	…	4.2	3.1	4.0	…	…	…	4.1	4.0	5.3

Notes: [a] IR5–IR34 and C4 series.
[b] IR36–IR62.
[c] IR64–IR74 and RC varieties.
[d] … stands for 'no case reported'.

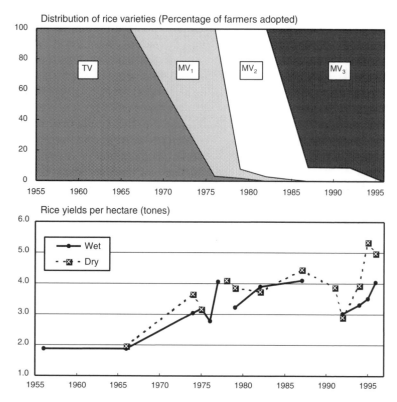

Figure 5.2   Distribution of rice varieties adopted by farmers, and average rice
yield per hectare harvested, East Laguna Village, 1956–96

the instructions of extension technicians with such inputs as fertilizers and
chemicals paid for by the office and, on harvesting the output becomes the
farmer's possession. According to this scheme, the planting of IR8 and
subsequent modern varieties was demonstrated on farms near East Laguna
Village. Paddy produced from these demonstration plots was sold to other
farmers in cash, or exchanged for paddy from old varieties.

Many other channels were also developed. For example, IRRI researchers
who tried to conduct on-farm experiments found that the best way to obtain
the farmers' co-operation was to give them a small pack of new seeds. Also,
there were cases in which the IRRI's local staff members of farm origin
propagated the new seeds on their farms, or their parents' farms, for distribution to relatives and neighbours.

Quantitative data are not available to identify the MV diffusion process in East Laguna Village before 1976. According to the memories of several veteran farmers, however, the rate of MV adoption as measured by the percentage of farmers adopting reached nearly a third by 1970, but held back somewhat for the next couple of years because of an outbreak of tungro virus disease; it then returned to a level of a third in 1973, and rose to about half in 1974, before our 1976 survey recorded the almost complete adoption.

Modern varieties distributed during this initial period – the IR series from IR5 to IR34 as well as the C4 series developed by rice breeders in the UPLB – were susceptible to pests, especially brown planthoppers and tungro virus disease. As pest-resistant varieties (MV_2) such as IR36 were developed, farmers quickly shifted to them, with the adoption rate for MV_2 reaching 92 per cent in the wet season and 96 per cent in the dry season by 1979. From the mid-1980s onwards, farmers shifted to MV_3, such as IR64 and subsequent RC series,[4] characterized by better grain quality and improved pest resistance. By 1996 the adoption rate of MV_3 reached 100 per cent in both wet and dry seasons.

In Table 5.2 the adoption rates for the three MV categories are compared with their average yields. It is hazardous to make an assumption based on single-year yield data subject to weather and other environmental variations. Yet it appears clear that yield margins of MV_1 and MV_2 over TV were much larger than those of MV_3 over MV_1 and MV_2. This indicates that the potential of yield growth opened up in the late 1960s had largely been exhausted by about 1980, when the adoption of MV_2 was completed. Subsequent improvement in varieties offered no significant contribution to yield growth, while some improvements were caried out in such aspects as grain quality and pest resistance to reduce the application of chemicals.

RICE YIELD TRENDS

How did rice yields change corresponding to the MV diffusion? The data of rice yields in East Laguna Village collected from our periodic surveys between 1974 and 1996 are assembled in Table 5.2 (columns 1–3). Considering the critical importance of observing pre-Green Revolution situations as a benchmark for comparison, we try to extrapolate our village data by the sample survey data on rice farms in Laguna Province conducted periodically by the IRRI's Social Sciences Division, entitled *Laguna Survey*. Concrete procedures of extrapolation to 1965 and 1966 of our

Table 5.2   Average rice yields per hectare by season and total/per capita rice production in East Laguna Village, 1956–96

	Yield per hectare per season (tons/ha)			Output per year (ton:	
	Wet	Dry[a]	Average[b]	Village total	Per capita
Average yield					
1956[c]	1.9	No crop	1.9	136	0.53
1966[d]	1.9	2.0[e]	1.9	401	1.00
1974	3.0	3.7[e]	3.4	704	1.28
1975	3.2	3.2	3.2	676	1.14
1976	2.8	n/a	n/a	n/a	n/a
1977	4.1	n/a	n/a	n/a	n/a
1978	n/a	4.1			
1979	3.2	3.9	3.5	636	0.90
1982	3.9	3.7[e]	3.8	610	0.82
1987	4.1	4.4[e]	4.3	761	0.93
1991	n/a	3.9	n/a	n/a	n/a
1992	3.0	2.9	3.0	550	0.56
1994	3.3	3.9	3.6	702	0.66
1995	3.5	5.3	4.4	958	0.84
1996	4.0	5.0	4.5	n/a	n/a
Growth rate[f] (%/year)					
1956–82	3.1[**]	–[h]	3.1[**]	6.1[**]	1.9
1966–82	4.4[**]	4.3[**]	4.2[**]	2.6	−1.4
1977–96	−0.3	0.7	0.6	1.3	−1.6
1977–92	−1.0	−1.1	−1.1	−0.6	−3.1
1956–96[g]	1.6[**]	–	1.9[**]	3.4[**]	−0.2
1966–96[g]	1.3[**]	1.8[**]	1.8[**]	1.5[*]	−1.9[*]

Notes: [a] Unless otherwise stated, records for the year the dry season begins: e.g. 199 for 1996/97 dry season.

[b] Weighted average using harvested areas as weights.

[c] Assumed to be the same as in 1966.

[d] Estimated by multiplying to the *Laguna Survey* data for 1966 the ratio c 1974–82 village average to 1975–81 *Laguna Survey* average for the wet sea son, and by multiplying to the *Laguna Survey* for 1965 the ratio of 1982–8 village average to the 1982–88 *Laguna Survey* average for the dry season.

[e] Recorded for the year the dry season ends.

[f] Estimated from semi-log time trend regressions: **significant at 5 per cer level; *significant at 10 per cent level.

[g] For total village and per capita rice output, up to 1995 instead of 1996.

[h] –stands for 'undefined'.

Source: Note(d) International Rice Research Institute, Social Sciences Division *Laguna Survey*, various years.

village data are as follows: for the wet season, the *Laguna Survey* data are available for 1966, 1975, 1978 and 1981, and our village data are available annually from 1974 to 1982 except for 1978, 1980 and 1982; for an estimation of the village yield data in 1966, we first took the ratio of the 1974–82 village average to the 1975–81 *Laguna Survey* average and then propagated this ratio to the 1966 *Laguna Survey* data. Similarly, for the dry season, the *Laguna Survey* data are available for 1965, 1982 and 1988, while the village data are available for 1978, 1979, 1982 and 1987; the ratio of the village average for 1982 and 1987 to the *Laguna Survey* average for 1982 and 1988 was propagated to the 1965 *Laguna Survey* data.[5] The wet season yield in 1956 is assumed to be the same as that of 1966, based on veteran farmers' recollections.

Similar to the yield data in Table 5.1, the data in Table 5.2 are subject to intrinsic weakness in identifying systematic trends in output and productivity through technological progress, because single-year data for specific survey years are subject to large annual fluctuations because of changes in environmental conditions such as inclement weather and pest infestation. For example, a major yield decline in 1976 resulted from the severe outbreak of brown planthopper and tungro virus disease. Another major drop in 1992 and 1994 was because of water supply cuts from the national irrigation system. On the other hand, a sudden boost in dry season yield in 1995–6 came about because the farmers purchased irrigation pumps in response to a deterioration in surface irrigation from the national system.

Despite the major influences of such environmental shocks, the impacts of new rice technology over time are unmistakable from a comparison between changes in average rice yield and distribution in rice varieties, as plotted in Figure 5.2. First, starting from a pre-MV level of about two tons per hectare, average rice yield in the wet season rose rapidly between the late 1960s and late 1970s to reach a level close to four tons per hectare, corresponding to the diffusion of MV_1 and MV_2, and thereafter became largely stagnant. An essentially similar growth pattern was observed for dry season yields. A rise in dry season yield to a five-ton level in 1995–6 corresponded to the diffusion of private irrigation pumps, but it is yet to be seen whether this level will be sustained in the future.

Recognizing major data limitations, Figure 5.2 shows unmistakably that a kink in the rice yield trend in this village occured some time in the late 1970s/early 1980s. Regression estimates of the average yield growth rates for both 1956–82 and 1966–82 were positive and statistically significant, while those for 1977–96 and 1977–92 were not significantly different from zero. The deceleration in rice yield trends in the ten to fifteen years after the advent of the Green Revolution is reflected clearly in our survey data for East Laguna Villages. Such a yield deceleration was commonly expereienced in irrigated areas in tropical Asia, such as Laguna and Central Luzon in the Philippines, Java in Indonesia and Punjab in India (Hayami and Otsuka, 1994; Pingali *et al.*, 1997).

Given such a dramatic innovation as the MV diffusion in this village that nearly doubled average rice yield within about a decade, it may be reasonable to expect that yield variations across farms increased as a result of a widened yield gap between early MV adopters and laggards. However, the ratio of average yield of top the 25 per cent of high-yielding farmers to the remaining 75 per cent of farmers stayed remarkably stable within a range of 1.5 to 1.8, except for abnormal seasons: for example, the 1975 dry and 1976 wet seasons with the infestation of brown planthoppers and the tungro virus; and from the 1992 dry season to the 1995 wet season because of the deterioration of the water supply from the national irrigation system (see Table 5.3). Correspondingly, the coefficient of variation in yield across plots also remained largely stable. Yield differences across both farmers and plots did not significantly widen in the major innovation process because there was little variation in the speed of adoption of new rice technology among farmers. The association between the stability in

Table 5.3 Rice yield per hectare of top 25 per cent high-yielding farmers, and yield variation among rice plots, East Laguna Village, 1956–96

Year	Average yield of top 25 % high-yielding farmers				Coefficient of variation across plots (%)	
	Average yield per hectare (tons/ha)		Ratio to the average of the rest			
	Wet	Dry	Wet	Dry	Wet	Dry
1956	2.6	n/a	1.5	n/a	29	n/a
1966	2.7	2.9	1.7	1.7	33	30
1974	4.6	4.8	1.8	1.5	37	28
1975	4.4	5.4	1.7	2.1	33	43
1976	4.2	n/a	1.9	n/a	48	n/a
1977	5.7	n/a	1.6	n/a	32	n/a
1979	4.8	5.8	1.6	1.7	40	36
1980	n/a	5.1	n/a	1.6	n/a	45
1982	5.3	4.6	1.7	1.5	33	34
1987	5.7	6.0	1.5	1.5	35	36
1991	n/a	5.3	n/a	1.5	n/a	30
1992	4.4	5.0	1.7	2.2	41	67
1994	5.2	6.8	1.9	2.1	47	56
1995	5.4	7.1	2.0	1.6	56	31
1996	5.9	7.0	1.7	1.6	33	33

the ratio of top-yielding farmers' average to the remainders' average yields (Table 5.3) and the very fast and uniform adoption of MV technology (Table 5.1) in East Laguna Village was also commonly observed in irrigated rice areas in the Philippines (Pingali *et al.*, 1997, p. 27).

Major increases in rice yield per hectare were recorded for both wet and dry seasons for the first decade of the Green Revolution. Rice output per capita in East Laguna Village, however, declined from 1 ton in 1966 to 0.8 of a ton in 1982, after slight increases in the early 1970s (see last column of Table 5.2). Despite its major yield-increasing effects, the diffusion of MV was not sufficiently powerful to overcome population growth at a rate of nearly 4 per cent per year, which resulted from large immigration into the village in addition to high natural growth among the native population. The decline in per capita output was also accentuated by transfer of some paddy fields from villagers' to non-villagers' cultivation (see Table 4.8). The same forces continued to operate after 1982 to depress per capita rice output to almost 0.6 tons in the early 1990s, even though this declining trend was somewhat reversed in 1995–96 through yield increases resulting from the diffusion of irrigation pumps.

Before the Green Revolution, however, per capita rice output nearly doubled between 1956 and 1966, because of the extension of a national irrigation system to the village in 1958 that converted all the rice fields from single to double cropping. This experience clearly demonstrated the high capacity of irrigation development to increase food supply, even compared with MV-based technology.

PURCHASED INPUTS FOR RICE PRODUCTION

How was the modernization of agricultural production, as epitomized by MV adoption, associated with purchased inputs from the market? Unfortunately, data are not available to ascertain the pattern of input changes in the village in the early phase of the Green Revolution because our survey covered the area of farm production inputs only from 1976. The 1965–66 levels have been estimated by applying the same method as applied to the rice yield, except that the years for which input data are available for the village are limited to 1976 and 1982 for the wet season, and to 1979 and 1987 for the dry season.

Fertilizers and Chemicals

What is commonly called 'seed-fertilizer technology', the new rice technology that supported major boosts in rice yields in tropical Asia during the first decade of the Green Revolution, was characterized, above all, by the association of MV diffusion with the increased application of fertilizers and chemicals.

This characteristic is clearly reflected in changes in current inputs in East Laguna Village (see Table 5.4). In 1966, the level of fertilizer input was very low, at only 13 kg of nitrogen (N) per hectare, and 15 kg of all plant nutrients (nitrogen – N, phosphate – P, potash – K) added together; this was almost one-tenth the level that prevailed in Japan in the

Table 5.4   Current inputs in rice production, East Laguna Village, 1965–95

	Fertilizer		Insecticide[c] *(litre/ha)*	Herbicide[d] *(litre/ha)*
	N^a *(kg/ha)*	NPK total[b] *(kg/ha)*		
Input level				
Wet season				
1966[e]	13	15	0.1	0.4
1976	58	67	2.6	0.9
1982	80	91	1.6	1.5
1987	92	103	1.9	1.5
1995	88	111	1.1	1.3
Dry season				
1965[f]	15	20	0.1	0.5
1979	63	84	1.3	1.3
1987	94	109	2.0	1.6
1995	106	132	1.0	1.5
Growth rate (%/year)				
Wet season				
1966–76	16	16	36	10
1976–82	5	4	−7	7
1982–7	3	3	3	0
1987–95	−1	1	−7	−1
Dry season				
1965–79	11	11	18	6
1979–87	5	3	5	3
1987–95	2	2	−8	−2

Notes: [a] N = nitrogen.
[b] NPK = nitrogen, phosphate, potash.
[c] In Brodan equivalent.
[d] In 2–4D equivalent
[e] Estimated by multiplying to the *Laguna Survey* data for 1966 the ratio of 1976–82 village averages to 1975–81 *Laguna Survey* averages.
[f] Estimated by multiplying to the *Laguna Survey* data for 1965 the ratio of 1979–87 village averages to 1982–88 *Laguna Survey* averages.

same period. Starting from such a low level, average fertilizer input in this village increased in the first decade of the Green Revolution (1966–76) more than fourfolds, as fast as 16 per cent per year.

It is important to recognize that during this decade the price of nitrogen did not decline, but increased slightly relative to the price of rice (see Table 5.5). Therefore, the dramatic increase in the application of fertilizer in the first decade of the Green Revolution is explained solely by a shift from traditional varieties (TV) characterized by low fertilizer responsiveness to highly fertilizer-responsive MV.[6]

After the first decade, however, the increase in fertilizer input decelerated sharply, and virtually no significant increase was recorded after nitrogen input reached a level of about 90 kg per hectare in the 1980s. The pattern of rapid rise and stagnation in fertilizer input paralleled the pattern of rice yield growth (Table 5.2), both reflecting the process of exploitation and the exhaustion of new production potential opened up by the transfer of a new rice plant types to tropical Asia through adaptive research.

Even more dramatic were changes in the use of pesticides. The rate of increase in pesticide application from 1966 to 1976 was more than twice as fast as that of fertilizer (Table 5.4). This extraordinary increase was induced, to a large extent, by the farmers' fear of the brown planthopper and the tungro virus disease, which caused a major loss to the crop of early IR varieties (MV_1). However, as IR36 and other varieties resistant to the brown planthopper (MV_2) were developed in the mid-1970s, pesticide application began to decline. This trend continued to be strengthened with the development and diffusion of MV_3. Increasingly, both farmers and scientists recognized that the benefit of increased pesticide dosage is low, or even negative, as it causes environmental degradation such as reduction in the population of the natural enemies to pests (Pingali *et al.*, 1997, chs. 5 and 11), not to mention external diseconomies such as water contamination and a hazard to human health. As a result, a major decline in the application of pesticides was recorded for 1987–95.

It is well known that the thinner leaf cover of short-stalked MV, together with increased fertilizer application, encourages the growth of weeds compared to TV. Despite the increased need for weeding, however, the use of herbicides increased much slowly than the input of fertilizers for the first decade of MV diffusion. This was mainly because this need was covered primarily by increased labour for weeding under the condition of stable wage rates relative to the price of rice during this period (Table 5.5). Later, as the real wage rate increased, corresponding to increases in non-farm employment opportunities – especially after improvements in the highways in the late 1970s – the application of herbicides increased much

Table 5.5   Farmers' purchase prices of inputs relative to their sale price of rice (paddy), East Laguna Village, 1966–96

Year	Real price in rice equivalent			Real price index (1966 = 100)		
	Labour wage (kg/day)	Tractor rental (kg/day)	Nitrogen (kg/kg)	Labour wage	Tractor rental	Nitrogen
1966	9.6	50	3.2	100	100	100
1974	8.5	51	3.0	88	103	94
1976	9.8	61	3.7	101	123	117
1980	11.4	72	3.5	118	144	110
1983	15.0	121	4.1	155	242	129
1987	13.2	88	2.1	137	176	67
1992	18.3	75	2.7	190	151	84
1994	21.4	78	2.6	223	156	83
1995	17.8	63	1.9	185	125	61

faster than did fertilizer input. It is a puzzle, however, that the input of herbicides dropped slightly from 1987 to 1995 despite a major increase in the real wage rate. This anomaly might be explained by the shift in the herbicide used by farmers from 2-4D to the more effective butachlor (locally called 'machete') during this period.

Use of Productive Capital Assets

In the use of capital assets for rice production, the first major change was a shift from *carabao* (water buffalo) to hand tractors (power tillers) for land preparation (see Table 5.6). Although *carabaos* continued to be used for supplementary tasks such as cultivation on the edges of fields, tractors had almost completely overtaken *carabaos* as the source of power for land preparation by the mid-1970s. However, this shift was not a result of MV technology. It began much earlier than MV diffusion, evidenced by the fact that by 1966 nearly 40 per cent of farmers used tractors, and as many as fourteen tractors (as compared with twenty-one *carabaos*) were owned by villagers (see Tables 5.6 and 5.7). Considering the early adoption of tractors by larger farmers, it seems reasonable to assume that well over a half of the paddy fields in East Laguna Village had been ploughed and

Table 5.6 Use of capital services in rice production, East Laguna Village, 1965–95 (% of farmers adopted)

Year	Carabao	Tractor	Thresher	Irrigation pump
Wet season				
1966[a]	93 (10.3)[b]	39 (1.2)[c]	...[d]	...
1976	78 (0.9)	100 (5.0)	...	...
1982	73 (1.6)	98 (3.5)	30	...
1987	96 (2.1)	98 (2.9)	92	...
1995	66 (0.5)	98 (3.6)	100	69
Dry season				
1965[a]	100 (9.3)	35 (1.4)	...	...
1979	94 (1.2)	100 (5.6)	33	...
1987	98 (2.1)	98 (3.2)	80	4
1995	64 (0.7)	95 (3.4)	100	83

Notes: [a] Estimates as Table 5.4.

[b] Numbers of carabao-service days per hectare in parentheses.

[c] Numbers of tractor-service days per hectare in parentheses.

[d] ... stands for 'not applicable'.

Table 5.7　Holdings of draft animals, machines and tools, East Laguna Village, 1966–96

Item	1966	1974	1976	1980	1983	1987	1995	1996
Owned by farmers	(46)[a]	(54)	(54)	(46)	(44)	(53)	(51)	(50)
Carabao	21	4	8	10	14	17	3	2
Hand tractor	14	21	24	20	16	21	16	16
Chemical sprayer	0	23	26	19	16	21	21	20
Rotary weeder	35[b]	80	84	65	51	55	32	26
Thresher	0	0	1	n/a	4	7	7	5
Irrigation pump	0	0	0	0	2	2	13	28
Owned by agricultural labourers	(20)[a]	(41)	(55)	(76)	(76)	(98)	(150)	(n/a)
Carabao	0	0	0	3	2	6	5	n/a
Hand tractor	0	0	0	2	2	0	1	n/a
Chemical sprayer	0	0	0	0	2	0	0	n/a
Rotary weeder	10[b]	23	43	45	66	71	43	n/a
Thresher	0	0	0	n/a	0	0	3	n/a
Irrigation pump	0	0	0	0	0	0	0	n/a

Notes: [a] Numbers of farmers and labourers are shown in parentheses.
[b] The total of 45 weeders owned by all villagers, as recorded by Umehara (1967), is allocated to farmers and agricultural labourers according to the ratio in 1974.

harrowed with tractors by the time MV was first planted. Several factors underlay the early adoption of hand tractors. First, tractors with floating wheels could operate more efficiently in deep water fields adjacent to Laguna de Bay, where even *carbaos* often got stuck. Second, the increased speed of land preparation by tractors was also advantageous, with a shift from single to double cropping for planting the dry-season crop soon after the wet-season harvest in order to avoid water shortage in late dry months (Umehara, 1967). It is also said that the use of tractors was induced by the increasing scarcity of grazing land as a result of expansion of rice cultivation frontiers as well as the frequent incidence of animal theft. Another underlying factor might be duty-free imports of tractors and the application of subsidized credits for tractor purchase through World Bank loans in the 1950s, under the slogan 'agricultural modernization' (Barker *et al.*, 1972).

In the first decade of MV adoption, the number of chemical sprayers increased in parallel with the increased use of pesticides. More significant, however, was the increased use of hand-pushed rotary weeders, corresponding to the increased need for weeding in MV cultivation (Table 5.7). The effectiveness of the use of rotary weeders increased sharply with the adoption of straight-row planting of seedlings. Straight-row planting had been recommended by the extension service office long before MV adoption, but it became a common practice with the diffusion of MV.

It is noteworthy that not only farmers but also many agricultural labourers owned rotary weeders; this corresponded to the spread of the new contractual arrangement called '*gama*', in which a labourer agrees to perform both weeding and harvesting of a plot for the reward of one-sixth of the rice harvest. Owning a rotary weeder was instrumental in obtaining these new contracts for agricultural labourers, as this assured them stable employment and income.

A dramatic development that took place in this village during the second decade of the Green Revolution (1976 to 1987) was the introduction of portable threshing machines. The use of axial-flow threshers designed by the IRRI spread very rapidly, and completely replaced hand threshing. This technological innovation induced major changes in contract labour relations. Traditionally, the labourer who cut rice plants with a sickle threshed the crop by beating the harvested plants on a bamboo stand or a wooden plate, and he or she received a certain share of output for both these tasks. With the use of a mechanical thresher, however, the task of threshing was contracted out separately to a machine owner, who provided a custom service of machine threshing with operators for a fee also paid as a percentage of the threshed paddy. This custom service operation was initially practised by large farmers. However, it was found in 1995 that three landless agricultural labourers were also operating a threshing business with machines they had bought (Table 5.7). Another dramatic change occurring in more recent years was the introduction of irrigation pumps as a response to the serious deterioration in the service of the national irrigation system to the village in the 1990s. In 1987 only two farmers owned pumps, but the number increased to thirteen in 1995 and further jumped to twenty-eight the following year.

A highly conspicuous aspect in this village (as well as in the surrounding villages) was an active rental market for animals and machines. It has been argued that markets are difficult to develop for the rental of draft animals and agricultural machines, because of the danger of damage that is likely to be caused by the reckless use of animals and machines by renters (Binswanger and Rosenzweig, 1986). In this village, also, the rental of animal or machine alone was seldom practised. But the market of custom services with operations handled by an owner or his/her employees was pervasive, as is evident from the very high dependency on hired capital services in the operation of farm tasks using animals and machines (see Table 5.8). The major role of custom service operation in the diffusion

Table 5.8   Dependency on hired capital services in rice
production, East Laguna Village, 1965–95[a] (%)

Year	Carabao	Hand tractor	Thresher	Irrigation pump
Wet season				
1966[b]	20	75	...[d]	...
1976	58	31	...	...
1982	61	44	68	...
1987	75	68	94	...
1995	82	49	78	9
Dry season				
1965[b]	17	71[c]	...	...
1979	61	32	n/a	...
1987	63	64	90	...
1995	90	51	78	11

Notes: [a] Percentage of area receiving hired services.
[b] Estimates as for Table 5.4.
[c] Estimated from the 1966 wet estimate by applying the
ratio between wet and dry in the *Laguna Survey* (see
p. 110).
[d] ... stands for 'not applicable'.

of portable threshers has already been explained. It also played a large role
in tractorization, especially in the early period, when the purchase of tractors was limited to large farmers; this was reflected in a very high percentage of the rice area that received tractor custom services in 1966 before the
percentage declined, according to subsequent tractor purchases by smaller
farmers. Because of this active market for capital services, even small
farmers whose operational sizes were economically too small to purchase
large, high-cost machinery, such as tractors and threshers, were not excluded
from the use of modern mechanical technology. Investments in these
productive assets by large farmers yielded significant cash incomes to
them as they were used for custom services.

In the case of irrigation pumps, the custom service has not yet been as
well developed, with the ratio of dependency on hired services remaining
at only 9 per cent in the 1995 wet season, and 11 per cent in the dry season
(Table 5.8); this should have underpinned the emergence of significant rice
yield differences between large and small farmers as well as the increased
yield variation across farmers (Table 5.3). It is yet to be seen whether such
variations in productivity across farm-size classes will be reduced with the
development of the custom service market for irrigation pumps.

LABOUR USE IN RICE PRODUCTION

How did the use of labour change in the process of the Green Revolution? During the first decade of MV diffusion, average labour input as measured by the number of days of work (workdays) applied to rice production per hectare increased by more than 15 per cent from the wet season total of 89 days in 1966 to 105 days in 1976 (see Table 5.9).

By task, a significant reduction was recorded for land preparation because of the progress of tractorization. Labour input in crop establishment, including seedbed preparation and transplanting, remained about the same. In this village, after its fields were converted from rainfed to irrigated conditions, the so-called *dapog* method was introduced. In this method, a seedbed is prepared on a dry clay or concrete floor covered by banana leaves, on which seeds are densely placed for germination (in some cases mixed with husks of paddy); about 10 days after seeding, the young seedlings are rolled up like a carpet and taken to the fields for transplanting. Compared with traditional seedbed preparation in a watered paddyfield (*punla*) in which seedlings are grown for about a month before transplanting, the *dapog* method saves significant labour in both seedbed preparation and transplanting, though it requires twice as many seeds and, more critically, good water control in the transplanted fields, so that young seedlings will not be drowned by floods or killed by drought. This

Table 5.9   Use of labour in rice production, East Laguna Village, 1965–95 (days/ha)

Year	Total	Land preparation	Crop establishment	Weeding	Harvesting and threshing	Other
Wet season						
1966[a]	89	28	10	13	32	6
1976	105	19	10	31	38	7
1982	80	16	10	18	29	7
1987	68	12	11	14	24	7
1995	73	12	10	15	27	9
Dry season						
1965[a]	75	27	9	5	27	7
1979	72	18	10	17	22	5
1987	69	12	11	15	24	7
1995	76	11	9	14	26	16

Note: [a] Estimates as for Table 5.4.

method had already been adopted by the majority of farmers in the village before 1966 (Umehara, 1967), and not much change in labour input for crop establishment was experienced after that. Only a modest gain was recorded in harvesting and threshing corresponding to yield increases, because traditional hand-harvesting and threshing continued during the first decade.

A major increase in labour input occurred for weeding with the spread of straight-row planting and rotary weeders, as explained before. A slight increase was also recorded in 'other', reflecting an increased labour use for water control, and fertilizer and chemical application associated with MV technology. The increase in these tasks outweighed the decrease in labour input for land preparation. In other words, the labour absorptive capacity of rice production enhanced by MV technology was able to more than offset the decrease resulting from labour-saving technologies such as tractorization, at least for the first decade of the Green Revolution. Underlying this process was the stability of labour wage rates relative to the price of output (Table 5.5).

However, as the wage rate rose relative to the price of output after the late 1970s, the power of labour-saving technology began to outweigh the labour-absorptive effect of MV technology. Increasingly, manual weeding with the use of rotary weeders was replaced by herbicides, and threshing by hand-beating was replaced by threshing machines. A reversal in this declining trend in labour intensity was observed in both wet and dry seasons from 1987 to 1997. This was primarily because of increased use of labour for the operation of irrigation pumps that farmers had introduced in order to counteract the deterioration in the service of the gravity irrigation system.

Throughout the three decades since the advent of the Green Revolution, dependency on hired labour in rice production continued to increase (see Table 5.10). Dependency on hired labour in irrigated rice farming in the Philippines as well as in many other South-east Asian economies had traditionally been much higher than in North-east Asia, such as Japan. The origin of this difference will be discussed in detail in Chapter 7. For the present discussion it is sufficient to point out that the dependency became even higher since the 1960s.

Before 1972, when land reform programmes began in the village, most farmers were sharecroppers, as explained in the previous chapter. The common form of land tenure contract then prevailing was to share both the outputs and the cost of inputs, including hired labour, 50:50 between landlord and tenant. However, not all the labour costs were shared. It was customary that payments to transplanting and harvesting labour were

Table 5.10   Dependency on hired labour in rice production, East Laguna Village, 1965–95 (%)

Year	Total	Land preparation	Crop establishment	Weeding	Harvesting and threshing	Other
Wet season						
1966[a]	49	20	78	16	90	20
1976	71	53	83	71	90	23
1982	70	47	77	69	89	32
1987	83	70	81	93	98	37
1995	84	78	85	86	98	42
Dry season						
1965[a]	56	20	75	21	93	11
1979	70	57	85	71	86	19
1987	83	71	83	93	97	39
1995	78	79	86	83	95	40

Notes: [a] Estimates as for Table 5.4.

shared equally, as dependency on hired labour for these two tasks at the seasonal peaks of labour demand was traditionally high, even before the introduction of MV.

On the other hand, land preparation with the use of *carabaos*; crop care activities, such as weeding, and fertilizer and chemical application; and water control were expected to be performed by tenants. Concurrent with MV diffusion, dependency on hired labour in land preparation rose as many small farmers who did not own tractors became dependent on the custom services of tractors operated by large farmers.

A major increase in the employment of hired labour was associated with the diffusion of *gama* contracts in the first decade of MV diffusion, in which the weeding and harvesting of a plot were performed by the same labourer in return for a share of the harvested crop from the plot, as explained before. However, despite significant declines in the incidence of these contracts from the 1980s, the use of hired labour continued to increase under the daily wage contract (*upahan*). Similarly, the use of daily wage labourers for such tasks as fertilizer and chemical application also increased. Thus since the 1960s farmers have continued to substitute hired labour for family labour in rice production.[7]

Underlying this substitution process were major increases in farmers' incomes. After the farmers were converted from sharecroppers into leasehold tenants or mortgaged owners with rents and mortgage payments fixed by land reform laws, they were able to capture all the yield gains from the new rice technology. As their incomes rose, disutility of labour also rose to reduce their own work. More importantly, as their children received a better education, they seldom returned home to succeed their parents in farming. Under the land reform laws that dictate removal of land reform beneficiaries' titles on farmland if it is rented to another person, farmers had no option but to continue to manage the farm themselves while relying to a greater extent on hired labour. Through this process, employment and income from the new rice technology spilled over to landless agricultural labourers, who not only received no direct benefit from land reform programmes but were also deprived by the programmes of the opportunity to ascend the 'agricultural ladder' to become tenant operators.

FACTOR INPUTS AND FACTOR SHARES

A broader perspective on the nature of technological change in East Laguna Village may be obtained by aggregating the inputs used for rice production per hectare. In Table 5.11, inputs are aggregated into three categories: (i) current input, including seeds, fertilizers and chemicals; (ii) capital, including services of draft animals and farm machinery; and (iii) labour, in workdays. These three categories of input are further aggregated into total input using as weights the factor shares estimated in Table 5.12. Both current and capital inputs are converted into real terms through deflation by item in each category.

For the entire three decades since the 1960s, current input increased more than four times and capital input increased two to three times, whereas labour decreased by about 20 per cent in the wet season but stayed nearly constant in the dry season. Consequently, the index of total input, including current input, increased much faster than the aggregate of capital and labour alone.

However, the patterns of input movements were very different between the earlier period (1966–82 for wet, and 1965–79 for dry seasons) and the later period (1982–95 for wet, and 1979–95 for dry seasons). In the first period, the rate of increase in current input was nearly three times higher than that of capital. In the second period, however, the rate for current input dropped precipitously, whereas the growth of capital input accelerated and exceeded the rate of increase in current input by a wide margin.

These movements reflect the process in which the major momentum of technological progress in the village shifted from increasing yield per hectare based on MV adoption and fertilizer application to substituting labour by machinery.

Table 5.11   Indices of real inputs in rice production per hectare, East Laguna Village, 1965–95 (1966 = 100)

Year	Current input[a]	Capital[b]	Labour	Total input[c]	
				Including current input	Excluding current input
Index					
Wet					
1966	100	100	100	100	100
1976	389	145	117	157	113
1982	418	152	90	155	104
1987	498	164	76	166	101
1995	458	237	82	173	115
Dry					
1965	100	100	100	100	100
1979	324	182	96	133	109
1987	461	156	92	147	104
1995	437	353	101	174	138
Growth rate (%/year)					
Wet					
1966–82	9.3	2.6	−0.7	2.8	0.2
1982–95	0.7	3.5	−0.7	0.8	0.8
1966–95	5.4	3.0	−0.7	1.9	0.5
Dry					
1965–79	8.8	4.4	−0.3	2.1	0.6
1979–95	1.9	4.2	0.3	1.7	1.5
1965–95	5.0	4.3	0.0	1.9	1.1

Notes: [a] Aggregate of seed, fertilizer (deflated by the price of nitrogen), pesticide (deflated by the price of Brodan) and herbicide (deflated by the price of 2-4D).
   [b] Include services of *carabaos*, tractors, threshers and irrigation pumps.
   [c] Edgeworth indices for respective intervals using factor shares in Table 5.12 as weights for aggregation are chain-linked.

This change in the nature of technological progress is also reflected in movements in the factor shares shown in Table 5.12. These shares are the shares of nominal input costs at the current value of rice output per hectare. The residual after subtracting all the input costs from output value per hectare measures returns to land and operators' entrepreneurship. As such, it is likely that an increase in the share of one input category reflects a bias in technological change to increase the use of this input category relative to other categories.[8] Relative increases in the share of

Table 5.12   Factor shares in rice production per hectare,
East Laguna Village, 1966–95 (%)

Year	Factor shares in output				
	Total	Current inputs	Capital	Labour	Residual
Wet season					
1966	100	8	10	36	46
1976	100	24	12	31	33
1982	100	18	17	30	35
1987	100	14	13	26	47
1995	100	14	15	35	36
Dry season					
1965	100	7	10	39	44
1979	100	15	13	27	45
1987	100	13	12	26	49
1995	100	11	16	30	43

current input in the earlier period and in the share of capital in the later
period are, therefore, consistent with the hypothesis on the bias of technological progress towards using more current input in the former and
towards using more capital in the latter.

RATES OF TECHNOLOGICAL PROGRESS

Overall, what were the rates of technological progress in East Laguna
Village? In economics, technological progress is defined as an upward
shift in production function; it means an increase in output for given
inputs. Under certain restrictive assumptions (such as linear homogenous
production function), it can be measured by taking a ratio of growth in
output to growth in the aggregate of inputs. So-called 'total factor productivity' (TFP), calculated as the ratio of total output to total input, is thus
commonly used as a convenient (though crude) index of technological
progress (Hayami, 1997, pp. 117–19).

In Table 5.13, two kind of TFP are calculated for rice production in
East Laguna Village – one taking the ratio of rice output to total input,
including all three categories of input, and another the ratio of value added
(output minus current input cost) to total input, including only capital
and labour. Since the cost of current inputs such as fertilizer are paid out to

Table 5.13   Estimates of total factor productivity (TFP) in rice production
per hectare, East Laguna Village, 1965–95 survey years (1966 = 100)

	Output terms			Value-added terms		
	Output	Total input[a]	TFP	Value added	Total input[b]	TFP
Index						
Wet						
1966	100	100	100	100	100	100
1976	175[c]	157	112	144[c]	113	128
1982	189[d]	155	122	168[d]	104	162
1987	218	166	131	203	101	201
1995	201[e]	173	116	187[e]	115	163
Dry						
1965	100	100	100	100	100	100
1979	198[f]	133	149	181[f]	109	166
1987	226	147	153	211	104	203
1995	263[g]	174	151	251[g]	138	182
Growth rate (%/year)						
Wet						
1966–82	4.1	2.8	1.2	3.3	0.2	3.1
1982–95	0.5	0.8	− 0.4	0.8	0.8	0.0
1966–95	2.4	1.9	0.5	2.2	0.5	1.7
Dry						
1965–79	5.0	2.1	2.9	4.3	0.6	3.7
1979–95	1.8	1.7	0.1	2.1	1.5	0.6
1965–95	3.3	1.9	1.4	3.1	1.1	2.0

Notes: [a] Including current input.
 [b] Excluding current input.
 [c] Average for 1974–7.
 [d] Average for 1979 and 1982.
 [e] Average for 1995 and 1996.
 [f] Average for 1978, 1979 and 1982.
 [g] Average for 1995 and 1996.

the non-farm sector, TFP in value-added terms is appropriate to analyze
the productivity of factors owned by farm operators. Because current input
was the fastest to grow among the three input categories, total input including current input increased faster so that TFP in output terms increased
more slowly than TFP in value-added terms. In order to avoid the influences of environmental factors, such as weather and incidence of the pests,
several years' averages are used for output and value added, where data are
available (see footnotes to Table 5.13). Yet our observations are too small

to eliminate these influences, with the result that major differences have arisen in the estimates of TFP between wet and dry seasons as well as between output and value-added terms.

Nevertheless, all the estimates are unanimous in showing that a significant deceleration occurred at some time around 1980. The TFP growth rates in output terms decreased from 1.2 per cent per year in 1966–82 to −0.4 per cent in 1982–95 in the wet season and 2.9 per cent to 0.1 per cent in the dry season. Meanwhile, the rates in value-added terms also decreased, from 3.1 per cent in 1966–82 to zero per cent in 1982–95 for the wet season, and from 3.7 per cent to 0.6 per cent for the dry season. These estimates are consistent with a hypothesis that a major advance in technology (defined as an increase in output for given inputs) in East Laguna Village was limited mainly to one to two decades following the advent of the Green Revolution. It is also indicated that significant mechanization in more recent years has represented a substitution of capital for labour along the surface of a fixed production function in response to relative price changes, rather than technological progress or an upward shift in the production frontier.

GREEN REVOLUTION ON IRRIGATION

However, it must be cautioned that a recent deceleration in the TFP growth rates has resulted not only from the exhaustion of technological potential created by the development of MV, but also from deterioration in the national irrigation system servicing the village. The estimates of total productivity had continued to rise until 1987, but they declined thereafter until 1995 because of a sharp increase in total inputs. This increase in total inputs from 1987 to 1995 resulted mainly from the purchase by farmers of irrigation pumps in response to the reduced water supply from the national gravity system and associated increases in labour input for operating pumps.

Indeed, the highly successful application of MV technology in the village, ahead of many other villages, not only in the Philippines but also in other economies in tropical Asia, was based on a well-developed irrigation system in addition to its proximity to the IRRI. Recent technological retrogression, as measured by a decline in TFP, clearly indicates critical complimentarity between MV technology and irrigation infrastructure.

6 Community and State in Irrigation Management[1]

The previous chapter ended with an emphasis on the critical role of irrigation in the effective use of new rice technology. It was also hypothesized that recent stagnation, or even retrogression, in rice production technology in East Laguna Village, as measured by movements in total factor productivity, was to a large extent the result of a deterioration in the national irrigation system servicing rice fields in the village. This chapter aims to examine factors underlying the deterioration, with a focus on interrelationships between village communities and government administration in the management of the irrigation system.

THE NATIONAL IRRIGATION SYSTEM SERVICING EAST LAGUNA VILLAGE

Paddy fields in East Laguna Village receive their water supply from one of the national irrigation systems under the jurisdiction of the National Irrigation Administration (NIA). Its construction began in 1953 and was completed in 1958. As has been emphasized repeatedly, the start of the NIA system's service opened a new epoch in the economy of East Laguna Village by converting its rice production from rainfed single-cropping to an irrigated, double-cropping system.

Profile of the System

The system is a gravity system based on surface flows of water diverted from the Sta. Cruz River that originates in Mount Banahaw, gathering several tributaries along the north-western side of the mountain (see Figure 6.1). Irrigation water diverted by a dam is sent to fields in the service area through a network of canals and laterals ending in Laguna de Bay. The network consists of a main canal, five laterals (A to E) and sixteen sub-laterals. East Laguna Village is located at the end of Lateral C (see Figure 6.2). The system was designed to serve about 4000 hectares cultivated by about 2500 farmers, with an average farm size of about 1.6 hectares, encompassing thirty-seven villages in five municipalities.

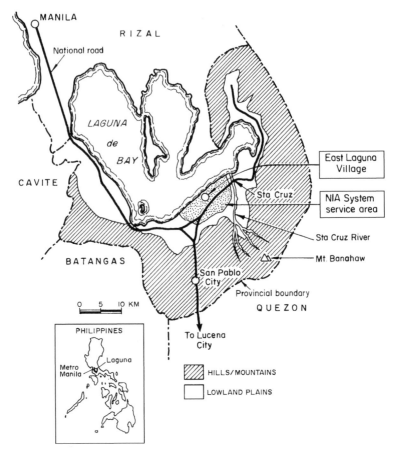

Figure 6.1   Location of the NIA System and East Laguna Village

It is a middle-sized system among 171 national irrigation systems under the NIA, with an average service area of about 4000 hectares. Within the system, most cultivable lands are paddy fields, apart from small elevated coconut groves on which houses are clustered – as is the case in East Laguna Village. Relatively more coconut groves and fewer paddy fields are found in the upper than in the lower reaches of the system. In fact, the main canal runs straight through a coconut belt, with scattered niches of paddy field. Five main laterals flow through the coconut belt for a few kilometres after the head gates on the main canal, which demarcates the western edge of a large, contiguous coconut area covering the foot of the

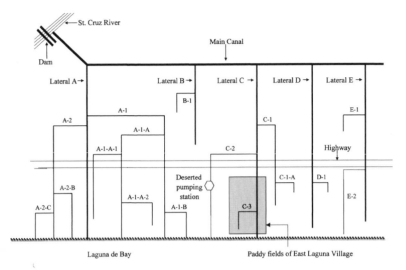

Figure 6.2   Canal layout of the NIA System irrigating East Laguna Village

Mount Banahaw and other small mountains in the region. In the coconut area, such tree crops as banana, lanzones, papaya and coffee are inter-cropped. Some farmers on the upper reaches of the main laterals use canal water for irrigating these tree crops, mostly without receiving permission from the NIA.

Attributes of the System

The NIA system is a simple gravity system of the type commonly found in tropical monsoon Asia. The supply of water is based on the diversion of current natural river flow with no reservoir and no pumping system being installed. Canals and laterals have banks of mud, except for concrete structures to support water gates and water-gauging facilities at the junctions of laterals with the main canal. Needless to say, there is no device of metering water intake into individual farms or fields. In fact, most fields are irrigated by direct flows of water from upper to lower paddy fields without being channelled through laterals and farm ditches. As a result, the total length of canals serving 4000 hectares is only 80 kilometres, implying that the average canal density is only about 20 metres per hectare.

The system is endowed with the attributes of 'local commons' or 'common-pool resources', similar to forests, pasture lands, and inshore fishing grounds which are allowed to be used by the people in the local

community but are soon exhausted if used in excess of their normal repro-
ductive capacity.[2] Since water resources for the system are limited by the
capacity of diversion from the river flow, this is exhaustible through over-
exploitation. Thus, an abuse by farmers in the upper reaches has a negative
effect on downstream farmers. Yet no incentive mechanism exists to prevent an individual user from abusing the water, because the water intake to
individuals' fields cannot be metered and, hence, cannot be chargeable in
proportion to consumption. It is costly to organize actions to save water
(by such means as rotating water supply among users) or to augment water
supply (by such means as removing silt and cutting weeds in canals),
because everyone is tempted to be a free rider on others' conservation
activities. This problem is exacerbated in the case of gravity irrigation systems by an asymmetry in the distribution of the means and benefits of conservation activities; typically, farmers at the head end of the system can
reduce abuse in their water use but receive no benefit from it, whereas those
at the tail end receive benefits from the head-enders' water savings but are
not in a position to reciprocate it (Ostrom *et al.*, 1994). The tendency for the
head-enders to abuse the water is especially serious in rice production,
because rice plants are intolerant of drought while being tolerant of excess
water application. In the absence of a mechanism to prevent resource users
from free riding, or to exclude from use of the resource those who do not pay
for its cost, local commons or common-pool resources will be exhausted.
This 'tragedy of the commons' predicted by Garrett Hardin (1968) is largely
applicable to gravity irrigation systems such as this NIA system.

As one way to escape this tragedy, Hardin proposed a conversion of
commons under communal ownership (hence, free access to community
members) either to state ownership and management or to private ownership and management, so that free riders can be excluded from use of
the resource. Considering the high costs involved in establishing private
property rights on irrigation water in gravity systems, such as installing
metering devices on all the small farms and plots, the option of privatiza-
tion does not seem feasible in the context of peasant farming in developing
economies. Thus the first option of state enterprise is a common organization for the management of relatively large gravity systems covering
a large number of villages, while small systems serving one or two villages are often managed communally by the associations of irrigator-farmers, commonly called 'communal systems'. Yet state administration has
often proved to be less than efficient in preventing water users from free
riding. Although rules are determined on collective action such as water
rotation and canal maintenance work, government agencies such as the

NIA find them difficult to enforce. For example, farmers located on an upstream portion of the system tend to take out a more than necessary amount of water in normal conditions from a canal to minimize the risk of possible water shortage, with the result that downstream farms have to face a problem of chronic water deficit. Compliance with the draft for collective work on canal maintenance as well as collection of irrigation fees are typically low.

The low efficiency of irrigation management by government agencies stems from (a) weak work incentives for government employees; (b) lack of practical enforcement means (for example, it is too expensive to litigate over the non-payment of irrigation fees by a large number of small farmers); and (c) the difficulty for government employees of obtaining grassroots information such as variations in the timing of water use among farmers corresponding to their different cropping patterns, which should be the basis of scheduling efficient water rotation.

For these shortcomings of government agencies, it has been argued that local communities could be a more efficient organization for managing local commons. Close personal relationships and intense social interaction in a local community provide the conditions for the efficient collection of grassroots information. Moreover, fear of social opprobrium or even ostracism in the community is considered to be an effective counter-force against temptation to become a free rider or benefit from the violation of the community's rules on collective action.[3] Indeed, cases have been illustrated in which common-pool resources have been managed adequately in the hands of local communities, contrary to Hardin's prediction of a 'tragedy of the commons' (Wade, 1990; Feeny *et al.*, 1990; Ostrom, 1990, 1992; Baland and Platteau, 1996). An emerging consensus is that it is indispensable for efficient management of national irrigation systems to incorporate local communities' initiatives and participation (Small and Carruthers, 1991; Uphoff, 1986). According to this new perspective, the NIA has endeavoured to promote irrigators' associations (IAs) in its systems and transfer some tasks previously shouldered by the NIA's employees to the associations.

Despite such efforts, it is a fact that East Laguna Village has experienced serious deterioration in the service from the NIA in recent years. Deterioration in the quality of gravity irrigation systems because of the difficulty of mobilizing adequate maintenance activities by government agencies and local communities is not specific to the NIA, but rather it is universal in developing economies (Chambers, 1988). What has been the mechanism of interaction between state and community that has resulted in a situation akin to the 'tragedy of the commons'?

DETERIORATION IN THE SERVICE OF IRRIGATION

From our first visit and until very recently, East Laguna Village has been characterized in our minds as a well-irrigated rice village. The major source of water supply to this village had been Lateral C of the NIA System, supplemented by a few small rivers and creeks which gather drainage water from the system. Apart for occasional interruptions in water supply caused by a major rehabilitation project during 1977–84, almost all the fields cultivated by the farmers in the village appear to have been fully irrigated during both wet and dry seasons, at least to our eyes. In fact, we had seldom heard complaints from villagers about the supply of water from the NIA.

Therefore, it was a great surprise to find a serious deterioration of the irrigation service to the village when we visited it in July 1995 for the preparation of the eighth full-enumeration household survey. Farmers said that the NIA's irrigation had reached only about 20 per cent of their fields in the present wet season as well as the previous dry season. We observed the major lateral buried under weeds, and the head gate was completely broken. Many farmers had bought irrigation pumps but, as late as July, which was already the middle of the wet season, several fields were still unplanted. In fact, we had witnessed signs of deterioration in the NIA system at the time of the 1987 survey, but we did not anticipate such a dramatic change to follow.

Structure of the System's Deterioration

Data on paddy fields cultivated in the dry season by the villagers of East Laguna Village by type of irrigation show that the deterioration of the irrigation service to East Laguna Village progressed very rapidly from 1987 to 1994, with a decline in the area served by the NIA's surface irrigation, from nearly 100 per cent to only about 20 per cent of the paddy fields cultivated by villagers (see Figure 6.3). Meanwhile, non-irrigated area (unplanted areas in the dry season) rose to nearly 40 per cent by 1993, but decreased thereafter with the diffusion of private pump irrigation.

A further investigation of system-wide performance was attempted in 1996 by means of interviews with the headmen (*barangay captains*) of the thirty-seven villages located within the system's service area. Results of the survey revealed the fact that the deterioration was not unique to East Laguna Village, but was common in the lower reaches of the major laterals. As shown in Figure 6.2, a national highway passes through approximately the middle of the system's service area. According to the headmen interviewed,

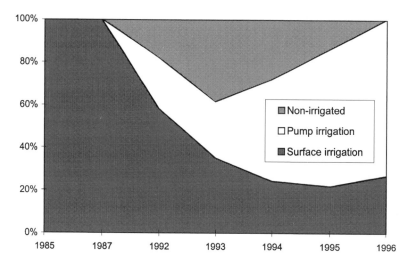

Figure 6.3   Percentage of paddy fields cultivated by the villagers by irrigation condition, East Laguna Village, 1985–96

most villages located above the highway did not suffer any water shortage even after the system's deterioration. The villages with assured water supply are classified as being in the upper reach, whereas those who suffered from water shortages are classified as being in the lower reaches of the system.[4]

The aggregation of village headmen's data indicates that the service area in the upper reaches continued to be well irrigated during both wet and dry seasons from the 1970s to the 1990s, maintaining the irrigation ratio (defined as the ratio of total area irrigated in a year to the service area) at a level between 180 per cent and 190 per cent (see Figure 6.4). In contrast, the ratio in the lower reaches was only about 150 per cent by the 1970–85 period, reflecting a much less satisfactory water supply to downstream farms. Moreover, the ratio went down sharply from 153 per cent in 1985 to 116 per cent in 1996. The decrease was especially large in the lower reaches of Lateral C, from 172 per cent to 91 per cent.

Decreased Public Support

What factors, then, did underlie the significant decline in water supply to the lower reaches? There was no suspicious environmental reason. Both the total amount and the seasonal pattern of rainfall remained the

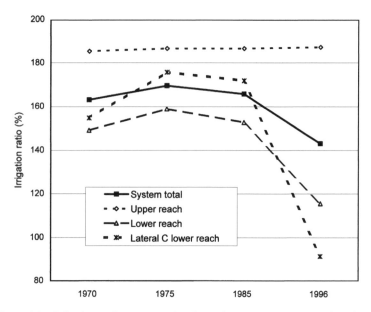

Figure 6.4   Irrigation ratio per year for the entire system, upper reaches, lower
                reaches and the lower reaches of Lateral C
Source: Our 1996 survey on the headmen of villages within the NIA system.

same, though subject to large annual fluctuations. Examination of satellite
images of the watershed area in Mount Banahaw revealed no appreciable
depletion of forests between 27 February 1976 and 11 February 1992.

It is therefore probable that degradation in the system's performance
was brought about mainly by a decline in operation and maintenance
(O&M) activities. Indeed, the NIA's expenditure on O&M in this system
declined by almost half from the early to the late 1980s (see Figure 6.5).
The number of NIA personnel engaged in O&M was also reduced sharply.
They say that eight 'water masters' in charge of water allocation and
scheduling, and twenty 'ditch tenders' in charge of manual operations used
to be allocated to this system by the mid-1980s, but by 1995, only two
water masters and eleven ditch tenders were employed.

Correspondingly, some physical structures of the system were seriously
dilapidated. In 1995, the spill gate at the dam was out of order and did not
shut properly, leaving a gap of about ten centimetres through which water,
which should otherwise have been diverted to the main canal, was running
away. Of the five head gates diverting water from the main canal to the laterals, four had some defects, with parts missing or damaged. Many turn-out
gates along the laterals were in a similar condition, and many sections of

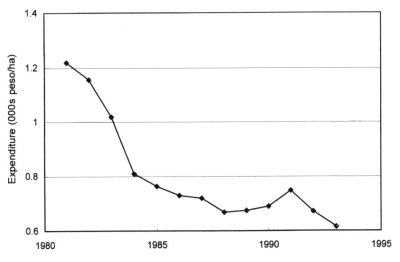

Figure 6.5   Operation and maintenance expenditures per ha in the NIA System, deflated by GDP deflator (1995 = 100), three-year moving averages, 1981–93

Source: NIA.

the main canal and the laterals were in obvious need of dredging and weed cutting. These observations leave little room to doubt the hypothesis that insufficient O&M activity since the early 1980s or even earlier has accumulated to produce degradation in the performance of the NIA system in recent years.

A low intensity of O&M activities was not unique to this system, but was pervasive in irrigation systems under the auspices of the NIA. It is only symptom of reduced public support for agriculture in the Philippines as well as in other developing economies in the world in recent years. Public investment in the infrastructure of agricultural production, such as irrigation and research in agricultural technology, were greatly intensified, especially for rice and wheat in the years of high food prices following the 'World Food Crisis' of 1973–4. However, in the 1980s, when these investments were transformed into high productivity, as epitomized by the success of the Green Revolution, world food markets entered a low-price regime; this is illustrated clearly in the movements of both the export price of Thai rice from Bangkok (as a yardstick of the international market), and the domestic price of rice in the Philippines (see the upper chart in Figure 6.6). The situation was exacerbated in the Philippines because of prolonged political instability from the 1980s to the early 1990s following the downfall of the Marcos Administration.

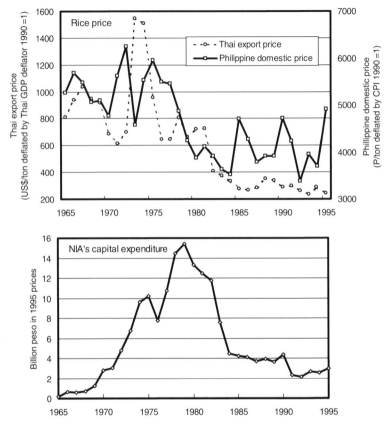

Figure 6.6   Rice price and NIA project expenditures, 1965–95
Source: Rice prices from IRRI (1995) supplemented by IRRI Social Science Division; GDP deflators from ADB (various issues); NIA capital expenditures from the NIA Headquarters.

The NIA's O&M budget was doubly hit by the decline in rice prices. It had been stipulated since 1974 that the NIA should be autonomous in financing expenditure for the O&M of existing systems from its revenue, consisting mainly of irrigation fees collected from farmers.[5] On the other hand, capital expenditure for the construction of new systems and major rehabilitation of existing systems were intended to be financed by government investments, based mainly on foreign aid. The irrigation fees are usually paid in paddy – 100 kg in the wet season and 150 kg in the dry season per hectare. Thus, the NIA's revenue for financing O&M decreased sharply, corresponding to the decline in the price of rice during the 1980s. Another significant revenue accruing to the NIA's current account is a 5 per cent set-aside for administrative overheads from the 'project fund' originally allocated for the construction of new systems. In addition, part of the project fund, which was specifically designated for the use of O&M projects (mostly foreign-funded), is allocated to existing systems, not on a project basis but in proportion to their service areas, to pay for the cost of small repairs. As both the international aid agencies and the national government became more reluctant to assist irrigation projects under an apparent oversupply of rice, the set-aside for administrative overheads from the new construction funds, as well as the project funds designated for small repairs, also shrank. The relationship between the decline in the project fund and the decline in rice prices in the 1980s will be evident from Figure 6.6.

Deterioration in the performance of the NIA system because of insufficient O&M activity was thus a reflection of the financial crisis of the NIA that emerged in the 1980s as a result of the very success of the Green Revolution.

Differential Performances across Laterals

Deterioration in the service of irrigation was, however, not uniform within the system, but varied greatly across laterals, as observed in the movements in the percentages of irrigated areas in the service areas based on the NIA's data (see Figure 6.7). Major decreases in the irrigation ratio occurred in Laterals C and D, showing that the system's performance deteriorated first in Lateral D during the 1980s, followed by Lateral C during the 1990s. In contrast, a significant improvement was recorded in the irrigation ratio of Lateral E. The irrigation ratio also increased slightly in Lateral B, especially in the 1990s, when Lateral C's performance deteriorated rapidly. The ratio in Lateral A was low, but remained relatively stable.

The differential performances across laterals were, to some extent, based on differences in their physical and geographical conditions. For example, the lower rate of irrigation in Lateral A than in Lateral B is explained by the fact that the former's service area extends widely in the lower reaches of the system below the highway, whereas the latter's service is limited to the area above the highway. However, no appreciable degradation occurred in Laterals A and B. It is understandable that the performances of Laterals C and D located below them along the main canal deteriorated relative to A and B, corresponding to the contraction in the

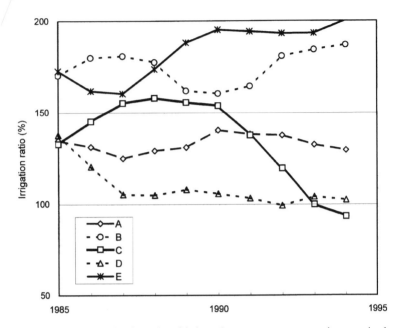

Figure 6.7   Changes in the ratio of irrigated area per year to service area in the
NIA system by lateral, three-year moving averages, 1985–94
Source: NIA.

water supply resulting from insufficient O&M activity. It is a major
puzzle, however, that the performance of Lateral E improved despite its
location in the tail end of the main canal.

IRRIGATORS' ASSOCIATIONS AND THE NIA

When public support for irrigation began to decrease significantly in the
1980s, the NIA tried to mobilize local communities' contributions to
O&M activities. For a given amount of water diverted from the river, water
supply to crops could be increased if laterals and ditches were cleaned by
farmers working collectively. Efficiency in the use of scarce water may be
enhanced if a rational water rotation was agreed upon and observed
by farmers. The deferential performances of the irrigation service across
the laterals seem to reflect successes and failures in the organization of
local initiatives for these activities.

Organization of Irrigators' Associations

When the NIA was pressed strongly to establish its financial autonomy in the 1980s under waning public support, farmers' participation in O&M activities was recognized as a necessary condition to prevent the system's performance from deteriorating. Taking this into consideration, the NIA began to organize farmer-beneficiaries into irrigators' associations (IAs). It was also believed to be more efficient to delegate the collection of irrigation fees to IAs. NIA's institutional development strategy consisted of two steps: first, to organize farmers in a turn-out service area group (TSA group); and, second, to federate TSA groups along each lateral into an IA. Both TSA groups and IAs in national systems are organized under the guidance of the NIA, each with a management team of five elected officers, including a president, a vice-president, a secretary, a treasurer and an auditor. IAs are categorized into three types in terms of O&M responsibility turned over from NIA – Type 1 if an IA agrees to take responsibility for cleaning canals; Type 2 if, in addition, the IA takes charge of collecting irrigation fees; and Type 3 if the IA agrees to take all the O&M responsibility on condition that the IA establishes property rights on the canal structures and finances their construction costs. In order to mobilize local participation and initiative, the NIA designed various incentive schemes for the IAs. First, if an IA agrees to take responsibility for cleaning canals within its territory, the NIA will pay 4800 pesos per month (equivalent to about 30 person-days of farm work) per kilometre of canal length. For repair work that costs more than 500 pesos, the NIA grants the contract to the IA. For a smaller repair costing less than 500 pesos, the IA is required to mobilize members' labour without pay, but materials and machinery are supplied by the NIA. When the IA enters a Type 2 contract, including fee collection, it is entitled to receive 2 per cent of collected fees if it is able to collect more than 50 per cent of the total invoice (and to receive 15 per cent if the collection rate exceeds 90 per cent).

Supported by the NIA, four IAs, one each for Laterals A, B and E, and another for Laterals C and D combined were created, covering about 70 per cent of the total service area. These were registered at the Security Exchange Commission, one in 1987 and the remaining three in 1991, to establish a legal person status. Among the four IAs, however, those of Laterals B and E continued to be active, of which only the latter advanced to the stage of being Type 2. Meanwhile, the IAs of Laterals A, C and D stopped functioning within a few years of their formation. There is little doubt that success and failure in the organization of IAs underlay the differential performances across laterals as observed in Figure 6.7.

The patterns and sources of the differential institutional performances will be examined through a comparison between Laterals C-D and E.

The successful IA in Lateral E was established in 1983, federating six TSA groups in the area above the highway, and in 1993 one TSA group below the highway joined the IA. While canal cleaning, small repairs and irrigation fee collection are important activities of this IA, an even more important function is to establish and monitor a water rotation schedule. The IA holds a regular monthly meeting at which IA officials and TSA leaders discuss prospective water needs to reach an agreement on a rotation schedule. The schedule is made in consultation with the NIA's field staff so that it remains consistent with the system-wide rotation. Leaders take turn in monitoring 24 hours a day during a crop season when violation of the rotation is likely to occur. Though specific penalties for violations are not stipulated, the leaders' warning and persuasion are usually sufficient to suppress illegal water take-out. As a result, conflicts and disputes on the use of water, which used to be common before the formation of the IA, were largely eliminated in the service area of Lateral E. As farmers recognized the benefit of the IA, their co-operation and participation were increased resulting in the enhanced rate of fee collection as well as additional contributions to O&M activities proportional to farm sizes. The increased revenue to the IA provided a basis for further improving the quality of irrigation to produce a greater satisfaction in members. Thus a virtuous circle operated between institutional development and irrigation service in Lateral E.

The case of Lateral C represents a sharp contrast to that of Lateral E. As in the case of Lateral E, the NIA tried to organize farmers in Lateral C into an IA in the early 1980s. This attempt failed, presumably because the water supply along Lateral C was relatively abundant, so that farmers did not feel the need to organize themselves for water allocation. Later, during the water shortage in 1990–1, the NIA was able to establish a combined IA for Laterals C and D. These were combined into a single IA because some of the service areas from the two laterals are intermeshed.

In organizing and activating farmers' participation, the NIA appointed eight farmers in the area as 'farmer-irrigators organizers' (FIOs) with an honorarium of 500 pesos per person for six months. The NIA's 'water masters' and the FIOs called farmers to meetings in each of sixteen turnout service areas in Lateral C, and fourteen in Lateral D, explaining the benefit of IAs and urging their active participation. Nevertheless, this IA was not able to advance even to a stage of handing over from the NIA the responsibility of cleaning laterals and ditches (a Type 1 contract). Rotation of irrigation was also tried under the guidance of the NIA but totally failed without being able to reduce rampant illegal water take-outs. The NIA's officials blamed low moral and lack of co-operative spirit among the people in Laterals C and D, compared with those of Lateral E. More concretely, the IA's president (who was formerly elected by TSA group leaders but *de facto* appointed by the NIA) complained that there was no participation by leaders, especially those in the lower reaches, in meetings, despite his repeated requests.

However, the perception of people in East Laguna Village, which is at the tail-end of Lateral C, was different. The president of the TSA group in the village explained that leaders in the village were eager to participate when the IA was created. Their enthusiasm waned, however, as the IA was incapable of enforcing the water rotation schedule. They complained to both the NIA and the IA about rampant illegal water take-outs by upstream farmers, which resulted in water shortages in the lower reaches. In fact, they padlocked water gates in the upper reaches to prevent upstream farmers from taking out water during the downstream turn of rotation. However, the chains and locks were soon destroyed. Despite knowing who carried out these illegal actions, neither the NIA nor the IA was able to stop them. Dismayed by such incidents, leaders in East Laguna Village (who were relatively large farmers) purchased pumps to cope with the deteriorating water supply from NIA, rather than wasting time and energy in activating the IA. Thus local participation and irrigation services in Lateral C deteriorated in a vicious circle.

Why, then, was Lateral E able to escape such a vicious circle and take part in a virtuous circle? Based on a field study of an irrigation system in India, Robert Wade (1990) advanced a hypothesis that villages at the tail end of a system tend to organize collective action better to economize on the use of water, because of higher rates of return to such actions under stronger constraints on water supply. This hypothesis seems consistent with the contrast between Laterals C-D and E. However, it does not explain why an IA was organized successfully in upper-stream Lateral B, if not as active as in Lateral E. Also, it does not explain why farmers in Lateral E were successful in organizing themselves when they faced a water shortage in the early 1980s, and why they failed in Lateral C when facing a similar problem in the 1990s. In Lateral E also, conflicts and disputes among farmers on the use of water were common and often fierce, culminating sometimes in bloodshed and even a murder case before the formation of the IA. Why was Lateral E, but not Lateral C, able to shift from the negative-sum to the positive-sum co-operative game?

We have examined several factors which might explain the difference between the area with active IAs (Laterals B and E) and the area with inactive IAs (Laterals A, C and D), such as the depth of the underground water table as a measure of cost for using irrigation pumps, and the distribution of farm sizes and the ratio of non-farm households as measures of homogeneity of communities. Differences in these variables are, however, not statistically significant at conventional levels (Fujita, 1998).

The factor found to be significant was the size of the system by lateral. As shown in Table 6.1, both Laterals B and E, with active IAs, are much smaller than those labelled A, C and D – less than a third on average in terms of the length of lateral (including sub-laterals) and service area as well as the numbers of farms and villages in the service area. A is distinctively larger than the others, but since C and D are combined to form one IA, both the territory and the member size of this IA is comparable to that of A. The structures of Laterals B and E (and also D) are simpler, with only one sub-lateral being attached, compared to A and C, with nine and three sub-laterals, respectively.

Technically, the larger and more complicated a system, the more difficult it is to monitor if the system is to be operated and maintained properly, including identification of where and by whom illegal water take-outs are practised. More serious is the greater difficulty of groups having larger membership to organize collective action for the supply of public goods, since it is easier and more profitable for members in larger groups to

Table 6.1   Length of laterals, service areas, and number of sub-laterals, villages and farms in the five laterals of the NIA system, 1996

	Length of lateral (km)	Service area (ha)	Number of sub-laterals	Number of villages	Number of farms
Active IA					
Lateral B	6.0	240	1	2	159
Lateral E[a]	4.9	227	1	3	121
Average	5.5	234	1	2.5	140
Inactive IA					
Lateral A	29.3	1602	9	17	1070
Lateral C	12.8	588	3	7	334
Lateral D	8.0	336	1	5	193
Average	16.7	842	4	10	532

Note: [a] Data at the formation of the IA in 1983, excluding the lower reach extended after 1993.
Source: NIA and our 1996 headmen survey.

become free-riders (Olson, 1965). In this respect, the IAs of A and C-D, including much larger numbers of irrigator-farmers than those of B and E, should have had a greater probability of failure in reaching a consensus on the rules of water use and public works as well as enforcing the rules for their systems' O&M by members.

It is likely that an even more critical determinant of the effective organization of an IA than the size of its membership is the number of villages in its territory. In the rural sector of developing economies, the village is the basic unit of life and work. It is a community characterized by strong social interactions among people tied closely by both blood and locational affinity. The community is ruled mainly by traditional norms and conventions, enforced by villagers' moral obligation to neighbours as well as their fear of social opprobrium and ostracism resulting from a violation of the rules. This community mechanism of rule enforcement is considered to be effective in conserving local commons, as discussed earlier. However, its effectiveness tends to be limited within a small community, typically one village or one tribe. While the solidarity of a village community may be effective in preventing its members from indulging in opportunistic and free-riding behaviour, it often encourages opportunism against outsiders (Hayami, 1997, pp. 266–8). Indeed, it is not uncommon to observe that local commons, such as forests and communal irrigation systems under the auspices of one village are relatively well maintained, whereas those encompassing several villages are seriously depleted, in a condition akin to the 'tragedy of the commons'.

This difficulty of organizing people across different communities should increase as the number of villages increases, even if a mutually beneficial scheme of co-operation can be envisaged. There seems to be little doubt that the organization of IAs in Laterals A and C-D was handicapped by having a large number of villages within each of the territories, compared with Laterals B and E.

Optimization of the NIA

The differential performances across laterals have been explained so far by the successes and the failures in organizing IAs. It must be recognized, however, that the differential performances were amplified by the optimizing behaviour of the NIA's bureaucracy. To understand this process, it is necessary to understand the position of an office directly in charge of the system's operation and maintenance within the organization of the NIA as well as the goals and means of the office.

As shown in Figure 6.8, the NIA's hierarchy, from its headquarters to the field level, is separated into two lines: one for the construction of new systems and major rehabilitation of existing systems, and the other for the operation and maintenance of existing systems. Each construction or major rehabilitation project was managed by a 'project office' established for the project period. The O&M of national irrigation systems are handled by 'irrigation systems offices', and the NIA's assistance to communal systems is administered by 'provincial offices'. Both of these are under the supervision of 'regional offices'. The system serving East Laguna Village is managed by a systems office located in Pila. This office also manages four other national systems and reports to the regional office covering the fourth region of the NIA.

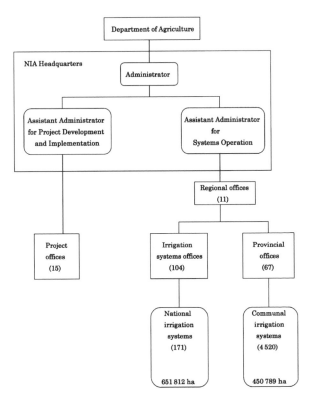

Figure 6.8   Organization of the National Irrigation Administration (NIA), as of December 1995

Note: This chart is simplified from the organizational chart prepared by the NIA Head quarters. Numbers of offices and systems are shown in parentheses.

As has already been explained, the NIA is required to cover its current expenditure, including administrative overheads and O&M costs, by its current revenue, consisting mainly of irrigation fees, administrative set-asides from project funds for construction projects, and special project funds for O&M. This financial autonomy on a current-account basis is also applied to each systems office. Collection of irrigation fees above a systems office's current expenditure budget is highly praised, since the excess adds to the revenue of the higher echelons of the NIA's hierarchy. On the other hand, a deficit results in a serious discredit against the executives of the systems office. The deficit of a systems office may be covered by a loan from a regional office based on surpluses in other systems. However, the loan cannot be easily obtained, because few systems are able to generate the surpluses. Therefore, because of the depressed rice market of the 1980s and 1990s, systems offices were forced to cut down on staff, and O&M expenditure. Even so, it was difficult for many offices to avoid a chronic delay in the payment of salaries to remaining staff for several months.

Under such conditions, it is no wonder that the systems office in Pila, similar to that in other offices, was hard pressed to increase the collection of irrigation fees. The willingness of farmers to pay the fees depends on the quality of irrigation service, yet, the option for the systems office to improve the service to farmers by increasing O&M expenditures was closed under stringent budgetary constraints. Thus the office opted to allocate more of the available water to the areas with high irrigation fee collection rates at the expense of the areas with low collection rates; this was achieved by a diversion of water to the laterals with active IAs from those with inactive IAs. Indeed, it is an open secret that NIA's water masters opened the head gates to Laterals B and E for longer hours at times of high water demand than the gates to other laterals. As a result, the water supply to the areas of active IAs increased further, and water shortage was aggravated in the areas with inactive IAs. Such behaviour by the NIA staff created distrust among farmers in the latter areas, and induced them to purchase irrigation pumps and stop payment of irrigation fees; and this motivated the diversion of more water away from those areas. Thus the vicious circle between inactive local participation and deterioration in the irrigation service in Laterals A, C and D was greatly amplified by the systems office's short-run optimization behaviour. The short-run optimization by the NIA office was not able to prevent its collection of irrigation fees from declining either. Instead, the rate of collection from the system's service area decreased, from 73 per cent in 1987 to 50 per cent in 1992, and further, to 38 per cent in 1995.

COSTS AND BENEFITS OF THE SYSTEM'S MANAGEMENT

Despite the major deterioration in the system, rice production in its service area including East Laguna Village was maintained, because in the areas in which the supply of water from the NIA was drained, farmers continued to irrigate their fields by purchasing private pumps. Because the underground water table in the areas adjacent to Laguna de Bay are shallow and easily replenishable, farmers in the lower reaches of the system could switch the source of irrigation at a modest cost with little worry about the exhaustion of the underground water supply. Yet the switch entailed a cost that could have been saved if the system was properly maintained. We shall attempt to illustrate by simple calculations the level of costs that may be involved in inadequate O&M activities in the system, and the level of benefits that may be forthcoming from appropriate expenditure on O&M.

Private Benefits and Costs to Farmers

First, private costs and benefits associated with farmers' switching from the NIA's gravity irrigation to pump irrigation are calculated on a per-hectare basis under several alternative assumptions in Table 6.2.

Farmers' cost in annual flow terms includes the interest and depreciation of capital investments for the purchase of a pump and the digging of a well, as well as operating expenses to pay for fuel and labour (row 1). Three alternative interest rates are tried in the calculation: 100 per cent per year is a typical rate in informal credits in the rural areas of the Philippines; 25 per cent is a modal rate of commercial banks' lending with collateral; and 12 per cent is the rate of concessional loans from the government.

Under a condition where the NIA's service has already been terminated, a benefit to farmers from the use of pump irrigation is an increase in farm income resulting from the shift from rainfed single-cropping to irrigated double-cropping. This benefit is calculated under two alternative assumptions: Case A assumes the same yields for the NIA's surface irrigation and pump irrigation (row 2); and Case B assumes increases in yield with a shift from the NIA's surface irrigation to pump irrigation (row 3). According to our farmers' survey in East Laguna Village, the average yields of pump-irrigated fields were higher by about 0.5 ton per hectare than those of the NIA-irrigated fields, for both wet and dry seasons. However, the differences were not statistically significant at conventional levels according to the data collected from village headmen in the system's service area.

Table 6.2   Benefits and costs to farmers of switching from surface to pump irrigation in the system service area [a]

		Interest rate assumed[b]		
		$i = 100\%$	$i = 25\%$	$i = 12\%$
›sts of pump irrigation (P/ha)[c]	(1)	21 607	12 607	11 047
ome increase with pump over ⠀infed case (P/ha):				
Case A[d]	(2)	40 832	40 832	40 832
Case B[e]	(3)	47 872	47 872	47 872
⠀gation fee saved (P/ha)[f]	(4)	2 000	2 000	2 000
nefit–Cost ratio				
⠀IA service terminated;				
Case A	(2)/(1)	1.9	3.2	3.7
Case B	(3)/(1)	2.2	3.8	4.3
⠀IA service continued;				
Case A	(4)/(1)	0.1	0.2	0.2
Case B	$(3-2+4)/(1)$	0.4	0.7	0.8

›tes: [a] Costs and benefits are all evaluated at 1995 prices.

[b] 100% per year is a typical rate in the rural informal money market; 25% is the typical lending rate (with collateral) of commercial banks; and 12% is the rate of government concessional loans.

[c] Investment costs $\times$ i + maintenance costs + fuel costs for wet and dry + operating labour cost.

[d] Assume the same yields per ha with NIA irrigation and with pump irrigation (3.9 tons in wet season and 4.8 tons in dry season) and rainfed yield (2.9 tons in wet season alone).

[e] Assume higher yields per ha with pump irrigation (4.4 tons in wet season and 5.3 tons in dry season) than with NIA irrigation.

[f] 2 *cavans* (1 *cavan* = 50 kg) for wet, and 3 *cavans* for dry season per ha, valued at P8.00/kg of rough rice price in 1995.

Division of rows (2) and (3) by row (1) produces benefit–cost ratios for introducing pumps where water supply from the NIA is not available, under alternative assumptions on the differences in yield between the NIA's gravity and private-pump irrigation. The results show that even for a farmer who has no access to anything but informal credits, the benefit from introducing a pump is twice as great as its cost; if he or she has a good collateral to enable him/her to receive credit from commercial banks, his/her benefit rises to about four times greater than his/her cost. Thus it is no wonder that many farmers, especially large ones having a fair amount of land and other real assets, were quick to purchase pumps when the NIA's water supply dwindled.

The situation is very different in the areas where sufficient water supply from the NIA continues to be available. In this case, the benefit of a farmer switching from the NIA's surface water to pumped underground water is only the saving of the irrigation fee (row 4), which he or she has to pay in the event of his/her continued reliance on the service of the NIA, in the absence of rice yield increases from the switch (Case A). If rice yields increase (Case B), a corresponding increase in the income of rice production (row 3 minus row 2), plus the saving of the irrigation fee (rows 4), would become his benefit.

The benefit–cost ratios calculated under these assumptions show that the benefit from the use of a pump is lower than its cost under the condition of continued water supply from NIA, even if concessional loans are provided for farmers by the government. So it is also no wonder that few farmers in the areas with adequate surface water supply purchased pumps. Clearly, farmers in the areas of deteriorated gravity irrigation service were worse off relative to those in the areas of continued adequate service, even though it was possible to recover their loss to a significant extent by the introduction of pump irrigation.

Social Benefits and Costs

What costs and benefits would the NIA's poor system maintenance produce to society? Calculations summarized in Table 6.3 may shed light on this question.

If the NIA had continued to supply sufficient water, it would have been unnecessary for farmers to change to pump irrigation. Therefore the cost of pump irrigation (row 1 in Table 6.3, same as row 1 in Table 6.2) can be considered as the benefit from an adequate water supply from the NIA system, if rice yields do not increase corresponding to the change from surface to pump irrigation (Case A). The cost of O&M activities per hectare that would enable the NIA system to continue supplying sufficient water to its service area is assumed to be the irrigation service fee set by the NIA intending to cover the system's O&M (row 2). Under NIA's financial framework, this is the maximum amount that can be spent for O&M. The level of actual O&M expenditure on the system in the 1990s was less than 40 per cent of this 'ideal level'.

Division of row 1 by row 2 produces a benefit–cost ratio for adequate maintenance of the system under the assumption of equality between rice yields under adequate surface irrigation and pump irrigation, while treating the investment in the system's construction as a sunk cost. The calculated ratios are very high, ranging from 5 to 11 for the different interest

Table 6.3 Social benefits and costs of NIA's maintenance of the system[a]

		Interest rate assumed[b]		
		i = 100%	i = 25%	i = 12%
Costs of pump irrigation (P/ha)[c]	(1)	21 607	12 607	11 047
O&M expenditure on the NIA system (P/ha)[d]	(2)	2 000	2 000	2 000
Capital cost of system construction (P/ha)[e]	(3)	79 196	9 783	3 983
Income increase because of pump (P/ha)[f]	(4)	7 040	7 040	7 040
Benefit–Cost ratio				
Case A: Assume no increase in yield with pump				
Excluding capital cost	(1)/(2)	10.8	6.3	5.5
Including capital cost	(1)/(2+3)	0.3	1.1	1.8
Case B: Assume yield increase with pump				
Excluding capital cost	(1−4)/(2)	7.3	2.8	2.0
Including capital cost	(1−4)/(2+3)	0.2	0.5	0.7

Notes: [a] Costs and benefits are all evaluated at 1995 prices.
[b] Same as Table 6.2.
[c] Same as Table 6.2.
[d] Assume the entire amount of irrigation service fee is spent on O&M.
[e] Initial investment costs for constructing the system in 1958 (including the interest for the average gestation period of 1.5 years).
[f] Income increase because of higher yields with a pump over NIA gravity irrigation.

rates assumed. Since the true social rate of discount is likely to lie some-where between the rates of the government's concessional loans and the commercial bank's lending – certainly much lower than the rate of infor-mal credit – the results seem to imply that one peso spent on the existing system's maintenance produces an additional income of as much as about six pesos to society. If the capital cost of construction (row 3) is included in the denominator, the benefit–cost ratio is reduced to less than 2, even at the concessional loan rate; this calculation, however, is not relevant in the present context, which is focused on the NIA's strategy within the existing system.

If rice yields are assumed to increase in response to the switch from sur-face to pump irrigation (Case B), the benefit–cost ratios are reduced to about a half of those under the assumption of no yield increase. Still, the conclusion remains unchanged that additional expenditure on the mainte-nance of existing NIA systems produces a large net benefit to society.

Although these calculations are very crude and somewhat over-simplified, the results unambiguously show that the NIA is investing in the O&M activities of existing systems at far less than a socially optimum level.

INSTITUTIONAL DEVELOPMENT VERSUS WHITE ELEPHANT

While it is evident that the NIA's O&M expenditure in the late 1980s and the early 1990s was much less than the social optimum, it does not follow that the NIA should return to the organization structure that prevailed until the early 1980s, in which the NIA's systems office, employing a large field staff, undertook directly the necessary O&M activities, with little effort to mobilize local participation and initiative. The NIA's attempt to orga-nize farmers in service areas into IAs and to hand over O&M activities to them represents a way to achieve greater efficiency in the maintenance of its systems.

As discussed earlier, the success has been limited to the small laterals with simple structures involving small numbers of farmers and villages, while the NIA's attempt to organize IAs in larger laterals with more com-plicated technical designs and social structures has largely failed. It is easy to understand that leaders in local communities have to face progressively greater difficulty in organizing IAs as potential membership and the num-ber of villages involved become larger. The time and energy involved in achieving consensus among a larger population in many different villages are often excessive for the leaders, who are usually busy with their own farming and other businesses. Assistance and advice from the NIA's staff with technical expertise as well as a certain discretion on the allocation of water and the O&M budget could be highly instrumental in enhancing co-operation and consensus among people in different villages.

The NIA has long recognized the importance of such institutional extension activities and employs specialists called 'institutional development officers' (IDO) mainly to assist with communal systems. Since the early 1980s, when the NIA tried to organize IAs into national systems, some IDOs have been allocated for that purpose. The NIA's manual specifies a standard that the full-time work of one IDO for one year should be allocated to each lateral to establish one IA. Yet, under stringent budgetary constraints, no full-time IDO has ever been allocated to any one of the five laterals in the system. Activities for the promotion of the IAs were left largely to the water masters. It is easy to imagine that the institutional extension activities by water masters who were busy with day-to-day operations were far from sufficient, especially when their numbers were reduced because of the systems office's financial crisis. In 1995–6, none of the IDOs were employed in the systems office, and only five IDOs were assigned to the Regional Office for Region IV that oversees thirty-five national systems. They are more than fully occupied by routine administrative work in support of existing active IAs, with little room to engage in field activities organizing new IAs or motivating inactive IAs.

While recognizing the limitation of government employees to promote the organization of local participation and initiative, is it not reasonable to expect that the IAs of Laterals A and C-D could have been somewhat more active, even if less active than in B and E, if the institutional extension activities by IDOs had been provided at the standard level specified in the NIA's manual?

Economic Returns to Institutional Development

In order to illustrate the potential of economic gains from public investments in institutional development, benefit–cost calculations are undertaken as shown in Table 6.4.

In this calculation, it is assumed that, in order to establish an effective IA in a lateral, which is difficult to organize by using the initiative of the local people alone, one full-time IDO must be allocated to the lateral for two consecutive years (instead of the one year specified in the NIA's manual). In addition, it is assumed that, in order to sustain the effective functioning of the IA after establishment, one IDO must continue to work for a third of his/her time in each lateral. According to several IDOs whom we interviewed, those assumptions are considered to include a fair amount

Table 6.4 Social benefits and costs of the NIA's institutional development investment for irrigators' associations (IAs) in the system

		Success probability = 0.5 Interest rate assumed		Success probability = 0.2 Interest rate assumed	
		$i = 25\%$	$i = 12\%$	$i = 25\%$	$i = 12\%$
Benefits					
Annual flow per ha (P'000s/ha/year)					
Case A	(1)	12.6	11.0	12.6	11.0
Case B	(2)	5.57	4.01	5.57	4.01
Total present value (P million)					
Case A	(3)	24.2	55.0	9.68	22.0
Case B	(4)	10.7	20.0	4.28	7.99
Costs					
Annual flow (P'000s/IDO/year)					
Case A	(5)	255	255	255	255
Case B	(6)	1.75	2.98	1.75	2.98
Benefit–Cost ratio					
Case A	(3)/(6)	13.8	18.5	5.5	7.4
Case B	(4)/(6)	6.1	6.7	2.4	2.7
Internal rate of return (%)					
Case A		338		173	
Case B		239		101	

Notes: (1) Row 1 in Table 6.3; assume no yield difference between NIA gravity and pump irrigation as in Table 6.2; assumed to emerge from the 3rd year.

(2) Row 1–Row 4 in Table 6.3; assume higher yield for pump than gravity as in Table 6.2; assumed to emerge from the 3rd year.

(3) and (4) Sum of total annual flows (annual flow/ha × 1500 ha × success probability), discounted to the 1st year.

(5) Salary and other supporting costs for one year of employing one institution development officer (IDO) for IA institution building.

(6) Sum of the costs of three IDOs for the first two years and one IDO thereafter, discounted to the 1st year.

of safety margin for calculating the cost needed to organize and maintain active IAs in most if not all the cases.

Our calculation assumes that, if effective IAs are to be organized successfully by those IDOs' institutional extension activities, the O&M of the system would be adequately performed, to assure a sufficient water supply to its service area, thereby eliminating the farmers' need to use pumps. However, success would be a matter of probability depending on many *ad hoc* elements such as the qualities of the IDOs and local leaders as well as personal matches (or mismatches) between them. Therefore, in our calculation in Table 6.4, two alternative probabilities are assumed, of 50 per cent and 20 per cent of the success of the institutional development project. One success out of five trials is considered to be a very conservative assumption according to the past experience of the NIA even with one full-time IDO allocated to a lateral for one year only.[6]

The annual flow of benefit from the NIA's investment in the institutional development project, if successful, will be the saving of pump costs arising from the return from the area presently irrigated by pumps to that served by the NIA's surface irrigation in Case A, assuming equality in yields between surface and pump irrigation (row 1 in Table 6.4), and the pump cost saving minus the value of increased yield in Case B, assuming yield increases because of the shift from surface to pump irrigation (row 2). These estimates of benefit per hectare are the same as in Table 6.3.

Multiplication of the annual-benefit flows per hectare to the area presently irrigated by pumps (1500 hectares of service area) produces the system-wide total benefit flows, which are converted into the total present values at the beginning of the institutional development project by discounting future annual flows that are assumed to emerge from the third year onwards by assumed alternative interest rates (rows 3 and 4). Note that this calculation is likely to produce conservative estimates of total benefit because it assumes the benefit to arise only in the area presently under pump irrigation. In fact, it is likely that, so long as the NIA's O&M expenditure remains at its present level, the system will continue to deteriorate, resulting in progressively larger areas diverted to pump irrigation in the future.

The cost of an institutional development project to organize IAs effectively in Laterals A, C and D is assumed to consist of the salaries of three IDOs for the first two years of the project and one IDO for subsequent years, plus other costs in support of their extension activities including transportation, holding extension meetings, honorariums for local leaders' assistance, and various logistics. More concretely, one IDO's salary per year is assumed to be 170 000 pesos and other costs to be 84 500 pesos per IDO per year, according to information collected from the NIA (row 5).

The total cost of three IDOs for the first two years and one IDO for subsequent years are discounted, and summed up to total present values at the beginning of the project (row 6).

The social profitability of the institutional development project can be assessed by the ratios between the total present values of costs and benefits as well as the internal rates of return calculated under alternative assumptions. The estimates of the benefit–cost ratio show that even under the most conservative assumptions (only one success out of five projects tried, the social rate of discount equal to the interest rate of commercial bank loan, and yield decreases corresponding to shifts from pump to surface irrigation) one peso spent for the support on IAs is expected to produce 2.4 pesos to society; this corresponds to the most conservative estimates of the internal rate of return to be as high as 101 per cent per year, nearly four times higher than the commercial banks' lending rate.

Despite such a high social rate of return being likely to be forthcoming, the NIA has invested very little in supporting the development of IAs. This under-investment may be explained partly by the much higher discount rate on future incomes held by NIA officials than the social rate of discount. It may also be explained by the low rate of private returns to the NIA. Private benefits to the NIA from the success of institutional development would be increases in the collection of irrigation fees corresponding to increases in the area serviced by the NIA system. If this benefit is compared with the NIA's cost as assumed in the calculation in the social rate of return, the private benefit–cost ratio for the NIA's institutional development investment is less than one if a commercial loan rate is applied for discounting, and is close to one even if the government's concessional loan rate is applied, both on the assumption of one success out of five trials; this corresponds to the internal rate of return being insignificantly larger than the concessional loan rate (Table 6.5). As has already been explained, the financial crisis of the NIA was created by the reduction in public support for irrigation from both external and internal sources. Under the crisis that meant even salary payments to its regular staff were often delayed, the NIA officials' future discount rate was likely to be much higher than the interest rate of concessional loans from the government. In such a situation it is no wonder that the NIA has neglected to invest in the institutional development of IAs.

Walang Silbi!

We emphasized earlier that the performance of this system deteriorated because it received insufficient maintenance. However, it must be pointed

Table 6.5 Private benefits and costs to NIA of institutional development investment for irrigators' associations (IAs) in the system

		Success probability = 0.5 *Interest rate assumed*		*Success probability = 0.2* *Interest rate assumed*	
		i = 25%	*i = 12%*	*i = 25%*	*i = 12%*
Benefit					
Annual flow per ha (P'000s/ha/year)	(1)	1.60	1.60	1.60	1.60
Total present value (P million)	(2)	3.07	7.97	1.23	3.19
Cost					
Annual flow (P'000s/IDO/year)	(3)	255	255	255	255
Total present value (P million)	(4)	1.75	2.98	1.75	2.98
Benefit–Cost ratio	(2)/(4)	1.8	2.7	0.7	1.1
Internal rate of return (%)		50		14	

Notes: (1) Row 4 in Table 6.2 × 0.8 (collection rate).
(2) Sum of total annual flows (annual flow/ha × 1500 ha × success probability), discounted to the 1st year.
(3) Row 5 in Table 6.4.
(4) Row 6 in Table 6.4.

out that the system received major investment for renovation for 1977–84, some twenty years after its construction. This rehabilitation project was funded by the Asian Development Bank. It was a very ambitious project including: (i) the replacement of an old sluice gate at the dam site made of wood by a new iron gate; (ii) the construction of an irrigation road for cars to pass next to the main canal to replace a footpath; (iii) the renovation of waterworks, including the replacement of all single-gated turn-outs by double-gated turn-outs; and (iv) the installation of ten large pumps to bring up water from Laguna de Bay with the construction of a new canal of a length of about twenty kilometres for the distribution of the pumped-up water.

The first and second components made some positive contributions: the irrigation road made operation and maintenance of the main canal much easier; and the old wooden sluice gate needed to be replaced in any case twenty years after its original construction. However, the third component's contribution is doubtful, because the sophisticated double-gated turn-outs have seldom been used as double-gated but only as ordinary, single-gated turn-outs.

And a magnificent failure occurred in the fourth component of the project. It was a very ambitious plan, exhausting most of the budget for this rehabilitation project. It aimed not only to augment water supply for the existing system's service area but also to expand the service area by as much as 3000 hectares, or 80 per cent of the existing service area, but the plan ended in a devastating failure. A new canal was dug, electric poles were raised, and pumps were installed in a large concrete station, but a 20-minute test after construction showed that the system did not work properly, and water available for pumping up in the channel connected with Laguna de Bay was soon exhausted. According to NIA engineers, this plan could be made technically workable, but was not likely to be feasible economically. They say its proper operation would be extremely costly, with both the heavy use of electricity and the constant need to dredge silt to a sufficient depth from the channel connecting the pump station and the lake. They estimate that in order to cover their operating expenses, the irrigation fee must be raised to as much as 500 kg of paddy per hectare per season from the NIA's standard rate of 100 kg in the wet season and 150 kg in the dry season.

In any case, the pumps, which were installed in the 'pumping station' as marked in Figure 6.2, did not operate beyond several test runs. All related structures were also unused. Today, one can see the ruins of the pumping station, with big pumps turned into junk, long canals used only as swimming pools for ducks, and a large number of electric poles fallen among the paddy fields. Such an outcome should have been seen as being inevitable because of the way this project was planned and implemented. The plan was drafted with no consultation with prospective farmer-beneficiaries and therefore with no due consideration of their needs either, and it was implemented in a totally top-down way, with no attempt to mobilize local participation. Thus, it was a 'white elephant', geared to demonstrating magnificent projects to impress government officials and donor communities rather than to meet the real needs of local people. It was destined to be called *walang silbi* (useless) by the local people.

It must be recognized that this white elephant was very costly. Total investment in this project amounted to 94.4 million pesos at current prices, which was nearly 495 million pesos at 1995 prices, with the unit cost per hectare of the service area being as high as 124 000 pesos. Note that this unit cost is more than sixty times higher than the adequate O&M cost per year needed to prevent the system from deteriorating, as assumed in the calculations in Table 6.3. More importantly, the total project cost was as much as 160 times higher than the highest estimate for the cost of institutional development as was assumed in the calculations in Table 6.4 (the present value at the beginning of the institutional development project under the discount rate of 12 per cent). One can only imagine how the system would look today if only one tenth of the money spent on this white elephant had been allocated to institutional development.

VOICE AND EXIT

Deterioration of the gravity irrigation system to which East Laguna Village belongs represents an organizational maladjustment to reduced public support for agriculture, which was a result of the very success of the Green Revolution. Although the system was under the auspices of a state agency, the NIA, its efficient management required the co-operation and participation of local beneficiaries because the system has attributes of local commons or common-pool resources. So long as the NIA was able to command abundant resources based on generous support from foreign donors and the national government, the system was operated and maintained decently, if not efficiently. However, as external support was contracted under the depressed rice market, the NIA faced a financial crisis. Pressed by the need to economize on the use of public resources, the NIA tried to hand over a part of resource-allocation functions to local communities by organizing irrigators' associations (IA). This attempt succeeded in relatively small areas but failed in many others, resulting in the deterioration of the overall system's performance.[7] The failure stemmed from the difficulty of organizing local communities sufficiently strong enough to prevent farmers from becoming free riders, involved in illegal water take-outs and non-payment of irrigation fees.

The failure implies a dysfunction of the organizational reform mechanism. According to Albert Hirschman (1970), deterioration in the performance of an organization may induce reforms either through members' collective protest or by action demanding appropriate reforms ('voice'), or the escape by individuals from the organization ('exit'). In the case of the irrigation system under our investigation, the voice was raised, for example, of downstream farmers in complaining to the NIA as well as protesting to upstream farmers against their abuse of water, or even padlocking the head gates channelling illegal water takeouts. Such a voice was effective in inducing the organization of active IAs in Laterals B and E characterized by small and simple system designs as well as the small numbers of farmers and villages involved. But the same voice totally failed to achieve the same kind of institutional development in Laterals A, C and D, involving much larger numbers of farmers and villages, thereby making it difficult to reach agreement and consensus among themselves. This contrast is consistent with a hypothesis that effectiveness of the voice in organizational reform may depend to a significant extent on the benefit that the reform is expected to produce, but it depends more critically on the inner structure of the organization to determine the cost of mobilizing a sufficiently strong voice.

The failure in the system's reform also resulted from the NIA's inability to respond appropriately to the voice of downstream farmers. The situation could have been very different if the NIA had advanced adequate support for institutional development to the communities in the larger laterals that are difficult to organize through the initiative of the local people alone. For the NIA officials, the urgent financial difficulties should have been more binding than the pressure of the farmers' voice; this adds to the evidence in support of the hypothesis that government officials' time discount rate on future incomes can be much higher than the social rate.

One of major factors underlying the weakness of the farmers' voice was the existence of a relatively easy exit from the system with the purchase of irrigation pumps. In the long run, this exit option will be very damaging to the NIA, as it will mean the diminution in irrigation fees. This long-run hazard, however, did not induce the NIA to undertake a reform for the provision of institutional development supports, because the short-run saving of current expenditure was an over-riding consideration under their financial crisis. Instead, they took advantage of the weak voice of farmers in the areas of deteriorated service to maximize their short-run revenue by diverting water to farmers with better service and, hence, higher rates of irrigation fee payment. This behaviour of the NIA further encouraged the exit of farmers with the purchase of pumps in the market.

If this market exit option had not been available, the farmers' voice could have been sufficiently strong in the long run to form effective IAs, even in the large laterals. When the NIA tried to form an IA in Lateral C, farmers in East Laguna Village protested by voice and by force to farmers in the upper reaches against their abuse of water. However, they soon gave up and opted to exit and buy pumps. However, if these pumps had not been available at a modest cost through the market, they would have had no other option but to escalate their 'voice' towards violence, possibly even involving major bloodshed. Such a negative-sum situation would have eventually forced upstream farmers to accept compromise and co-operation with downstream farmers. In fact, this was the process in which villages in Japan established detailed rules and their effective enforcement on the use of common-pool resources, such as forests and irrigation water, in the seventeenth century when natural resources became scarce under continued population pressure on closed land frontiers (Tamaki and Hatate, 1974; Tamaki, 1983; Hayami, 1997, pp. 252–3).

The problem is that, until very recently, farmers in East Laguna Village as well as in many other villages under this NIA system had had little chance to learn how to organize collective action for water management. Before the NIA irrigation was extended in 1958, farmers had practised rainfed rice production, for which co-ordination in the use of water had been unnecessary. After that time, the irrigation system was operated and maintained by the NIA with little involvement of farmer-beneficiaries except for irrigation fee payment. It was quite natural, then, that farmers were not able to organize adequate collaboration across the many villages along the lateral within a short time when the NIA's maintenance activities contracted rather abruptly; this is a common situation in many villages in South-east Asia, where the traditional abundance of natural resources has been eroded rapidly by explosive population growth. The social structure of village communities plus the availability of the exit option through the market makes it very difficult to organize rural people to manage local commons in South-east Asia as well as in many other developing economies in the world today.

7 Community and Market in Labour Relations[1]

In the previous chapter, the relative roles and interrelationships between village communities and state agencies in the development and management of local infrastructure were investigated in a case study of the national irrigation system covering East Laguna Village. This chapter aims to examine interrelationships between communities and markets in East Laguna Village. In order to shed light on this highly complicated and elusive issue to which little economic analysis has yet been applied, our analysis is concentrated on changes in labour employment contracts for rice harvesting. Common to rural villages in developing economies, labour employment in East Laguna Village has been embedded in traditional community relationships. Clearly visible in changes in harvesting labour contracts are villagers' efforts to adjust institutions in response to major changes in market conditions under the constraints of their traditional community norms.

COMMUNITY VERSUS MARKET: A REVIEW OF CONTROVERSIES

The relationship between community and market has been the subject of major controversies encompassing economics, sociology and political science. Before proceeding to the case study of rice harvesting, it will be useful to develop a conceptual framework through a review of the controversies.

The classic image of 'community' from Karl Marx (1953) to Ferdinand Tönnies (1922) and Max Weber (1924) is a small group of people linked by blood and locational ties, where different economic principles operate compared to those of the capitalist market economy. In this view, while the prime motivation in the capitalist economy is private profit-seeking by individuals, the principle of community existence is the provision of mutual help to ensure the subsistence of all its members. Economic rationality in terms of individual profit and utility maximization does not operate in the community that is thus defined. It has been presumed that the altruistic community norms geared to ensuring all the members' subsistence are bound to be destroyed and replaced by profit-orientated market relations as economic modernization proceeds.

162

Built on this traditional premise was the so-called 'moral economy' perspective regarding the behaviour of peasants in South-east Asia put forward by political scientists and sociologists, including James Scott (1976) among others. This theory assumes that social relations in pre-capitalist peasant communities are geared towards securing minimum subsistence for all the community members. Normally, peasants eke out a living at a near-subsistence level and are exposed to the constant danger that their income may decline below the subsistence minimum because of external variations such as weather, or internal incidents such as sickness among family members. The compelling demand of the peasants to avoid subsistence crises is said to have resulted in a 'subsistence ethic', by which the social arrangements designed to insure against such crises are considered fair and legitimate.

Common features of village communities such as the exchange of labour, the use of communal property for the livelihood of the orphaned or the widowed, the gifts given by a patron at the birth of a child or the death of a father, and rent reductions by landlords in years of crop failure are institutionized patterns developed under this ethic. The basic principle 'claims that all should have a place, a living, not all should be equal' (Scott, 1976, p. 40). To the extent that a landlord or a large farmer protects the poor members in the community (tenants or landless labourers) against ruin in bad years, he or she is considered as a legitimate patron.

Thus the theory of moral economy assumes a pervasive tendency in village communities to place informal social controls on the better-off members to redistribute wealth, or to impose specific obligations to provide for the minimum needs of the poor. It presupposes that the cohesive community organization based on social interactions and moral principles tends to break down as the market economy or the capitalist system penetrates into the subsistence-orientated peasant economy. With the intrusion of the market economy, the moral principle of securing minimum subsistence for community members is replaced by the hard economic consideration of maximizing profit. The well-to-do members of a community tend to rely more on external legal means to protect their property and become more concerned about increasing their incomes in order to purchase modern goods from outside than about buying respect and goodwill among their fellow villagers. The mutual-help and patron–client relationships are weakened and the poorer members are exposed to the risk of subsistence crises. Some of the small landholders are compelled to sell their land and become landless workers selling their labour in the labour market; and others accumulate land to become market-orientated farmers.

The moral economy perspective has been challenged by Samuel Popkin (1979). He denies the view that the pre-capitalist peasant community is moral-orientated to protect the poor. He insists that traditional village institutions and patron–client relationships have been neither motivated nor effective to guarantee the subsistence needs of community members. It is his essential contention that even in a traditional peasant community people are predominantly motivated to seek personal gain rather than to support group interests; peasants rely on their families or groups smaller than the village community for their subsistence guarantees, since a village-wide scheme to insure against risk is bound to be ineffective because everyone tries to claim profit from the group action without sharing the cost – the free-rider problem raised by Mancur Olson (1965). Moreover, he argues that elites exploit village institutions such as community property for their own profit rather than to protect the poor and, as a result, village procedures reinforce, rather than level, differences in income and wealth. Therefore the market system can be more beneficial to the majority of peasants to the extent that it emancipates them from the control of the elites and enables them to engage in transactions based on their own economic calculations. In short, according to Popkin, community is a yoke on the poor, and the market is the liberator .

A major controversy in development economics in the 1960s raged around the question of whether labour employment and wage determination in Third-World agriculture follows the neoclassical principle of marginalism or the classical principle of 'total employment' under the institutionally-determined wage rate. This controversy reflected the opposing perspectives of two Nobel Prize laureates: W. Arthur Lewis (1954) and Theodore W. Schultz (1964). In the formal theorizing of the two-sector development model, Gustav Ranis and John Fei (1961) were the major contenders for the classical camp, and Dale W. Jorgenson (1961) represented the neoclassical camp.

The key assumption for the classical dual economy model of the Lewis–Fei–Ranis variety is the existence of a horizontal labour supply curve to the modern sector (industry) based on 'surplus labour' in the traditional sector (agriculture), given the latter's lower marginal productivity compared with the institutional wage rate. Underlying this assumption is the mechanism by which social norms operate in rural communities, compelling employment of all community members ('total employment') at an institutional wage rate, even if they contribute less to output than the wage rate. This institutional wage rate is itself considered a norm established as an equal share of the community's output (or average product) before industrialization begins.

If the community principle is, in fact, based on mutual help and income-sharing instead of profit or utility maximization by individuals, community organizations should fail to achieve efficient resource allocations in the neoclassical criteria. However, many empirical studies, following the lead of Schultz, indicate that the wage rates in the rural sectors of developing economies are not significantly different from the marginal value product of labour, implying efficient resource allocation resulting from profit maximization by individuals (Schultz, 1964; Hopper, 1965; Paglin, 1965; Massell, 1967; Yotopoulos, 1968). Does this mean that the community principle of mutual help and income-sharing is an illusion, or a mere spoken moral code having no tangible power to control economic activities? Or have traditional communities already been destroyed by the introduction of the market economy into rural villages in developing economies? Despite accumulated evidence in support of the Schultz–Popkin perspective, that peasants in traditional rural society are rational and calculating egoists, we also often observe their apparently altruistic behaviour, as assumed by Lewis and Scott. According to the theory of Gary Becker (1974), in a village community characterized by a high degree of social interaction, an elite would probably try to simulate the behaviour of a benevolent patron in terms of traditional norms if the patron is a wise egoist. Being considered a legitimate patron by fellow villagers can be critical in avoiding malicious gossip, protecting prestige and property, and maintaining village procedures in order to maximize long-run profit. To the extent that production externalities are pervasive and that the market is characterized by high information and transaction costs, the advantage of non-market institutions is greater. A farmer may prefer to employ neighbours under the mutual-help or the patron–client relationship rather than to employ workers in the spot labour market, even if the nominal wage rates are the same or higher, because the cost of supervision or the cost of preventing shirking or stealing of crops may be lower for the former. Thus, conforming to village norms and institutions can be an efficient way of economizing on the cost of policing and enforcement.

However, we do not consider that social interactions in the village are always sufficient to compel villagers to conform to traditional norms and institutions. According to Becker, a person is altruistic to the extent that the return to his/her altruism exceeds the cost of behaving as an altruist. The theory implies that villagers will violate the village institutions if they see opportunities where the gain from the violation exceeds the cost. Changes in production relationship resulting from changes in technology, resource endowments and market structure may produce such opportunities. Whether the village institutions will be maintained depends on the balance between changes in production relations and the solidarity of the village community.

WORK AND INCOME SHARING

So what kind of community norm may be binding people in East Laguna Village?

As already pointed out in Chapter 5, rice production in East Laguna Village is characterized by high dependency on hired labour. This characteristic is typical of irrigated rice areas in the Philippines as well as South-east Asia, in contrast with North-east Asia.

Indeed, when people familiar with agriculture in North-east Asia, including China, Korea and Japan, visit rice villages in South-east Asia, such as Indonesia, Malaysia and the Philippines, they are intrigued by the observation that peasants and family members worked for relatively little time on their own farms, leaving many of the tasks to hired labour. In recent years in Japan, the reliance on hired labour for farm operations has increased as a result of increased off-farm employment opportunities. In the past, however, farm tasks were predominantly shouldered by family members, with hired and exchange labour used only as a minor supplement in peak seasons. According to a nationwide survey by Japan's Ministry of Agriculture for the period 1934–36, when the traditional pattern prevailed, the ratio of hired labour (including exchange labour) in the total number of workdays used for rice production was less than 10 per cent for owner-run farms and less than 8 per cent for tenant farms (see the top two rows in Table 7.1).

In contrast, according to our survey in East Laguna Village, the ratio of hired labour amounted to as much as 50 per cent to 80 per cent, despite the fact that the average operational farm size in the village was not significantly different from Japanese farms, while the level of labour input per hectare was significantly smaller than in Japan. This is not unique to our study village, it is a common situation in Laguna Province (Table 7.1). Farms dependent on hired labour for more than two-thirds of total labour input are not consistent with the traditional image of 'peasants' – small, subsistence-orientated farms mainly dependent on family labour – as stated by Alexander Chayanov (1966). This high dependency on hired labour is common in the irrigated rice-farming areas in the Philippines as well as the other parts of South-east Asia such as Indonesia (Halyami and Kikuchi, 1981).

Table 7.1   Labour inputs per hectare of rice crop area in Japan and the Philippines

		Workdays/hectare			Ratio of hired labour (%)	Operational farm size (ha/farm)
		Total	Family	Hired		
Japan 1934–36						
Owner		200	181	19	10	1.6
Tenant		198	183	15	8	1.4
Philippines						
E. Laguna Village	1976	105	31	74	70	2.3
	1982	80	24	56	70	1.8
	1987	67	12	55	82	1.7
	1995	75	12	63	84	1.9
Laguna Province	1965	86	40	46	53	2.4
	1975	100	24	76	76	2.1
	1981	93	22	71	76	2.1
	1994	84	13	71	85	1.8

Sources: Japan: Japan Ministry of Agriculture and Forestry (1974); East Laguna Village: our *East Laguna Village Survey*; Laguna Province: IRRI Social Sciences Division, *Laguna Survey*.

How is such a large amount of external labour employed in small farms? Almost all the external labour is hired for casual work on a daily contract basis. Hired labour is used mainly for peak-season activities such as rice transplanting and harvesting. Both activities demand large quantities of labour over short periods and are visible in terms of work-effort outcomes (that is, transplanted areas and harvested quantities). In contrast, family labour is used mainly for the tasks that require care and judgement without immediately visible outcomes, and for which physical labour requirements are not so large, such as water and pest control, fertilizer application, and seed-bed preparation. Land preparation with the use of *carabao* is traditionally the task of family labour. However, in recent years, this has increasingly been contracted out to tractor custom services.

This division of labour between family (and exchange) and hired labour is understandable in view of seasonal fluctuations in labour demand as well as the relative ease of monitoring work efforts. It is the common practice in Japan and elsewhere. A unique aspect in the Philippines, however, is that family members rarely work in transplanting and harvesting. Seedlings are prepared and brought to fields by family members, but the transplanting itself is performed by a labour crew organized by a contractor called *kabisilya*. More intriguing is the system of harvesting, which requires nearly 40 per cent of total labour input in rice production. The traditional system called *hunusan* (a Tagalog word for 'sharing') is a form of contract by which, when a farmer specifies a day of harvesting in his/her field, anyone can participate in the harvesting and threshing, and the harvesters receive a certain share (traditionally one-sixth in East Laguna Village) of the output. By custom, the farmer can deny no one the opportunity of harvesting the crop. Neither the farmer nor other family members may go to the harvesting field, even to monitor the work being performed, before the harvested paddy (rough rice) is piled on the ground ready for sharing.

So why do poor peasants employ external labour without fully utilizing family labour on their own farms? This behaviour is inconsistent with Chayanov's concept of peasants as small-farm producers who try to maximize the utilization of family labour even up to the point of zero marginal productivity.

Akira Takahashi (1969) developed a theory to explain this apparent anomaly by a system of absentee landlordism prevailing in the Philippines since Spanish colonial rule. A common form of land tenancy contract in rice areas was a sharecropping contract, by which both output and input costs (including hired wage cost) were shared $50:50$ between tenants and landlords. Under this contract, the larger the payment to hired labour, the smaller the landlords' share of output. The tenants' share also became smaller with the larger payment to hired labour. However, this reduction in tenants' income could be recovered by the receipt of output shares from neighbours. So mutual employment among tenants would maximize their output share at the expense of the landlords, who typically lived outside the village.

This hypothesis of 'tenants' collusion' is apparently plausible in terms of the agrarian history of the Philippines. However, when a similar survey was conducted in West Java, Indonesia, where most farmers were owner-operators rather than of tenants, it was found that dependency on hired labour was equally high, despite an average farm size significantly smaller than in the Philippines (Hayami and Kikuchi, 1981, chs 7–9).

An alternative hypothesis may be that a social norm of income- and work-sharing prevails in the rural sector of South-east Asia. This norm dictates that well-to-do members in a village community should provide income-earning opportunities to poorer neighbours by retreating from work, a community principle of mutual help to guarantee minimum subsistence to the poor. This hypothesis is consistent with the observation that dependency on hired labour has increased since the 1960s despite significant labour saving through mechanization corresponding to increased incomes of rice farmers, who benefited from land reform programmes and the new rice technology (Table 7.1).[2]

A rural community characterized by the principle of income- and work-sharing may sound like an altruistic utopia. However, this principle is not necessarily inconsistent with economic rationality based on egoism. A condition for the original establishment of the sharing principle could have been a low level of agricultural productivity with high risk. Until fairly recently, South-east Asia was characterized by sparse population relative to the available land for cultivation. Before the introduction of modern, high-yielding rice varieties in the late 1960s, rice farming was typically extensive, with very little fertilizer application and weeding, so that yield differences between diligent and idle farmers were much less pronounced than they were in Japan. Therefore, whether a farmer worked hard on his/her fields or left the work to hired labourers did not much affect the level of yield.

On the other hand, production risks were high, especially in the absence of irrigation and drainage systems. During times of drought, crops in elevated locations could be destroyed, whereas bumper crops could be harvested from lower-lying, marshy fields, and the reverse would probably be the case during a season of heavy rain and flooding. Similarly, an outbreak of pests may eliminate crops in a certain area, while other areas might be little damaged. In other words, it is hazardous to rely on production from a single plot for subsistence, and it is therefore common for a peasant to hold land in small parcels scattered over a wide area. Similarly, it greatly reduces risk, if the peasant farmer allows other villagers to share the work on and output from his/her farm, while the farmer is allowed to share work and output on others' farms. This insurance mechanism of work- and income-sharing would be especially valuable in economies where the market is underdeveloped, and therefore providing villagers with no other means of insuring against risk in farm production, such as off-farm employment opportunities, or formal insurance and credit systems. This is one of many insurance mechanisms in traditional societies, which generally involve diversifying family members' economic activities widely across different locations (Rosenzweig, 1988a, 1988b; Stark and Lucas, 1988).

Thus it is hypothesized that the sharing principle observable in South-east Asian villages emerged from people's need to secure subsistence at a low level of land productivity: that is, not very responsive to the work efforts of cultivators. It was established because it was mutually beneficial to sharing parties. As such, egoists should have found it profitable to observe this principle in terms of their rational economic calculations. However, the sharing system would not have been elevated to a social norm, and maintained as such, unless violations from this norm (for example, receiving shares from neighbours without reciprocating) could be expected to receive social sanctions such as social opprobrium (which may eventually escalate to ostracism) in the small village community characterized by intensive personal interaction (Becker, 1974; Akerlof, 1984).

FROM *HUNUSAN* TO *GAMA*

If the community principle of work- and income-sharing originated in rational choice under certain economic and technological conditions, its practice would have changed corresponding to changes in these conditions.

In the traditional *hunusan* system, every villager could participate in harvesting and normally receive one-sixth of harvested paddy. In the past, when rice farming was associated with low yields, one-sixth of output could well be close to the harvesting labour's contribution to output (or labour's marginal productivity). However, as the use of modern rice varieties and chemical fertilizers was promoted, yields per hectare rose sharply, with parallel increases in harvesters' receipts. On the other hand, the market wage rates remained largely stable under the pressure of labour force growth. As a result, the rate of return to labour under the traditional *hunusan* contract increased cumulatively above the market wage rate. Thus this community-type employment contract became a disadvantageous system for employer-farmers relative to the market-type daily wage contract, since the market wage rate remained constant in real terms between 1966 and 1976. Moreover, unlike the old days when *hunusan* harvesters had largely been neighbouring farmers, the majority of them were landless agricultural labourers, many of whom were migrants from outside the village (Chapter 3). It therefore became difficult for an employer-farmer to recover his/her high payment to harvesting labourers above the market wage rates from reciprocal employment.

Corresponding to these changes, the new system called *gama* (a Tagalog word for 'weeding') emerged and rapidly replaced *hunusan* in the 1960s and 1970s (see the first two columns in Table 7.2). As explained earlier, *gama* is an output-sharing contract similar to *hunusan*, except that employment for harvesting is limited to workers who weeded the fields without receiving wages. In other words, in the *gama* system, weeding labour is a free service provided by workers to establish the right to participate in harvesting and to receive one-sixth of the output. To the extent that weeding labour is additionally required to receive the same share of output, the implied wage rate is lower in *gama* than in *hunusan*. Although this adjustment reduced the rate of compensation to labour per hour, it was accepted

ble 7.2   Changes in the rice harvesting system in East Laguna Village (percentage of farmer adopters)

r	Hunusan	Gama				*New* Hunusan					*Family labour*[a]	Total
		1/6	1/7	1/8	1/9	1/6	1/7	1/8	1/9	1/10		
50	100	...	...	...	...	...	...	...	...	...	...	100
60	97	3	...	...	...	...	...	...	...	...	...	100
55	78	22	...	...	...	...	...	...	...	...	...	100
70	55	45	...	...	...	...	...	...	...	...	...	100
76	...	87	...	...	...	4	...	...	...	...	...	100
82	...	70	2	...	...	5	14	...	...	...	...	100
87	...	4	18	47	...	...	2	19	2	2	...	100
94	...	0	4	39	4	...	...	24	18	2	...	100
95	...	0	2	22	9	...	...	38	17	5	...	100
96	...	0	2	9	6	...	...	40	18	7	18	100

te: [a] Harvesting done by family labour alone.
   [b] ... stands for 'no case reported'.
urce: Data before 1976 are based on farmers' recall during the 1976 survey.

by villagers because it maintained the traditional sharing arrangement as well as the sharing rate, thereby remaining consistent with the norm of the village community.

Economic forces underlying the shift from *hunusan* to *gama* are illustrated by the following calculation with respect to 1976 (see Table 7.3). First, dividing the harvesters' share of output (row 4) by the number of workdays for harvesting and threshing (row 3) produces an imputed wage rate in terms of rough rice under a *hunusan* contract (row 5). Comparison between this imputed wage rate and the market wage rates deflated by the farm-gate price of rough rice (row 6) shows that the rate of compensation to *hunusan* labour was about 40 per cent higher than the market wage rate (row 7). This calculation indicates that a major disequilibrium between the rate of compensation for harvesting labour under the *hunusan* contract and labour's marginal productivity had accumulated by the mid-1970s thanks to the rice yield increases resulting from developments of irrigation infrastructure and new rice technology, under the assumption that the market wage rate approximates the marginal productivity of labour. Note that in this calculation the market wage rate for land preparation was used as a proxy for the harvesting wage rate, because both land preparation and harvesting constitute seasonal peaks in labour demand for rice production.

It can be seen that the major disequilibrium arising from the use of *hunusan* in 1976 was eliminated with the adoption of *gama*, according to

Table 7.3   Imputation of wage rates for rice harvesting work under different labour contracts and threshing technologies, East Laguna Village, 1976–96 survey years

		1976 Hand	1982 Machine		1995 Machine		
Threshing technology →							
Threshing cost shouldered by →		Harvester	sharing[a]	Farmer	Farmer		
		(1)	(2)	(3)	(4)	(
(1) Rice yield (ton/ha)[b]		3.2		3.8		4.0	
Hunusan							
(2) Harvesters' share rate		1/6	1/8	1/8	1/8	1/
(3) Number of *hunusan* workdays (days/ha)		33.6[c]		18.0[d]		18.5[d]	
(4) Harvesters' share (kg/ha)	(1) × (2)	533	323[e]	475	500	4
(5) Imputed wage rate (kg/day)	(4)/(3)	15.9	17.9	26.4	27.0	2
(6) Market wage rate (kg/day)[f]		11.4		16.7		21.8	
(7) Wage dis-equilibrium (%)	((5) − (6))/(6)	39	7	58	24	–
Gama							
(8) Harvesters' share rate		1/6	1/6	1/8	1/8	1,
(9) Number of *gama* workdays (days/ha)[g]		54.5		32.3		34.5	
(10) Harvesters' share (kg/ha)	(8) × (9)	533	481[e]	475	500	6
(11) Imputed wage rate (kg/day)	(10)/(9)	9.8	14.9	14.7	14.5	1
(12) Market wage rate (kg/day)[h]		10.1		15.2		19.8	
(13) Wage dis-equilibrium (%)	((11) − (12))/(12)	−3	−2	−3	−27	–

Notes: [a] The cost for machine threshing is shared equally between farmers and harveste[r]
[b] Average yield over the two seasons. For 1995, average over the four seasons 1994 and 1995.
[c] Workdays of harvesters for harvesting and manual threshing.
[d] Workdays of harvesters for harvesting, excluding those for threshing
[e] Net harvesters' share after deducting harvesters' threshing cost share (4%) fr[om] the gross share.
[f] The market wage rate for land preparation, divided by the farm-gate price [of] rough rice.
[g] The sum of (3) and the number of workdays for weeding by *gama* workers.
[h] The weighted average of wage rates for land preparation and transplanting usi[ng] harvesting and weeding workdays as weights, divided by the farm-gate price [of] rough rice.

the following calculation. Dividing harvesters' output share (row 10, the same as row 4) by the number of workdays, including not only those for harvesting and threshing but also for weeding (row 9) produces the imputed wage rate of *gama* harvesters (row 11). A comparable market wage rate in rice terms is obtained from deflating the weighted average of land preparation and transplanting/weeding wage rates by the rough rice price (row 12). A comparison between the imputed and market wage rates shows that no significant disequilibrium existed in 1976, if *gama* was adopted (row 13). Essentially the same results were obtained from broader samples of the IRRI's *Laguna Survey* during the 1970s (Kikuchi and Hayami, 1983, pp. 252–3).

These findings are consistent with the hypothesis that the *gama* contract represents an institutional arrangement designed to reduce disequilibrium between the remuneration rate of labour and its marginal productivity within the framework of work and income-sharing in the community. Relative to other methods to recover equilibrium, such as lowering the harvesters' share rate, or replacing the sharing contract with the fixed-wage time-rate contract, the *gama* contract should have entailed lower transaction costs for its greater congruence with the traditional arrangement. The cost arising from a change in the long-established custom, such as the one-sixth share of harvesters, would not have been small.

Further, the *gama* contract by nature tends to promote a patron–client relationship among villagers, because it links harvesting with weeding and continues to be renewed over the seasons. Wages are not paid at the time of weeding. In the minds of villagers, weeding with no direct payment is considered not to be a part of a contract based on economic calculation, but rather an expression of gratitude by labourers for the goodwill of a farmer-patron who provides them with the guarantee of a stable income from contracted plots at a time-honoured share rate, thereby reducing their subsistence risk. Such a personal relationship is further strengthened through exchanges of gifts, credit and personal services. Both the sense of moral obligation and the fear of losing the patron–client relationship motivates labourers to exert conscientious work effort and to refrain from committing misdemeanours such as stealing the harvested rice. For these merits, *gama* was preferred to the other alternatives and soon met wide acceptance during the Green Revolution period.

DIGGING OUT OF TRADITION

An interesting finding was that, even though *gama* represented a new arrangement for the lowland rice belt along Laguna de Bay, it was an old institution practised in small paddy plots scattered amidst hills and mountains surrounding the rice belt. This traditional institution in the highlands was transferred to the lowlands by migrant labourers.

While the new rice technology significantly increased labour demand in the lowland rice belt, no comparable technological advance occurred in coconut production, the major source of livelihood for highlanders. Under strong population pressure, labour was forced to flow from the coconut areas to the rice belt (Chapter 3). Typically, a labourer in the highlands commuted seasonally to a lowland rice village, at first to participate in *hunusan* harvesting. Then, the labourer asked a rice farmer to grant an exclusive right of harvesting a plot in return for the service of weeding, explaining that this was the traditional practice in his home village. As the proposal was accepted by several farmers, so the labourer was able to have a *gama* contract for a sufficient number of plots for subsistence, and he/she settled in the rice village permanently, building a bamboo-nipa hut.

Based on a number of surveys conducted between 1978 and 1982, a map can be drawn to show the geographical distribution of the villages in which *gama* had traditionally been practised (before the Second World War) and those that adopted *gama* with the introduction of the new rice technology (see Figure 7.1). It is clear that the traditional *gama* villages are clustered in the north-western hills of Mount Banahaw, from where labourers have migrated, while the new *gama* villages are distributed in the lowland rice belt along Laguna de Bay, to which the labourers flowed in. The observed pattern is consistent with the hypothesis that the concept of *gama* was brought down from the hills to the lowland rice belt by migrant labourers.

Why was the *gama* contract traditionally practised in the hills before the introduction of modern rice technology? The answer appears to be the unique topography of the hills. The undulating rice terraces there can be irrigated only with a minor communal effort to modify the natural water flows. Under such conditions, weeding is effective in increasing rice yields. In contrast, in the lowland plain, water control was difficult prior to the development of a major national irrigation system. Before that time, the lowland rice fields were typically flooded with deep water, and consequently weeding was unnecessary. A number of farmers in the lowland rice villages reported that they adopted the *gama* contract once the irrigation systems had been instituted and weeding had become profitable.

Although the undulating topography is a probable factor underlying the early adoption of *gama* in the hilly areas, the form of contract also undoubtedly had sociological and anthropological origins. Historically, the hilly area was settled earlier than the lowland area, because upland

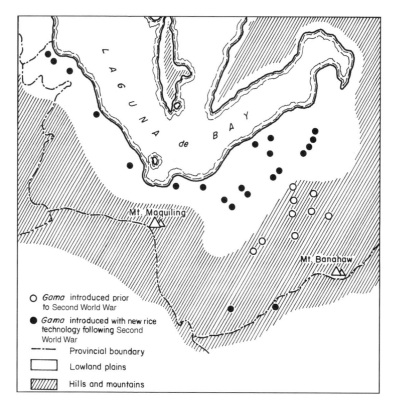

Figure 7.1   Distribution of sample villages by period of the adoption of the *gama*
contract in the Province of Laguna
Source: Kikuchi and Hayami (1983, p. 255).

dwellers suffered fewer outbreaks of malaria than did residents of the
marshy coastal plain. Therefore population pressure was traditionally
stronger in the hills. Social change in response to growing population
pressure on limited land resources during the early, less-commercialized
period could have represented what Clifford Geertz (1963) called 'involution'
and 'shared poverty'. That is, the development of *gama* represented a
social adjustment for work-sharing in response to population pressure
in the hill communities, which was associated with the development of a
cultural norm to consider the patron–client relationship such as *gama* to be
fair and just.[3]

In any case, the transfer of *gama* from the highlands to the lowlands in
Laguna represents an example of the digging out from the storehouse of

traditional institutions an appropriate one to use to better co-ordinating the division of labour under a new economic environment. It also illustrates the importance of migrants as the agents of institutional experimentation or mutation in the evolution of economic and social systems.

PEASANTS AND ESTATES IN MULTIPLE EQUILIBRIA

By the early 1980s, *gama* had thus been established as a new social norm among peasants operating small family farms, representing the dominant mode of production in the rice belt of Laguna. However, it was found not to be practised in large estate farms. An exceptional village was found on the south coast of Laguna de Bay, about 15 kilometres from East Laguna Village, where three large estate farms held 135 hectares, or as much as 65 per cent of paddy land in the village, and the remaining 74 hectares were cultivated by fifty three small farmers, averaging in 1977 only 1.4 hectares per farm. The area where the village is located was part of a large land grant by the Spanish Crown but had been left as a wild, marshy jungle adjacent to Laguna de Bay until as late as the 1930s. At the time, two landlords cleared the jungle and installed drainage and irrigation facilities. In this way, small *haciendas* (small compared with those in Central Luzon, but large in Laguna) were developed in the village. As the infrastructure was created by the *haciendas*, marginal areas were settled by smallholders and squatters.

Unlike small peasant farms, in which farm tasks are performed either by family members or a few hired labourers in a long-term intimate relationship with the farmers, the large estates have to employ overseers and foremen to supervize a large number of labourers. A small peasant who has a long-term *gama* contract with a few labourers may need to supervize the labourers' weeding and harvesting work very little because he/she can rely on enforcement of the contract by means of mutual-trust and the patron–client relationship. A key to the effective working of this mechanism is the sense of belonging (for both employers and labourers) to the same community, and of sharing the same social and cultural norms; this makes social sanctions credible against possible opportunistic behaviour.

Because of the difficulty in developing such a community relationship between a wealthy *haciendero* and a large number of poor labourers, labour management in the estate farms had to exercise costly supervision and command. Instead of adopting *gama*, they continued to use *hunusan* for harvesting, but with the harvesters' share rate lowering, from one-sixth to one-seventh and then to one-ninth, at which the rate of compensation for harvesting labour was nearly equal to the market wage rate.

Violation of the time-honoured sharing rate created strong indignation among labourers, as evident from an incident where standing crops in some plots of the estates were burned during the night. In these circumstances, labourers would not hesitate to engage in opportunistic behaviour such as cheating and stealing harvested paddy, so, the management employed overseers on harvesting operations with the use of mechanical threshers to measure paddy output accurately, at a time when threshing in small family farms was done by hand. [4] On large farms, weeding was also done by daily-wage contract labourers under the supervision of overseers.

As a result, labour input per hectare in person days, including management and supervision labour, was about 20 per cent higher in the estates than in small family farms. Large farms also used more capital than did small farms. The larger labour requirements in the estates were compensated for by the lower rates of wage payment. In the case of small farms, labourers employed at a fixed daily wage rate *(upahan)* were provided with snacks *(merienda)* in addition to cash wages. For example, standard daily wages were ten pesos in cash and a snack worth about two pesos for land preparation. However, the large farms paid only the cash wages of ten pesos, implying that the effective rate of their wage payment was lower by about 15 per cent than small farms' payments. The serving of snacks by small farmers can be considered as a payment to purchase the goodwill of the labourers, and thereby to reduce the cost of labour enforcement. This was replaced by direct supervision in the estates.

Relative efficiency of the estate versus the peasant system in rice production is illustrated by cost–return comparisons between two large estates (holdings of 80 and 41 hectares, respectively) and fifty-three peasant farms. According to the calculations in Table 7.4, for the same level of rice yield per hectare, the cost of inputs (excluding land) was about 15 per cent higher, and therefore the residual (which is supposed to accrue to land and operators' entrepreneurship) was about 20 per cent lower in estates than on peasant farms. A major cost difference arose in capital cost, while the cost gap was relatively minor for labour because of the lower wage rates applied to estates, as explained previously. However, if the same wage rates were applied, the total input cost would have been nearly a-quarter higher, and the residual as much as a-third lower for estates than for peasants, implying that social inefficiency of the estate system was even greater than private inefficiency. The cost difference, either private or social, represents peasants' advantage over estates in saving labour transaction costs with their effective use of traditional community norms. It can be considered an economic return to mutual trust, or 'social capital' in the Putnam (1993) sense, existing among the members of the peasant community as opposed to distrust between estate management and labourers.

Table 7.4   The cost–return structures of rice production, estates versus peasants in a polarized village in Laguna, Philippines, 1977 dry season

	Estate (1)	Peasant (2)	(1)−(2) (1) (%)
Number of farms	2	53	
Average farm size (ha)	61	1.4	
Rice (paddy) yield (kg/ha)	3960	3996	−0.9
Input costs:[a]			
Current inputs	540	477	11.7
Capital[b]	531	333	37.2
Labour[c]	1143	1085	5.1
Total	2214	1895	14.4
Residual[a]	1746	2101	−20.3

Notes: [a] Measured in rough rice equivalents.
     [b] Sum of paid and imputed rentals of draft animals, tractors, threshers and other machines.
     [c] Sum of hired labour wages and imputed family labour costs.
Source: Hayami and Kikuchi (1981, pp. 130 and 139).

Why, then, did the estate management not subdivide their holdings into small parcels for renting out to peasant producers? In the initial land-opening stage, the large-scale operational unit should have had an advantage as it enabled the internalization of large-scale investment, such as irrigation and drainage systems, but the system tended to sustain itself thereafter despite its growing relative inefficiency because of inertia stemming from various institutional complementarities, as is common in large commercial plantations in Asia. Ironically, Philippine land reform laws have been working as a force to sustain the estate system, because the confiscation of land from landlords and its distribution to tenants are applicable only to tenanted lands, while lands under the direct administration of landlords are exempted (Chapter 4). Therefore, it was rational for landlords to continue to operate the estate system for the sake of evading the land reform programmes, even if it was economically less efficient than renting out their land to small producers.

Evolution of two different institutional arrangements (that is, *gama* in the peasant system and *hunusan* with a reduced share rate in the estate system) represents a case of multiple equilibria emerging under different cultural, social and legal norms, even if the economic forces inducing institutional change are the same. We were thus able to confirm, on the basis of purposively collected microeconomic data, the nature and mechanism of emerging multiple equilibria, which had hitherto been inferred based on broad historical observations (Greif, 1994).

FROM *GAMA* TO NEW *HUNUSAN*

After the late 1970s, however, the incidence of *gama* contracts with the traditional harvesters' share of one-sixth declined. At the same time, *gama* was replaced by *hunusan* at reduced share rates of up to one-tenth (Table 7.2). The *hunusan* contract that became widespread in the 1980s and 1990s was different from the traditional *hunusan* that prevailed before 1970. In the traditional *hunusan* that everyone could participate in harvesting and receive an output share, but in the new *hunusan* only the labourers who received specific invitations from employing farmers were allowed to participate.[5] By its nature this is no different from ordinary piece-rate contracts found in market economies, compared with the traditional *hunusan*, which is consonant to the community norm of village-wide sharing.

Underlying the shift from the community-type to the market-type of contract were (a) diffusion of mechanical threshers; and (b) expansion of non-farm employment opportunities associated with increased wage rates. The development of portable threshing machines by the IRRI began in 1974, but their dramatic diffusion took place in the 1980s. Until towards the end of the 1970s threshing had been done in Laguna and its surroundings primarily through hand-beating of harvested rice plants on bamboo stands or wooden plates. In East Laguna Village, the rate of adoption by farmers of machine threshing rose from 6 per cent in 1976 to 87 per cent in 1987, and up to 100 per cent in 1995 (Table 7.5).

Table 7.5   Farmers adopting threshing machines by type of cost sharing, East Laguna Village, 1976–95

Year	Number of machine adopters		Thresher cost sharing			
			Sharing 50:50		Farmer 100%	
	No.	*%*	*No.*	*%*	*No.*	*%*
1976	3	6	3	100	0	0
1982	13	30	13	100	0	0
1987	46	87	24	52	22	48
1995	51	100	3	6	48	94

In traditional *hunusan* as well as *gama*, it is the same labourer who cuts the rice plants by sickle and threshes them by hand. The one-sixth of output was a renumeration to him/her for both the tasks. With the introduction of mechanical threshers, the threshing was contracted out separately to the custom service of threshing machines, with the operators employed by the machine owner, except for a few large farmers who owned their machines. A part of the harvesters' share hitherto attributed to hand-beating was transferred to those who provided the machine custom services. When threshers were first introduced, the custom service fee for threshing, including winnowing, was 8 per cent of total threshed paddy, which was shared equally between farmers and harvesting labourers.[6] Farmers had an incentive to introduce machine threshing at the additional expense of 4 per cent of output, partly because of increased paddy recovery of the order of 3 per cent to 6 per cent of output (Toquero and Duff, 1985) and partly because of the prevention of harvesters' moral hazard (such as the stealing of threshed paddy). On the other hand, it was acceptable for harvesting labourers to pay the equivalent charge out of their output share to save their labour in a situation where there were increased non-farm employment opportunities brought about mainly by improvements in the highways in the late 1970s.

Despite there being a major innovation in the form of mechanical threshing, the traditional *gama* contract with the harvesters' share of one-sixth continued to be dominant in the early 1980s, so long as the 50:50 cost sharing for thresher custom services was maintained. Indeed, a calculation for the case of *gama* employing threshers under a machine cost-sharing arrangement in 1982 (column 2 in Table 7.3) produces the result that the imputed wage rate (row 11) obtained from dividing the 'net share' of harvesters after deducting their payment to a machine services (row 10) by the number of workdays for harvesting and weeding, not including those for threshing (row 9), indicates no significant disequilibrium compared with the market wage rate (row 12).

It appears to be an anomaly that, despite the equilibrium under the traditional *gama* system, in the 1980s some farmers began to shift to new *hunusan* at reduced share rates for harvesters (Table 7.2). The imputation of an implicit wage rate in the new *hunusan* contract with the harvesters' share of one-eighth for the case of machine threshing under cost sharing shows that there was only a slight gap between the imputed wage rate (row 5) and the market wage rate (row 6). If traditional *gama* and new *hunusan* could result in a similar equilibrium, why was it necessary for farmers to shift from the former to the latter?

Several farmers who adopted the new *hunusan* contract cited unsatisfactory weeding by *gama* workers as the reason for their contract shift. It is understandable that, as non-farm employment opportunities expanded, low-income labourers, whose time discount rate was high, were strongly tempted to divert their labour to currently-paid daily employment from weeding, which does not command an immediate remuneration. It is also understandable that community norms and patron–client relationships, which used to be effective in preventing moral hazards by labourers, such as shirking, within a relatively isolated rural village were weakened under increased exposure to urban economic activities. Therefore, it should not be surprising to observe that some farmers opted to shift from *gama* to the new *hunusan* at a reduced share rate to harvesters, while employing daily-wage labourers for weeding. Reductions in the share rate from the traditional one-sixth, which should have met with strong criticism as it violated the community norm of work and income sharing, became socially accept-able because of increasing non-farm employment opportunities.

In this shift away from *gama*, farmers did not return to the traditional *hunusan* contract of village-wide voluntary participation. This was because farmers became uncertain as to whether a sufficient number of labourers would show up voluntarily in their fields on the day of harvest under the conditions of relative labour scarcity. Thus farmers found it necessary to adopt the new *hunusan* in which specific labourers are invited in advance.

Another change that occurred in the 1980s was a reduction in the har-vesters' share rate to one-eighth under the *gama* system. This change cor-responded to a change in the mode of payment to custom threshing services, from equal sharing between farmers and harvesters to full-cost shouldering by farmers alone, at the rate of 10 per cent of threshed paddy after deducting the *gama* harvesters' share of the one-eighth. Essentially, this reduction in the harvesters' share rate was equivalent to a shift of the threshing cost previously shouldered by havesters to the farmers' expense. Therefore, the imputed wage rate of *gama* workers under this system was almost exactly the same as for the traditional *gama* contract with the one-sixth share under threshing machine cost sharing, hence it was not subject to disequilibrium (lower parts of columns 2 and 3 in Table 7.3)

Of course, if the one-eighth share had continued under new *hunusan* despite the shift from threshing cost-sharing to the farmers' sole payment, the imputed wage rate would have turned out to be far larger than the mar-ket wage rate. The major disequilibrium would have remained even if the share rate was reduced to one-ninth and one-tenth. It was therefore not sur-prising that the new *hunusan* contract practised during the 1980s was lim-ited to the cases of thresher cost-sharing.

Although the real market wage rate began to rise in East Laguna Village from the late 1970s early 1980s, the growth trend was interrupted in the mid-1980s because of economic retrogression under political turmoil following the downfall of Marcos's regime. However, upon the rapid recovery of the Philippine economy in the 1990s under President Ramos, the wage rate in this village and its surroundings began to rise very rapidly, associated with a major expansion in non-farm employment opportunities.

Correspondingly, the rate of return to labour under the *gama* contract with the harvesters' share of one-eighth, which was dominant in the 1980s, became lower than the increased market wage rate; this was illustrated by the calculation that produces the imputed wage rate for *gama* with the one-eighth share being exceeded by the market wage rate by nearly 30 per cent in 1995 (lower part of column 4, Table 7.3). This disequilibrium could have been eliminated by raising the harvesters' share rate back to one-sixth (lower part of column 5). However, this adjustment did not take place. What happened in fact was a shift to the new *hunusan* at reduced share rates under the arrangement that farmers shouldered the cost of threshing. Calculations shown in the upper parts of columns 4 and 5 of Table 7.3 illustrate that equilibrium was restored when the *hunusan* harvesters' share rate was reduced from one-eighth to one-tenth. It appears that the farmers' contract choice in the mid-1990s was moving towards this equilibrium.

Underlying the farmers' choice of the new *hunusan* contract at a reduced share rate over the *gama* contract at the traditional share rate should have been the difficulty of enforcing proper weeding work, which was implicitly agreed upon in the *gama* contract, under loosened personal ties and weakened traditional norms as the result of integration of the village economy with the wider market.

EFFICIENT PEASANTS

The evolution of rice harvesting contracts in East Laguna Village in the three decades since the advent of the Green Revolution shows, above all, the remarkable ability of small farmers to achieve efficient resource allocation through adjustments in contractual agreements in response to major technological advancements, such as the introduction of modern high-yielding rice varieties, and threshing machines, as well as changes in market wage rates. Specific forms of contract were chosen, in a direction consistent with community norms, so as to save transaction costs. Such abilities in these peasants must underlie the efficient resource allocations in Third-World agriculture attested by T. W. Schultz (1964) and his followers. Thus changes in labour contract relations in this village add to the evidence in support of the hypothesis that rural people in developing economies have the ability to achieve efficient resource allocation if their contract choice is not unduly restricted (Hayami and Otsuka, 1993).

A serious doubt has been expressed that informal contracts based on traditional norms and personal ties in small subsistence-orientated communities might be difficult to adjust to bring them in line with modern market relationships, and thereby work as an impediment to the adoption of modern institutions in support of a wide division of labour (North, 1994). However, the evolution of rice-harvesting contracts as observed in this chapter clearly shows the ability of small farmers and agricultural labourers in Philippine villages to develop efficient institutions in response to the growing integration of their community with the urban market, in addition to their effective use of traditional community norms and relationships under the more isolated conditions of the earlier stages of development.

8 Farmers and Middlemen in Rice Marketing[1]

The previous chapter elucidated the process of change in rice harvesting contracts in East Laguna Village through interactions between community relations and market forces. Although changes in the conditions of the wide labour market have been a major influence on the evolution of harvesting labour contracts within the village, the linkage of villagers with agents in external markets was not analyzed explicitly. In contrast, with a specific focus on the relationship of villagers with outside market agents, this chapter traces the channels of rice marketing from the farm gate in East Laguna Village to consumers.

APPROACH

Unlike the other chapters of this book, this chapter does not attempt to document the historical developments in East Laguna Village based on periodic village-wide surveys. Instead, this chapter tries to identify the position of farmers in this village *vis-à-vis* wide market with a special focus on their relationship with middlemen and processors (the rice mills). Instead of tracing changes over time, our investigation in this chapter traces market linkages during 1995–7.

The basic reason why such an approach is necessary is the lack of availability of data on marketing from our previous surveys. From its beginning, our study has concentrated on activities and relationships within East Laguna Village. Hence, our investigation was seldom extended outside the village; we tried to capture the influences of external forces from the data of within-village activities obtained from the village surveys. It was only towards the end of this long-term project that we realized that a critical gap remained in our knowledge about the village with respect to its linkages with external markets, especially for rice.

In general, however, relative to farm production and rural life, agricultural product marketing in developing economies has received much less intense scrutiny from economists. Although substantive economic studies have been accumulated in this area, including the classic work on export cash crops in West Africa by Peter Bauer (1964) followed by major studies for food crops in India by Uma Lele (1971) and in Africa by William Jones (1972),

184

their quantitative analyses were mainly based on the broad observations of price spreads across various markets over a wide region. Few exercises have been performed to collect microeconomic data to identify the relationships between farmers and middlemen at a local level. In the absence of solid empirical evidence, a popular perception persists of greedy middlemen exploiting poor peasants. As Leon Mears (1981, p. 133) wrote about Indonesia, 'it is not unusual to hear judgement ... that farmers or consumers are exploited by the market control exercised by ethnic Chinese middlemen. At times one even hears that all private traders are exploitive and discouraging to producers'.

Part of the reason why less than sufficient research has been done on agricultural marketing than on agricultural production is the much greater difficulty of collecting information from traders than from farmers. Information is one source of success in the trading business, so traders are understandably hesitant to disclose details of their businesses. They are also suspicious about interrogation by outsiders about such matters as marketing margins and costs which impinge on tax and government regulations. These conditions defy an approach based on a large sample survey over a wide area with a standardized questionnaire. The investigation must rely on informal contacts and discussions with traders, possibly through an introduction by someone they trust, and checking their data and explanations with several informed people in the same community, akin to the approach taken by anthropologists (Dewey, 1962).

We tried to apply such an approach to rice marketing as it pertained to East Laguna Village. Our exploration covered mainly Pila and its neighbouring municipalities Victoria and Calauan, and San Pablo City, which is a major trading centre in this area.

We first interviewed all the farmers in East Laguna Village to identify how much of their paddy was sold and to whom. We then followed the marketing chain through a sequence of marketing agents up to end-users, noting prices, transportation and processing costs, trade practices and contracts. When inconsistencies were found in data and explanations among transacting parties, we visited them again for verification. This 'pedestrian approach' based on our own observations gathered through walking around rural villages and towns proved to be effective in grasping the elusive behaviour and organization of the informal marketing agents in developing economies (Hayami and Kawagoe, 1993).

A reconnaissance of the marketing system in Laguna was attempted in August 1995, and the first-round farmer survey was conducted in July 1996. Utilizing the farmer survey data as a benchmark, the marketing survey in March 1997 traced the marketing channel from farmers to retailers.

In July 1997, the second-round farmer survey was conducted, for the 1996 wet season and 1996/97 dry season.

SALES OF RICE FROM FARMERS

Table 8.1 shows how paddy outputs in East Laguna Village were disposed in 1995 and 1996.

In this village, nearly 100 per cent of the rice fields were double-cropped, in both dry and wet seasons. The average yield per hectare, and hence total output, were significantly higher for the dry than for the wet season. For both seasons the share of payment in kind for land rent, harvesters' labour wage (*hunus*) and loan repayment in total paddy (rough rice) output was about the same on average for all the farmers. However, the share of the market sale in the dry season (47 per cent) was higher than in the wet season (42 per cent), reflecting seasonal yield differences. As expected, larger farmers with larger output per household had higher marketable surplus ratios than did small farmers. However, the difference in the ratio of sale to output between large and small farmers was reduced by much a larger home consumption by large than small farmers, mainly because of the larger grants of paddy from large farmers to children and relatives, classified as home consumption in Table 8.1.

Market sales by farmers followed the seasonal pattern of paddy harvest. As shown in Figure 8.1, as much as 60 per cent to 90 per cent of the harvested crop was sold during the two months of peak harvest: October and April, in the wet and dry seasons, respectively. One would expect the price of paddy to decline during the harvesting months and rise in the lean months. However, the price in East Laguna Village was at its lowest in November and May instead of the expected October and April. This was presumably because of a delay in the harvesting peak in the larger rice-producing area of Central Luzon, which is about a month behind Laguna. Increases in paddy prices by about two pesos per kilogram (kg) both from the wet season trough in November to the peak in February–March, and from the dry season trough of May to the peak of July–August, were a relatively normal pattern.

To whom did farmers sell their marketable surplus of paddy? Part was shipped directly to the rice mills, and the rest was assembled by small traders called 'collectors' for procurement by the rice mills. Typically, a collector is the wife of a farmer or a landless labourer who engages in paddy collection within her village and nearby villages. Two types of collector can be distinguished. One type is what we call a 'commission agent', who identifies farmers willing to sell paddy, makes a contract of sale with them at a

Table 8.1 Average output and disposal of paddy per farmer in East Laguna Village, 1995–6 average

	Large farmer (2 ha and above)		Small farmer (below 2ha)		All	
	kg/farm	%	kg/farm	%	kg/farm	%
Wet season						
Number of farmers planted	14		27		41	
(Number of farmers with no sale)	(2)		(8)		(9)	
Output	11 417	100	3 647	100	6 332	100
Payment in kind[a]	4 267	37	1 403	38	2 357	37
Home consumption[b]	2 202	19	830	23	1 340	21
Sale	4 948	43	1 414	39	2 635	42
Dry season						
Number of farmers planted	15		29		44	
(Number of farmers with no sale)	(1)		(2)		(3)	
Output	15 716	100	4 680	100	8 359	100
Payment in kind[a]	5 653	36	1 711	37	3 048	36
Home consumption[b]	2 193	14	964	21	1 350	16
Sale	7 870	50	2 005	42	3 960	47
Year total						
Number of farmers planted	16		29		45	
(Number of farmers with no sale)	(0)		(0)		(0)	
Output	27 133	100	8 327	100	14 691	100
Payment in kind[a]	9 920	37	3 114	37	5 405	37
Home consumption[b]	4 395	16	1 794	22	2 690	18
Sale	12 818	47	3 419	41	6 595	45

Notes: [a] Includes not only rice production costs paid in kind, such as land rent and harvesting labour wage, but also other payments, such as consumption loan repayment.
[b] Includes grant.

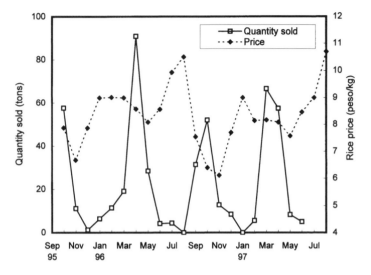

Figure 8.1   Monthly average price of paddy rice and quantity sold, October
1995–August 1997

price approved by the miller, and then lets the miller undertake the hauling
of paddy and the payment to farmers. For this task, the collector receives a
commission. Another type is an 'independent trader', who finances the purchase of paddy at her own risk, and assembles it into bulk storage for shipment for sale to the rice mills. While these two transaction modes are
categorically different, they are often practised by a same collector.

Table 8.2 shows that 75 per cent of paddy procured from farmers in East
Laguna Village was assembled by collectors, of which about two-thirds
were handled by those of the independent-trader type. It is amazing to
find that as many as thirty-seven buyers, including twenty-four collectors
(twelve commission agents and twelve independent traders) and thirteen
mills, operated for procurement of the paddy produced by only forty-five
farmers, each holding an average farm size of 1.9 hectares, and whose
average marketable surplus was less than 3.5 tons per farm per season. All
the buyers were private traders. Although eight farmers in East Laguna
Village belonged to an agricultural co-operative operating a rice mill in a
nearby village, none of them sold his paddy to the co-op, despite the
announced policy of collective marketing by co-op members. None of
these private buyers had a disproportionately large share. As we shall explain
later, their incomes and profits are largely proportional to the volumes of
paddy they procure. They are therefore bound to compete strongly with

Table 8.2   Marketing outlets of paddy produced by farmers in East Laguna Village, 1995–6 average

| | Collector | | Rice mill | Total |
	Commission agent	Independent trader		
Wet season				
Number of buyers	8 (36)[a]	8 (36)	6 (27)	22 (100)
Number of sales by farmers	7 (19)	21 (58)	8 (22)	36 (100)
Total quantity sold (kg)	16 340 (18)	54 438 (60)	19 844 (22)	90 622 (100)
Average quantity per sale (kg)	2 334	2 592	2 481	2 517
Dry season				
Number of buyers	6 (21)	12 (41)	11 (38)	29 (100)
Number of sales by farmers	6 (11)	31 (62)	14 (27)	51 (100)
Total quantity sold (kg)	13 674 (9)	88 795 (59)	48 225 (32)	150 694 (100)
Average quantity per sale (kg)	2 486	2 819	3 445	2 955
Year total				
Number of buyers	12 (32)	12 (32)	13 (35)	37 (100)
Number of sales by farmers	13 (15)	52 (60)	22 (25)	87 (100)
Total quantity sold (kg)	30 014 (13)	143 233 (59)	68 069 (28)	241 316 (100)
Average quantity per sale (kg)	2 401	2 728	3 094	2 774

Note: [a] Percentages of total are shown in parentheses.

each other, leaving little room for any buyer to impose lower prices on farmers than the prevailing market prices. In a small village where so many middlemen are operating, it should not be difficult for a farmer to find out if a price offered by a buyer for his product is appropriate, simply by checking with his neighbours who deal with other middlemen.

A stereotyped view assumes that a middleman advances credits to peasants at the crop-establishment stage and binds their supply at harvest to him or her at a reduced price, implying exorbitant rates of interest. However, in the case of our study village at least, the middlemen's paddy procurements in 1996 involving advanced credits were less than 20 per cent, and those involving production loans for longer than three months were less than 10 per cent (see Table 8.3). Transactions in cash were the most common (48 per cent), followed by delayed payment by middlemen to farmers (34 per cent). The incidence of delayed payment being almost twice as high as that of credit advance seems to imply that farmers were net lenders to middlemen rather than borrowers.

Another stereotype is to assume a double squeeze on peasants by a middleman engaging in both monopsony purchases of farm product at low prices and monopoly sales of farm inputs at high prices. However, in the case of our study village it was only one of many rice buyers who sold fertilizers and chemicals to farmers (see Table 8.4). Only three farmers purchased fertilizers from this middleman (who was an independent trader) and only five purchased chemicals during 1996, though all the cases involved production loans of longer than one month. Thus the cases of double squeeze by middlemen would have been very limited, if they ever existed. All the other farmers purchased fertilizers and chemicals, also on credit, from specialized agricultural input suppliers (as many as fifteen suppliers).

ORGANIZATION OF MARKETING

A local flow of rice from producers to consumers is illustrated in Figure 8.2. Paddy retained for home consumption by farmers is milled at small *kiskisan* (steel huller) mills within their village or its neighbourhood, with payment in kind, often in the form of rice bran. Some large mills typically located in the suburbs of cities or along highways also engage in custom milling, with a charge of 35–40 pesos per 50 kg bag of white rice. Older, and relatively small-scale, mills in local towns still use the so-called *cono* system equipped with iron disc-shellers and cone polishers. Larger and more modern ones use rubber rollers instead of iron discs (Timmer, 1973; Barker and Herdt, 1985, pp. 174–7). Most mills were privately owned and

Table 8.3 Modes of transaction in the sale of paddy by farmers in East Laguna Village, 1996 total

	Collector		Rice mill	Total
	Commission agent	Independent trader		
Total number of sales by farmers	14 (100)[a]	46 (100)	24 (100)	84 (100)
Cash	11 (79)	16 (35)	13 (54)	40 (48)
Delayed payment				
Shorter than 1 week	2 (14)	15 (32)	2 (8)	19 (22)
1 week to 1 month	1 (7)	4 (9)	4 (17)	9 (11)
Longer than 1 month	0 (0)	0 (0)	1 (4)	1 (1)
Total	3 (21)	19 (41)	7 (29)	29 (34)
Credit advance				
Shorter than 1 week	0 (0)	3 (7)	1 (4)	4 (5)
1 week to 2 months	0 (0)	2 (4)	0 (0)	2 (2)
Longer than 3 months	0 (0)	4 (9)	3 (13)	7 (8)
Unknown	0 (0)	2 (4)	0 (0)	2 (2)
Total	0 (0)	11 (24)	4 (17)	15 (18)

Note: [a] Percentages of total are shown in parentheses.

Table 8.4   Purchase of fertilizers and chemicals by farmers in East Laguna Village, 1996

	Fertilizers			Chemicals		
	Agricultural supply store	Rice trader	Total	Agricultural supply store	Rice trader	Tota
Number of sellers	13	1	14	16	1	1
Number of farmers purchasing	35	5	40	39	3	4
Average purchase per farmer						
Quantity (kg)	593	555	588			
Value (peso)	4 302	4 262	4 297	1 663	468	1 57
Payment mode (no. of farmers)						
Cash	13	1	14	17	0	1
Credit[a]						
Shorter than 1 month	0	0	0	0	0	
1–3 months	6	3	9	4	3	
Longer than 3 months	22	2	24	19	0	1
Total	28	5	33	23	3	2

Note: [a] Some farmers get credit from more than one source.

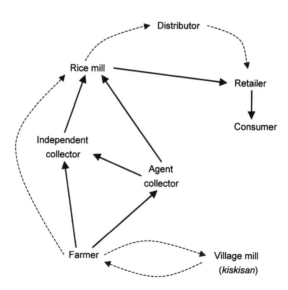

Figure 8.2   Channels of local rice marketing in Laguna, Philippines

operated. Out of thirty-one mills licensed by the National Food Authority (NFA) within the study area, only three were operated by agricultural co-operatives. According to the estimates of both co-op and private mill managers, the share of co-ops in rice marketing in this area is probably less than 5 per cent.

Paddy sold by farmers reaches consumers after being milled at large commercial mills. These mills have the function not only of processing paddy into white rice; they also act as wholesalers in the collection of paddy and the distribution of milled rice to retailers.

As inferred from the data in Table 8.2, a relatively small portion of paddy processed by the mills was purchased directly from farmers, the majority being assembled through collectors. Not single collector intermediates between a farmer and a mill; it is common that a collector of the independent-trader type employs several commission agents in his/her operation. There are even cases in which a commission agent operating on a relatively large scale receives assistance on a commission basis from inexperienced village wives in developing contacts with neighbouring farmers. The commission to this subcontractor is slightly lower than the commission to the primary contractor; for example, three pesos per *cavan* (bag) of paddy goes to the subcontractor out of five pesos that the primary contractor receives from the mill.

Independent traders are usually a husband and wife team working together. The fixed capital requirement is large for an independent trader as the collection operation means the purchase of a truck. Although the truck can be chartered, it is much more convenient to own it for speedy operation, such as hauling wet paddy from farmers' fields immediately to a mill before it spoils. Also, considerable experience is needed to develop the necessary skill in judging qualities of paddy to offer. Since the sale price to mills varies for different varieties and moisture content, miscalculation of the quality of paddy when offering prices to farmers can result in major losses. On the other hand, working capital requirement is not very high, because independent collectors usually pay the farmers after receiving payments from the mills when they deliver their collected paddy (Table 8.3). But having some additional working capital is useful, as it helps them to keep their word to farmers in the event of a miscalculation of paddy qualities or market conditions.

In contrast, the operation of a commission agent is entirely free from such trade risks. Capital requirement is low because it is the miller's truck that hauls paddy from the farmers' fields. Therefore, if villagers enter the collection business, they usually start as commission agents and work towards becoming independent traders.

The hierarchy of traders in paddy collection from commission agents to independent traders, and further up to rice mills, is a common form of marketing organization for farm products in peasant agriculture (Hayami and Kawagoe, 1993). It stems from the fact that each small producer sells only a small amount, which tends to increase the transaction cost per unit of product collected by middlemen. For an independent trader who is anxious to increase the volume of collection for the sake of increasing the rate of utilization of his/her truck and trade skills, it is more economical to let poorer village wives, who have a lower time opportunity cost, to search for and make contracts with their neighbour farmers than for the trader to do the job him/herself.

This condition applies even more strongly to the operators of large rice mills. For the sake of increasing the utilization rate of large fixed capital consisting of milling and drying facilities together with a fleet of trucks, they must endeavour to maximize the procurement of paddy. In order to keep a mill running over the months beyond the local harvesting season, it is necessary to procure paddy from different areas with different harvesting seasons. Assemblage of a large amount of paddy from small producers over a wide territory makes it inevitable that the mills rely on collectors in various localities.

For the critical importance of maintaining assured supply of paddy, rice millers make various efforts to develop long-term trade relationships with large suppliers. Credit tying is one method used for this purpose. Application of this practice is rather limited, however, as observed in Table 8.3; it applies only to some large farmers who continue to sell large amounts directly to the mills. Such direct sales offer a higher price to the farmers as they do not have to pay commission to collection agents. Where a regular customer relationship (*suki*) is established, the mill is said to advance production loans at an interest rate of 8 per cent for three months or so, which is deducted from the proceeds of the paddy they supplied. This rate of about 2.5 per cent per month, or 35 per cent per year, is significantly higher than the banks' lending rates of around 25 per cent for collateral loans, but is much lower than the rates for informal credit, which are usually higher than 50 per cent.[2]

Credit tying is also practised by independent traders. They sometimes advance credit not only to large but also to small farmers, with interest rates ranging between 2 per cent and 5 per cent per month, depending on credit-worthiness of the borrowers, with an average of 3 per cent. And 3 per cent per month is a common rate applied to farmers' purchases of fertilizers and chemicals on credit from agricultural supply stores. The interest rate of 5 per cent per month (80 per cent per year) sounds exorbitant, but it is still lower than a typical rate of 7 per cent per month (125 per cent per year) charged to non-collateral consumption loans for poor rural people by informal moneylenders.

An interesting remark by a commission agent is that, once he/she introduces a farmer seller to a mill, he/she will continue to receive a commission of two pesos per *cavan* even if the farmer sells his/her paddy directly to the mill. This is an incentive payment to the agent to enhancing his/her efforts to find long-term suppliers with low transaction costs for the mill.

One collector usually has transactions with several mills. Yet it appears to be common that a patron–client relationship is established between a certain collector and a certain mill. In that case, the mill provides interest-free trade credit from which the collector advances payment up to ten days before harvest to farmers with whom the collector has a *suki* relationship. This cash advance also applies to the operation of commission agent, where the advance is distributed through the agent but is deducted from the payments that farmers will receive directly from the mill at the time of hauling paddy.

In the local context of Laguna, rice mills usually act as wholesalers for the distribution of their milled rice directly to retail stores. However, large mills located in the vicinity of Metro Manila distribute a large part of the milled rice through specialized wholesale agents to a large number of retailers in the metropolis. In the case of a mill located on the border between Laguna Province and Metro Manila, to which several independent traders operating in East Laguna Village regularly haul collected paddy, about half of its milled rice is sold to the wholesale agents, a third sold to retailers, and the rest sold directly to consumers at a large retail store owned by the mill.

In our local setting, a stable flow of demand from retailers is of vital importance for the rice-milling business, therefore each miller makes major efforts to attract the interest of retailers. One such effort is to advance interest-free loans to regular-customer retailers in the form of sales on credit with delayed payment for two to four weeks. This credit operation is said to be risky, because relatively small amounts of credit to typically small retail stores in local town markets are difficult to recover by legal means. It is said that it is more difficult to establish a mutual trust relationship with town retailers than with farmers and village-based collectors, presumably because it is easier for the former to shift the source of supply.

Significant skill seems to be needed for the effective operation of such trade practises to attract trade from retailers. A manager of a co-operative owning a rice mill remarked that the co-op milling operation was often interrupted by shortage of demand. This remark might reflect the institutional

rigidity or the lack of an incentive mechanism in the co-op system to prac-
tise such risky trade activities *vis-à-vis* local retail stores. Co-op managers
are usually appointed by the elected board of trustees. In addition to fixed
salaries, they also receive perfomance-related bonuses. However, a strong
egalitalianism characteristic of the co-op organization prevents their
receiving a disproportionate share of residual profit. Correspondingly, their
incentive to take risks for high profits is low. It is understandable that they
hestitate to engage in informal credit transactions with private traders,
which are not officially mandated. Co-op mangaers tend to allocate more
of their efforts towards obtaining subsidies from the government and from
foreign aid agencies than towards gaining a larger slice of the market than
private traders.

PRICES AND MARKETING MARGINS

The March 1997 survey attempted to collect information on marketing
margins and profits of paddy collectors, rice mills and retail stores.
Because the number of our observations was small and the questionnaires
involved issues sensitive to respondents, rough calculations shown in this
section and the next are based on highly simplified and conjectural assumptions. They should be taken as illustrative (or even anecdotal) examples.

Before proceeding to the calculation of profit, underlying assumptions
must be made explicit.

In the calculation we attempt to estimate prices per kilogram in milled
rice terms at different points of the marketing channel, from farmers to
consumers, so that profit margins can be calculated for the various segments of marketing. In this calculation, a vital factor is the conversion rate
from paddy to milled rice. The commonly-used rate in the Philippines is
0.65, but this applies to dry paddy. As most paddy hauled to mills is wet, a
conversion factor of 0.58 should be assumed.

Another important factor is the contents of each *cavan* (bag). One *cavan*
is usually assumed to contain 45 kg of paddy but, according to our observations, its content varies from 40 kg to 45 kg, with an average of 42 kg.
Thus, we assume that one *cavan* of wet paddy hauled from the farmer to the
miller contains the equivalent of 25 kg of milled rice. One bag of milled rice
distributed from mills to retailers commonly contains 50 kg.

The prices of rice and paddy vary widely for different qualities but,
for the sake of simplification, our calculation is limited to the case of
ordinary rice, which was sold at a retail price of 20 pesos per kilogram at
the time of our survey.

Table 8.5   Average prices and profit margins in various segments
of the rice marketing channel in Laguna, observed March 1997

	Wet paddy peso/kg	Milled rice equivalent	
		peso/kg	Percentage of retail price
Price			
Farmer to collector[a]	8.0	14	70
Collector to mill	8.5	15	75
Mill to retailer	...[b]	18	90
Retailer to consumer	...	20	100
Margin			
Collector[a]	0.5	1	5
Mill	...	3	15
Retailer	...	2	10
Total	...	6	30

Notes: [a] Collector of the independent trader type.
[b] ... stands for 'not applicable'.

The average prices we observed at various points of the rice marketing channel in March 1997 are summarized in Table 8.5. For the grade of rice commanding a price of 20 pesos per kilogram at retail stores, the millers' wholesale price was typically 18 pesos, with the margin of two pesos for retailers being attested by both retailers and millers.

To produce this grade of rice, mills paid to collectors prices between 350 and 360 pesos of wet paddy per *cavan*, with an average price being about 8.5 pesos per kilogram. The corresponding price at the farm gate procured by collectors was typically eight pesos per kilogram, implying a collector's margin of 0.5 of a peso per kilogram of wet paddy, or approximately one peso per kilogram of milled rice equivalent. Note that this margin is applied to independent traders, and that the commission for agents of five pesos per *cavan* of paddy implies only about 0.2 of a peso per kilogram of milled rice equivalent. The five-times higher margin for independent collectors than the commission rate corresponds to trade risk and capital costs shouldered by the independent traders.

If an independent trader employs commission agents for paddy collection, his/her margin declines by 0.2 of a peso per kilogram of milled rice equivalent. On the other hand, if a miller hauls paddy directly from farmers through commission agents, his/her margin is higher by 0.8 of a peso than the margin of 3 pesos per kilogram of milled rice under the assumption of paddy supply through independent traders, as illustrated in Table 8.5. This increase in the millers' profit margin by shifting the source of supply to commission agents from independent traders is, to some extent, balanced by the cost of hauling the paddy from the farmers that he/she has to shoulder.

The calculation in Table 8.5 illustrates that out of 20 pesos per kilogram of rice paid by consumers at retail stores, 70 per cent goes to farmers, and 30 per cent comprises the profit, of which 5 per cent goes to collectors, 15 per cent to the rice mills, and 10 per cent to retailers.

It must be noted that this calculation relates to the case in which paddy procured in the first two weeks of March 1997 was processed and distributed to retail stores within the same period, during which the same prices are assumed to have prevailed. Early March is towards the end of a lean season during which the farmers' paddy harvest is small and its price is high. The price received by farmers in the previous peak harvest period (October–November 1996) was said to have ranged from 5 to 7 pesos per kilogram, with an average of 6 pesos per kilogram of paddy, or a little above 10 pesos per kilogram per milled rice equivalent, which is consistent with the data in Figure 8.1.

The difference of about 2 pesos per kilogram of paddy (or 3.5 pesos per kilogram of milled rice equivalent) should have accrued to the marketing agents who stored the paddy from harvest to the lean months. If this sum is added to the marketing profit margin, the farmers' share of the consumers' peso decreases to about 50 per cent, and the marketing profit margin rises to about 50 per cent. The average share of the total marketing profit margin over a season should be somewhere between 30 per cent and 50 per cent, because farmers sold paddy not only during harvesting months but also in the lean months.

This inventory carryover is operated mainly by the rice mills. However, some large independent traders also engage in storage operations. The storage charge for paddy was typically 5 pesos per *cavan* per month. Thus, if we assume an interest rate of 2.5 per cent per month, the total cost of the three-month storage period from harvest to the lean months, including both storage and interest charges, amounts to about 1 peso per kilogram. Therefore, the net profit obtained by deducting this 1-peso cost from the 2-peso profit margin is estimated to be 1 peso per kilogram of paddy stored. Much of this profit is considered to be a reward for millers' or traders' risk-taking. And the storage operation is indeed risky: those who stored paddy from the harvest of the 1994/5 dry season gained much more than a 1-peso profit. On the other hand, they incurred losses in the next wet season because the price dropped in the lean months because of major rice imports from abroad by the National Food Authority (NFA). Procurement of domestic rice at a floor price and its discharge at a ceiling price, though officially mandated to the NFA, did not operate to any significant extent during our study period. It appears that the NFA's price stabilization operation relied mainly on the control of imports by means of state trading. It is not quite so clear, however, if discretionary imports by bureaucrats contributed positively to domestic price stabilization.

There are often complaints that the retail market price of rice does not decline in the harvesting months at the same rate as the farm-gate price. It is said that in the mid-1990s the retail price of rice has seldom declined below 18 pesos per kilogram from a seasonal peak of 20 pesos, implying a rate of decline of only 10 per cent. In contrast, the rate of decline in the farm-gate price of paddy from 8 pesos to 6 pesos was 25 per cent. This relative fixity of the retail price reflects the fixity of the absolute marketing profit margin, which was argued by Vernon Ruttan (1969) as being evidence for the proximity to perfect competition in rice markets instead of monopoly/monopsony by millers and traders.

INCOME AND PROFIT

How much income and profit are generated from marketing activities? 'Income' is defined here as value added, including returns to operator's labour, which can be calculated by subtracting paid-out costs from the marketing profit margin. 'Profit' is obtained by subtracting the imputed value of the operator's labour from the income, which supposedly includes returns to the operators' owned capital and entrepreneurship (or human capital). In small-scale business operations heavily based on family labour, income and profit are significantly different. However, the difference is negligible for large enterprises (such as large commercial rice mills) which are based mainly on hired labour.

Because of the small sample size as well as the sensitive nature of information we sought, our data are much less than sufficient to estimate the incomes and profit of various marketing agents; therefore the following calculations are highly conjectural and anecdotal by nature.

Commission Agents

The estimation of commission agents' income is simple and straightforward. Their commission at a rate of 5 pesos per *cavan* of wet paddy (roughly equivalent to 0.1 of a peso per kilogram of paddy, and 0.2 of a peso per kilogram of milled rice equivalent) is deemed to consist entirely of the income of their labour. Thus, the larger the collection an agent arranges, the higher is his/her income. In general, the scale of collection by collectors acting as agents of rice mills is larger than the scale of those acting as agents of independent-trader collectors. The former generally ranges between 100 and 500 *cavans* per crop season, implying that their income from this business ranges between 1000 and 5000 pesos per year, involving two crop seasons. This income range is equivalent to about 7–35 days' farm labour wage.

The collection by commission agents working for independent collectors, however, seldom exceeds 100 *cavans*. They collect paddy in small lots, not only from small farmers but also from landless agricultural labourers who have worked during the harvest and received a share of the harvested paddy as their wage. Thus their income is likely to be below 1000 pesos per year. These commission agents' activities cannot be a major source of household income; they are generally seen as a small sideline revenue from the use of housewives' spare time and commanding a very low opportunity cost.

Independent Traders

The scale of the independent traders' collection is considerably larger, often more than ten times larger than that of commission agents. A wife of a *kiskisan* mill owner in East Laguna Village used to collect about 300 *cavans* per season when she was a commission agent before 1996. In 1996, she and her husband purchased a truck and began to undertake paddy collection as independent traders. Their procurement for the 1996 wet season was about 2000 *cavans*.

Assuming that they were able to collect the same amount for the dry season and applying the 0.5-peso profit margin per kg of paddy for independent collection (Table 8.5), their total margin per year would have amounted to 84 000 pesos. It is difficult to estimate their operational cost, however. But if we assume that the capital and operating cost of their truck was equivalent to a typical transport charge of 5 pesos per *cavan* of paddy, then 0.1 of a peso per kilogram of paddy could be assumed. In addition, if they employed commission agents to search for sources of supply (in fact, they did employ one in the 1996 wet season), the same charge should have been paid.

Under these assumptions, their net income per kilogram of paddy is estimated to have been 0.3 of a peso, implying that their income from paddy trading amounted to 60 per cent of the gross margin, or about 50 000 pesos per year. This was a respectable income in this village, about equivalent to that of a middle-sized full-time rice farmer cultivating about 1.5 hectares of irrigated double-crop paddy field under leasehold tenure with a low rent controlled by land reform laws.

The independent trader's income increases in parallel with the size of the paddy collection. A case was observed in a local town adjacent to Pila in which a couple owning a truck and a *jeepney* collect 4000 *cavans* in the wet season and 5000 *cavans* in the dry season, employing seven commission agents in various villages. If we apply the same calculation as before, it can be estimated that their income from paddy collection amounted to about 110 000 pesos per year.

Moreover, they also engage in a storage operation, holding about 700 *cavans* for about three months per season. If the profit on this was 1 peso per kilogram of stored paddy, they would have obtained an additional income of nearly 60 000 pesos from this operation over two seasons. Their total income would thus have amounted to nearly 170 000 pesos per year, about equivalent to the farm income from the cultivation of 5 hectares of irrigated paddy fields (normally about 35 000 pesos per hectare).

Rice Mills

The rice mills' profit margins were calculated in Table 8.5 as being 3 pesos per kilogram of milled rice. This calculation counts only the sale of rice on the revenue side. In fact, they received additional revenue from the sale of bran and germ produced in the milling process. Assuming that 8 kilograms of a byproduct is produced for each bag (50 kg) of milled rice, and its price is 5 pesos per kilogram, the byproduct's value per kilogram of milled rice amounts to 0.8 of a peso. By adding this value to the revenue side the total margin per kilogram of milled rice increases to 3.8 pesos.

The costs involved in the millers' operation after purchasing the rice from the collector (independent trader) are for drying, milling and distribution to retailers. The operational cost of drying is commonly considered to be 1 peso per kilogram of milled rice. Assuming that the cost of milling is equivalent to the custom-service milling fee, it is estimated to be 0.8 of a peso per kilogram of milled rice; but this may be an overestimate to the extent that the custom service charge includes a profit. However, it seems reasonable to assume that the profit from custom milling is slight, since it involves no risk. Note that this estimate of milling cost turns out to be the same as the value of the byproduct that is commonly used as a payment in kind to custom services by *kiskisan* mills, indicating that a single market integrates both small village mills and large commercial mills.

Distribution to retailers involves the costs of shipment and of interest for sales on credit to retailers for two to four weeks (with possible loss from defaulting), which we would estimate to be about 1 peso per kilogram. These costs add up to 2.8 pesos in total. The total margin of 3.8 pesos, including the value of the byproduct minus this total cost, results in an estimate of the millers' profit of 1 peso per kilogram of milled rice.

What will be the magnitudes of total profit and the rate of profit relative to the amount of capital used in rice mills? Illustrative calculations are attempted for two mills with very different characteristics.

The first calculation pertains to a large mill in San Pablo City, equipped with a modern milling machine using rubber rollers, three dryers and three trucks. Its total capital, including fixed and working capital, would amount to 10 million pesos, according to our rough estimation. Its milling capacity is 300 bags or 15 000 kilograms of rice per day. It runs for six days a week for ten months. In order to maintain utilization of the milling facility at this rate, paddy is hauled not only from Laguna but also from outside the province as far as Northern Luzon, Bicol and Mindoro. It also stores paddy procured in harvesting months for milling in the lean months. But it is still forced to operate below capacity as paddy supply decreases in the lean months and shut down altogether for about two months of the year. Assuming that a ten-month operation for twenty-five days a month produces 200 bags of milled rice a day, the total amount of rice produced and sold would amount to 2500 tons a year, implying a profit of the order of 2.5 million pesos. This estimate is based on the assumption that the miller's profit is 1 peso per kilogram, which relates to the milling of paddy (procured in previous harvesting months) in March 1997. In fact, however, a considerable amount of paddy milled in this month was procured at lower prices. Assuming that this mill stores 5000 *cavans* of paddy for three months per season, or 10 000 *cavans* per year, and that price appreciation exceeds storage cost by 1 peso per kilogram of paddy (as calculated in the previous section), the profit from the storage operation comes close to half a million pesos per year.

Thus, the total profit of this mill, including that from storage operation, would amount to about 3 million pesos per year. If the total capital being used is indeed 10 million pesos, the rate of return to capital is of the order of 30 per cent per year. This rate, when compared with commercial banks' typical lending rate of 25 per cent, suggests that the operator of this mill was able to produce a respectable return to his entrepreneurship and managerial ability.

The second case in our illustrative calculation pertains to a relatively small mill in the *poblacion* of Pila. It is an old *cono* mill purchased by the father of the present owner some forty years ago. Its milling capacity is said to be 120 bags of milled rice per day. However, it operates for only six months a year, presumably milling 100 bags or less per day on the average. Since this mill owns no truck, its paddy is hauled by *jeepney* from nearby villages. Also, it does not engage in a storage operation to any significant extent.

Assuming that this mill operates for 150 days per year with a daily milled rice output of 80 bags, and that the profit margin is 1 peso per kilogram, its total annual profit would amount to only about 60 000 pesos or so. However, the mill owner claimed that his mill, including machines, buildings and land could command the price of 6 million pesos if sold at the time he was interviewed (March 1997). If he is correct, the rate of return to capital is only about 10 per cent, equivalent to the banks' time deposit rate.

In this case, the mill-owner may be content with a low rate of return, presumably because his machines and buildings are long past depreciation, while he can continue to enjoy the rapid appreciation of land value in the Pila *poblacion* along the highway from Manila to Sta. Cruz. His case appears to be typical of the many mills in Laguna, including as many as nine mills within Pila alone.

Retailers

The major route of rice retailing in Laguna, as well as in the Philippines in general, is via specialized rice stores usually operating inside local town markets, although small grocery stores (*sari-sari*) also sell rice to consumers. The retail margin of the rice stores in markets was commonly 2 pesos per kg at the time of our March 1997 marketing survey. However, it is difficult to estimate their operating costs. Averages differ widely for different scales of operation, which range from less than 100 kg to more than 1000 kg of rice sold per day. In addition to store rental, utility charges and helpers' wages, implicit interest from sale on credit to customers appears to be a significant cost component.

An old lady who operated a relatively large store in the Pila market selling between 400 kg and 700 kg per day said that she assumes her income to be 1.5 pesos out of the profit margin of 2 pesos per kilogram sold. Her calculation does not appear to include the implicit interest incurred. It is likely that her income, after deducting interest and defaults, comes close to 1 peso per kilogram. Thus, if she is able to sell an average of 500 kg for 300 days, her income amounts to around 150 000 pesos. This level of income is comparable to that of a large rice farmer cultivating around four hectares, or of a large independent paddy collector. It was our impression, however, that the average scale of operation and income of retailers could well be less than half of this case. Obviously, the major risk involved in the retail rice trade is customers' default on their credit purchases. It is not uncommon that retail stores are forced to close down because of accumulated bad debts.

THE EVOLUTION OF THE RICE MARKET

Our reconnaissance survey of the Laguna rice belt, despite major limitations, revealed the highly competitive nature of local rice marketing in this area. Indeed, the countless number of middlemen competing in the procurement of paddy from farmers (illustrated by thirty-seven buyers operating in a small village with only forty-five rice farmers, each having an average farm size of 1.9 hectares), entry to the paddy collection business is open to virtually any villager.

Not only small, village-based collectors but also rice mills compete intensely for procurement of paddy so as to ensure a sufficient paddy supply to maximize the utilization of their capital. Mills in Laguna are not only large in number; they also have to contest with mills in other provinces and regions to procuring paddy at different harvesting seasons in order to even-out paddy supply over time; this rules out the possibility of any large mill exercising local monopoly power.

Intense competition also applies to the wholesaling of rice by mills to retailers as well as retailing to consumers. The fact that as many as nine mills operate in the one municipality of Pila alone, and many others in neighbouring municipalities within a short distance makes it difficult for any one mill, or even several in collusion, to exercise a private monopoly. The possibility is even smaller for retailers, whose number is indeed countless, and includes not only specialized rice stores but also small grocery stores.

Long-term continuous trade relationships are commonly observed between farmers and collectors, collectors and rice mills, rice mills and retailers, and retailers and consumers, with the relationships often being reinforced by credit tying. Such relationships do not seem to be driven by monopoly-seeking or monopsony profits being sought by any side involved in transactions. Rather, it seems to stem from the motive to save transaction costs arising from possible moral hazard or opportunism occurring under the asymmetry of information, as well as to reduce risk. Farmers, middlemen and consumers continue to maintain long-term trade relationships so long as it is beneficial to them, but it is very easy to switch trade partners if the present relationship is found to be unsatisfactory. Thus the market is highly 'contestable' if not perfectly competitive.

Since the Second World War, major changes have occurred in the means of transportation around East Laguna Village (such as shifts from *carabaos* and pony-drawn carts to *jeepneys* and trucks), as well as improvements in roads, highways and telephone systems, and large-scale modern mills have increased their market share relative to traditional *kiskisan* and *cono* mills. Yet, according to the memories of veteran farmers, traders and mill operators, the structure of rice marketing surrounding the village has remained essentially unchanged. Why has the market mode of transaction prevailed so long for rice, compared with a shift from the community to the market mode in labour transactions observed in the previous chapter?

One major reason appears to be that information asymmetry stemming from quality uncertainty is much smaller in rice than in labour transactions. It is well known that labour employment is characterized by a high degree of information asymmetry, with employers (buyers of labour) having difficulty in monitoring employees' work efforts; this difficulty is especially serious in agricultural production, which is performed across wide areas and subject to large variations in environmental conditions (Brewster, 1950; Binswanger and Rosenzweig, 1986; Hayami and Otsuka, 1993). This difficulty is considered to underlie the use of community-like contracts such as *gama*, and community relationships such as patron–client bonds (Chapter 7).

In contrast, it is not difficult for traders to develop through modest experience the ability to check the quality of paddy they procure. Similarly, under intensive competition among so many buyers, it should be easy for farmers to know the market prices for their products through casual conversations with neighbours. Long-term trade relationships between farmers and traders may help to save transaction costs in rice marketing, too, but they are likely to be much less important than in labour employment.

A more basic factor underlying the early development of market for rice might be a legacy of the colonial rule. Economies in South-east Asia including the Philippines were closely integrated into the international division of labour in the late nineteenth century to the early twentieth century under Western colonial powers backed by the high competitive strength of industry originating from the Industrial Revolution. As comparative advantage dictated, South-east Asian economies specialized in the production of export cash crops and minerals (Myint, 1965). As export-orientated plantations and mines were developed, the subsistence food sector was also commercialized as a supplier of foods to workers in the export-orientated sector. Through this process, household and cottage industries for the production of manufactured commodities geared for consumption by indigenous population were destroyed by the competition from industrial products from the West (Resnick, 1970).

Thus it seems reasonable to expect that lowland areas in South-east Asia, such as Laguna, specialized in rice production from their early stages of development, and sold a significant portion of rice to earn cash for the purchase of industrial goods as well as other agricultural commodities such as sugar. Commercialization of the rice sector should have been accompanied by the development of market institutions, including informal contracts and conventions. It is our hypothesis, yet to be tested by future research, that commercialization of the rice sector in the Philippines, under the pressure of the international division of labour, underlay the early development of the market for rice. In this respect, the history of market development in the area surrounding East Laguna Village might not be different from rice villages in South-east Asia.

9 The Emergence of Rural-based Industries[1]

The previous chapter ended with the hypothesis that household and cottage industries in rural villages in the Philippines were destroyed in the process of integration of its economy into the vertical division of labour with industrial economies in the West under the colonial rule. Indeed, until very recently, it was usually difficult to find significant manufacturing activities in rice villages in the Philippines, with East Laguna Village being no exception. Growing urban economic influences, which accelerated in the late 1970s and operated throughout the 1980s, mainly as a force to pull labour out of the villages as well as to increase employment in service activities, such as *sari-sari* stores, and *jeepney* and tricycle driving within the villages.

A dramatic change that occurred in East Laguna Village in the 1990s was a sudden surge of cottage manufacturing, which not only increased employment opportunities for villagers but also pulled a significant amount of external labour into the village. This chapter traces this new development, based on the three surveys on the industries within the village and its surroundings, as well as the marketing chains linking the activities with foreign markets. The first reconnaissance survey was conducted during July–August 1995; the second main survey was in August 1996; and the third, follow-up, survey was in March 1997.

THE NATURE OF NEW VILLAGE INDUSTRIES

When we first visited East Laguna Village in 1974, we were struck by the virtual absence of indigenous manufacturing activities for consumption at home or for sale to local markets, such as weaving, handicraft making and blacksmithing, which used to be very common in Japanese villages before Japan's rise to a high-income stage in the 1960s. This impression was shared by the Japanese investigator who surveyed this village in 1966 (Umehara, 1967). The low reliance of the village economy on manufacturing continued throughout the 1970s and 1980s. Indeed, the share of manufacturing in the total household income in East Laguna Village remained at only 1 per cent between 1974 and 1987, but to our great surprise, the

207

eighth-round village survey in 1995 recorded that this share had suddenly increased to 13 per cent.

This change resulted from the establishments of one paper mill and seven metalcraft factories during the period 1991–5. The paper mill produced folk art papers and paper crafts from local materials such as banana stems and cogon grasses, mainly to meet domestic demand; and the seven metal factories produced Christmas ornaments (such as candle holders) and other crafts from tin plate and wire, based on subcontract orders from export contractors operating in Metro Manila.

A subsequent search around neighbouring villages and surrounding municipalities found that similar manufacturing enterprises based on subcontract arrangements with export contractors had been springing up widely since the late 1980s. The most numerous were activities related to the production of ready-made garments, such as sewing and embroidery (Kikuchi, 1998). Metalcraft, paper, plastic and woodcraft industries manufacturing ornaments, gifts and toys followed the spread of the garment industries after a time lag of a few years. They were based on simple, highly labour-intensive technologies. The new wave of labour-intensive industrialization stemmed from foreign demand and has been progressing at such a rate as to become a significant income source, not only in towns but also in hitherto purely agriculture-based villages.

Further exploration in Metro Manila found that the waves of foreign demand for these labour-intensive, low-technology products began to reach the Philippines in the late 1970s/early 1980s. This was the period when newly industrializing economies (NIEs) in Asia, such as Taiwan, Korea and Hong Kong, began to shift in a major way to more sophisticated, high-value products corresponding to their sharp wage increases. The diversion of international demand for the labour-intensive products away from the NIEs spilled over into ASEAN and other low-wage Asian economies. However, the political turmoil associated with the downfall of the Marcos regime delayed Filipino entrepreneurs from capitalising on this opportunity. As the turmoil subsided, however, they began to recover the lost opportunity from the late 1980s, based on low wages relative to rich endowments of human resources, and especially the high level of education in the Philippines. In fact, the export contractors in Metro Manila whom we interviewed started their business mainly in the late 1980s.

These urban-based entrepreneurs tried to meet orders from foreign buyers initially by establishing their own factories. Later, as foreign demand continued to expand, they found it advantageous to contract-out parts of the production process to outside agents, especially those located in rural areas, where cheap labour is more abundantly available. They continue to maintain their own workshops for final adjustments and brushing-up, but the crude fabrication process has increasingly been handed out to subcontractors as this industry is easy to separate into accountable units. Some subcontractors are located within Metro Manila, but most are located in neighbouring provinces within a radius of about 100 kilometres. It is common that workers employed in an exporter's workshop return to their home towns and carry on the business on subcontract terms with the former employer.

COTTAGE WORKSHOPS AND RURAL FACTORIES

How are these rural-based industries organized under subcontacting arrangements with the export contractors? According to our observation it seems to be convenient to classify them into 'cottage workshops' and 'rural factories.' Typically belonging to the former are metalcraft workshops found in East Laguna Village. They operate either in the operators' houses or in neighbouring shanties with mud floors, unprotected by solid walls. Their production is based on highly labour-intensive technology requiring very little capital consisted only of soldering irons, cutters and hammers.

The first cottage workshop in East Laguna Village was established in 1993 with an initiative by the highly enterprising wife of a landless but relatively well-to-do villager. She operated a small rice mill (*kiskisan*) and used a *jeepney* to haul rice. She developed a contract with an exporter through an introduction from her daughter's godmother and started manufacturing by employing a village boy who had work experience in an exporter's factory in Metro Manila. At the time of our interview in August 1996, her crude workshop built next to her house was manned by nine labourers, including a couple who specialized in product quality control. The boy who assisted her with the start up of her business later became an independent manufacturer in the village, employing five workers in addition to his brother and himself.

In the mode of working as well as in the use of labour-intensive technology the 'rural factories' are similar to cottage workshops. Their scale of operation is, however, larger, employing between thirty and seventy workers, whereas the cottage workshops rarely reach this scale, typically employing fewer than twenty workers. But a more important distinction is their relative independence from the export contractors. Each cottage workshop relies on the orders from only one export contractor, while a rural factory receives orders from several; this is effective in insuring against the possible loss of orders from any one exporter. In fact, cottage workshops in East Laguna Village suffered from an interruption for a few months because of the business failure of a major customer in the USA. Another distinction is that a rural factory usually operates more than one workshop, either under the direct administration of an owner-operator or by subcontracting to small manufactures.

Also, important is the difference in the access to government assistance and institutional credit. The rural factories are usually covered by industrial extension activities by the Department of Trade and Industry (DTI), often benefiting from subsidized credits related to the extension programmes. The cottage workshops, however, are outside the reach of these government programmes. This difference stems, to a large extent, from a difference in the educational level of operators. Most operators of rural factories are college graduates, while those of the cottage workshops have attended only elementary school or, at most, high school. This difference underlies the difference in their ability to apply for government assistance and other institutional support.

While cottage workshops are located mostly inside villages, rural factories tend to be located in the more urbanized parts of municipalities. However, some rural factories are located within villages. The paper mill in East Laguna Village is one such exception. This mill was founded by a couple who both used to work in the administrative office of the University of the Philippines at Los Baños. After retirement, they returned to the wife's native village, where she had inherited a relatively large residential plot. They started the paper mill operation with technical assistance and a subsidized loan provided under the Small and Medium Industry Technology Transfer Programme of the DTI.

Subcontracts with Export Contractors

Both the cottage workshops and the rural factories producing metalcrafts operate as subcontractors of the export contractors. Typically, a subcontractor receives an order from his/her principal contractor specifying the product design, the unit price, the quantity and the delivery date. The products are usually delivered using a chartered *jeepney* once every two to three weeks. The delivered commodities are inspected within a week and paid per piece for those that pass the quality inspection. The subcontractor goes with his workers to the principal's warehouse one day before payment to correct defects found by the inspector, to minimize the rejection rate. The payment is usually made by dated cheque, though a post-dated cheque is sometimes used. Advance payments of the order of 10–20 per cent of the product value are often given.

This contract, which we shall call the 'advanced-order' contract, is different from the 'putting-out' contract commonly used in the garment industries, in which materials for processing are supplied by the export contractors to subcontractors. If a metalcraft subcontractor so wishes, he or she can receive from the export contractor a supply of materials such as tin plate and wire as a trade credit in kind. However, the prices of such material in advance are set at about 10 per cent higher than the cash purchase prices in the market. Considering that the production period is about three weeks from material purchase to product sale, the 10 per cent mark-up amounts to an exorbitant rate of interest, reaching as high as 360 per cent per year. Therefore, except for a few who are desperately short of working capital, most subcontractors prefer to buy their materials from local hardware stores.

The reason why the putting-out system is commonly used in garment subcontract arrangements is the need to make the products homogeneous, to be consistent with the demands of foreign buyers. Supply of material of a specific type is a vital means by which the export contractor can collect a sufficient amount of a standardized product from subcontractors to meet to the specifications of foreign buyers. In contrast, materials for metalcrafts, such as tin plate, are sufficiently homogeneous that the choice of the material does not significantly affect the product quality. This contrast between the garment and metalcraft subcontracting industries is consistent with the hypothesis that the putting-out system is induced more by the need of the principal contractor to achieve product standardization than the need to mitigate the working capital constraint of the subcontractors.

This contractual model applies to both cottage workshops and rural factories. The difference arises in the specification of product design. The job of a cottage workshop is simply to multiply the sample product supplied by his/her principal contractor. On the other hand, a rural factory often makes the sample product from a rough sketch drawn by its contractor. In this case, the product development is a collaborative venture between the rural factory and the export contractor. There have even been cases where a rural factory has produced original sample products which have been demonstrated to foreign buyers at such occasions as trade fairs. The product development capacity in rural factories seems to operate as a force both to strengthen their collaborative relationship with the principals on the one hand, and to promote their independence on the other.

Organizational Characteristics

The industrial organization, in terms of labour management and co-ordination over various tasks, is surprisingly similar between the cottage workshops and the rural factories, despite differences in firm size and product development capacity. They both depend heavily on piece-rate contracts. High-order managerial tasks beyond production activities, such as negotiations with exporters and procurement of materials, are handled by operators and family members. The maintenance of workshops and packing/unpacking of materials and products are shouldered by the family in small enterprises, with a few labourers being employed on daily (or hourly) wages in larger enterprises. Cutting and twisting tin plate and wire into appropriate sizes and forms are done either by family labour or contracted out to neighbouring families at piece rates. By far the largest task in terms of labour requirement is the assembly of these intermediate products into final product form, mainly with the use of a soldering iron. This task is performed in workshops by workers employed at piece rates. Some operators said this process could be carried out better within the workshop because of the convenience of quality control, but it has increasingly been contracted out, as will be explained later. The inspection and counting of the final products is the major task of operators and family members, often assisted by a few experienced workers who are given fixed sums in addition to their piece-rate remuneration for their own produce. In the case of cottage workshops in the East Laguna Village, almost 90 per cent of the workers are hired (see Table 9.1). This dependence on hired labour

Table 9.1   Workers in cottage workshops in
East Laguna Village, 1995

	Male	*Female*	*Total*
Number of workers			
Family	9	7	16
Hired	88	51	139
Total	97	58	155
Origin of workers			
East Laguna Village	53	49	102
Other villages in Pila	14	1	15
Other provinces	30	8	38
Total	97	58	155
Educational level of workers			
(school years)			
East Laguna Village	8.3	7.3	8.0
Other villages in Pila	9.2	8.0	9.1
Other provinces	8.3	9.5	8.6
Total	8.5	8.3	8.4

is somewhat higher than, but not much different from, that of the rural factories, because of their practice of contracting-out to other workshops.

This form of organization, based heavily on piece-rate contracts, is common in other rural-based industries such as garment manufacture, and plastic and paper crafts. However, for some cultural reasons we are not able to identify, the metalwork industry is characterized by a heavy reliance on young male labour relative to other industries, especially garment manufacture, in which almost all workers are women. Metal fabrication using a soldering iron is considered to be a man's job, though it can be performed physically by women. Regardless of the reason, however, the very rapid growth in this industry in less than five years has created a bottleneck in the local labour market, so that rural entrepreneurs have been forced to recruit labourers from other regions, such as Bicol and Zambales.

In the case of cottage workshops in the study village, the labourers recruited from outside the local community amounted to about 30 per cent of male labour according to the 1995 survey (see Table 9.1). They were housed in a corner of the workshop in very poor living conditions. They were paid at ordinary piece rates in addition to their transfer expenses from home. Food was cooked either individually by themselves or centrally in the operators' kitchen. In the latter case, meal charges were deducted from wage payments at a rate of about 27 pesos, equivalent to about US$1 per day.

The piece-rate payment per male worker is between 70 and 150 pesos for an eight- to ten-hour day. This wage earning per day is comparable with most farm tasks, though usually less than eight hours are spent on hired farm work per day. While the wage rate per hour is therefore lower than that of farm work, a major advantage of the metal workshop is year-round steady employment. Another attraction is that it is less arduous and less 'dirty' work than drudgery in the rice fields. Workers receive a wage payment every two weeks.

Hourly rates range from 6 to 15 pesos per hour depending on experience and skill, with average wage receipts per day being around 70 pesos. The capacity to mobilize labour at much lower cost than the official minimum wage rate of 145 pesos per day is considered to be one of the major factors underlying the development of the rural-based metal industry through subcontracting to the urban-based exporters.

Labour management is the most difficult task, especially for larger-scale operators. Managers are relatively free from monitoring workers' efforts because of piece-rate payment schemes, as well as the relative ease of inspecting the quality of crude metalcrafts. Training labourers for piece-rate tasks is also not difficult, as the needed skill of fabricating crafts by use of a soldering iron can be learned through apprenticeship in a week or so.

However, absenteeism and/or hopping to other jobs, often after receiving advanced wage payments, cause of headaches to operators, especially when they are under pressure to meet a delivery date. In addition, labourers recruited from distant places tend to create friction with the local community through drunkenness and violence.

These problems are much rarer in small workshops, where it is easier to develop an intimate personal relationship between the operator's family and hired workers. For this reason, some rural factories have been contracting-out part of their production to small workshops under the putting-out system. In fact, as we visited the cottage manufactures in East Laguna Village several times during 1995–7, we found that many of them reduced hired labour from outside to their own workshops and increased putting-out operations with other villagers during this period. Several workshops that failed in this organizational adjustment were forced to close down.

PRODUCTION STRUCTURE OF THE METALWORK INDUSTRY

The advantage to rural-based entrepreneurs of mobilizing cheap labour is especially beneficial in the metalwork industry because it uses extremely labour-intensive technology. Capital requirements are small, even compared with other labour-intensive activities in rural areas such as garment manufacture and rice farming, as illustrated in Table 9.2. Capital–output ratios calculated by dividing the value of capital stock (including both fixed and working capital) by value added (output minus current input value) in metal manufacturing are only about one-fifth that of garment manufacturing, and about a third that of rice farming. Even larger differences are observed in the capital–labour ratio (capital stock per worker). These data unequivocally show the high labour-absorptive and income-generating capacity of the metalcraft industry in capital-scarce economies, whatever margins of statistical error are assumed.

Cottage Workshop versus Rural Factory

A striking similarity is found between the cottage workshops and the rural factories in their production structure, despite different scales of operation. Both the ratio of value added to total output and the relative shares of factors in value added are almost identical. The slightly smaller capital–output ratio and larger labour productivity of the rural factories (as measured by value added per worker) reflect the fuller utilization of capital stock and labour force because of the more stable flow of orders they are able to receive than the cottage workshops, instead of the difference in technology used. The rates of return to capital are almost the same.

These observations are consistent with the hypothesis that the cottage workshops and the rural factories share a common production function with constant returns to scale. This characteristic must relate to the similarity in their internal organization, as explained in the previous section. It is no wonder that, in the absence of scale economies, rural factories prefer to contract out part of their production to smaller workshops as their operations grow above a size efficiently manageable by the owner and his/her family, instead of building a manager/foreman system in the expanded workshop. In this way the risk arising from demand fluctuations can also be reduced.

The only major indivisible input for the operators of rural factories is their entrepreneurial ability concerning product development and marketing, as well as access to the government's industrial extension services. Utilization of entrepreneurial ability can be no less efficient under the decentralized subcontracting system than under the hierarchical command system in the large workshops.

Comparison with the Garment Industry

The major difference between the metalwork and garment industries is the much smaller requirement for fixed capital in the former. This can be seen clearly from the comparison between the cottage workshops producing metalcrafts and the garment factories. Their scales of operation are not much different in terms of the average number of workers per enterprise, yet an average garment factory uses as much as fourteen times more capital stock than the average metal workshop. The operation of the garment factory requires the purchase of high-speed sewing machines, one for each worker. In order to protect these high-cost machines, the workshop must be enclosed by solid walls and a roof, and have a cement floor. In contrast, the metalcraft workshop needs only rudimentary tools such as a soldering iron, bull hammer and metal cutter, which can be operated in a crude structure with a mud floor and no walls. Thus, the average fixed capital stock per metal workshop is only 13 000 pesos. If the business is started on a modest scale with ten workers, the initial funding requirement, including both fixed and working capital, could be less than 15 000 pesos. This amount of capital can be mobilized by landless agricultural labourers, by such means as sale of livestock, as the prices of cattle and pigs are about 10 000 and 2 000 pesos per head, respectively.

Thus, five out of seven metal workshops in East Laguna Village are operated by landless households. In contrast, the fixed capital requirement

Table 9.2 Production structure of rural industries compared to rice farming (averages per firm/farm per year)

| | | Metal[a] | | | | Garment[a] | | Rice farming[b] | |
| | | Cottage workshop | | Rural factory | | | | | |
		(000s pesos)	(%)	(000s pesos)	(%)	(000s pesos)	(%)	(000s pesos)	(%)
Year of survey		1995		1996		1994		1995/6	
Sample size		7		2		37		51	
Output value	(1)	330		1081		630		142	
Current input		131		416		50		17	
Value added	(2)	198	100	665	100	580	100	125	100
Labour income		141	71	487	73	372	64	46	37
Capital income[c]	(3)	9	5	29	4	129	22	22	18
Operators' surplus[d]	(4)	48	24	149	22	79	14	57	46
Rate of return to capital	((3)+(4))/(5)	154%		156%		40%		126% (8%)[h]	

Capital stock	$(5)=(6)+(7)$	37	114	515	63 (963)
Fixed capital[e]	(6)	13	34	480	46 (946)
Working capital[f]	(7)	24	80	35	17 (17)
Capital–output ratio	(5)/(2)	0.19	0.17	0.89	0.50 (7.2)
No. of workers per firm[g]	(8)	22	51	17	7
Labour productivity	(2)/(8)	9	13	34	18
Capital–labour ratio	(5)/(8)	1.7	2.2	30	9.0 (138)
(P'000s/worker)					

Notes: [a] Assume rejection rates of 20% for metal and 5% for garments.
[b] For an average farmer cultivating 2 ha; data are from East Laguna Village survey.
[c] Assume interest rate of 25%.
[d] For rice farming, includes land income.
[e] For rice farming, the value of total rice-farming-related assets owned by villagers per 2 ha of rice land cultivated by farmers in East Laguna Village.
[f] For metal and garment production, one month costs for current inputs and labour. For rice production, 50% of the cost of current input, hired labour and capital rental per season.
[g] For rice farming, the number of labour force engaging in rice farming, both self-employed and employed, per 2 ha of rice land cultivated by farmers in East Laguna Village.
[h] Figures in parentheses show the case including land value (P450 000/ha at 1995 prices) in fixed capital.

of 480 000 pesos for a garment factory is roughly equivalent to the value of one hectare of well-irrigated rice land (see Table 4.7 on page 93), which is clearly beyond the reach of landless agricultural labourers. Therefore, its operation is limited to either landed households with collateral, or those who had accumulated money from trade and/or formal employment, such as in government offices.

It is interesting to observe that the requirement for fixed capital is much higher in the garment industry than in metal manufacture, but the reverse holds for the working capital requirement. Also, the cost of current inputs is much lower for the garment industry. This difference reflects different forms of subcontract: that is, the putting-out system commonly used in garment subcontracting and the advance-order contract used for metalcraft subcontracting, as explained earlier.

A striking finding is the extremely high rate of return to capital in the metal industry relative to the garment industry. This might be because of the higher risk involved in the metal industry as it is a very new industry within the study area. The garment industry is more mature and well established, as it began to spread earlier and more widely. It appears that the incidence of failure is higher in the metal industry than in the garment industry, even within our limited observations.

The high rate of return in the metal industry over the garment industry may thus include innovators' excess profit in the Schumpetarian sense as a reward for entrepreneurs' risk-taking. However, it must be recognized that, to the operators of cottage workshops who have no access to institutional credits, the effective rates of informal credits may well be close to 100 per cent per year. The extremely high rates of return to capital of the order of 150 per cent may barely be sufficient to induce landless labourers having no collateral to undertake this risky new business.

On the other hand, the rate of return to capital of the order of 40 per cent for the garment industry might be sufficient to maintain investment, since entrepreneurs in this industry have access to institutional credits from commercial banks at an interest rate of the order of the about 25 per cent per year. It seems reasonable to expect that the rate of return in the metal industry will soon decline to the level of the garment industry, as the initial high return will attract followers to enter this business.

Comparisons with Rice Farming

The labour-using and capital-saving nature of the metal industry is also evident from comparisons with rice farming with an operational size of two hectares. The capital intensity of rice farming measured in terms of capital–output and the capital–labour ratios is higher than in metalcraft manufacturing but lower than garment manufacturing so long as land is not included in the capital stock. However, if the value of rice land is added to the value of capital stock (as calculated in parentheses in Table 9.2), the capital intensity of rice farming exceeds that of garment manufacturing by a wide margin. Moreover, the rate of return to capital also declines to 8 per cent.

The very high capital intensity and the low rate of return from the inclusion of land value in capital is, to a large extent, the elevation of land prices far above the capitalized value of rice farming income because of the expectation of future conversion of farmland for urban use, though the conversion has as yet been rather limited in the eastern part of Laguna relative to the western part. New entry to rice farming has therefore been limited largely to those who have accumulated savings from non-farm professions and sought the social prestige and security associated with land ownership in addition to a future appreciation of land value.

Clearly, rice farming in this area does not represent an enterprise such as the metalcraft manufacture, in which poor landless labourers can participate and improve their income and living conditions by exploiting their enterpreneurship.

THE ACTIVITIES OF EXPORT CONTRACTORS

The export contractors of metalcrafts as well as paper, plastic and wood crafts operate widely in Metro Manila and its surroundings. Typically, they receive orders from foreign buyers who have offices in Manila and act as agents for US supermarkets and department chains. Some receive orders directly from abroad. The contracts between foreign buyers and export contractors are similar to those between export contractors and rural subcontractors: namely, advanced-order contracts specifying the quantity, unit price, product design and delivery date. Advance payments and credit guarantees are practised to some extent, but not the supply of materials characteristic of the putting-out contract. The degree of independence of the export contractors from the buyers seems to depend on their product development capability, which is similar to the relationship between the export contractors and the subcontractors. In fact, many export contractors started their businesses as subcontractors and then advanced to their present status. Almost all operators have university degrees. They are thus located in a continuous spectrum with operators of the rural factories.

Relative to the rural factories, however, the organizational models or management styles appear to vary much more widely across the export contractors. Three contrasting models may be illustrated by examining case studies of three contractors among those we interviewed in the August 1996 survey.

Towards the Modern Factory

One model represents a development towards the modern factory system. An export contractor based on the southern outskirts of Metro Manila has a workshop with about 150 workers employed at hourly rates and with a manager/foreman hierarchy. In addition, the fabrication of crude craft objects is mainly contracted out to some forty subcontractors. However, the final processes such as painting, and assembling the metal and wooden items, and packaging them in gift boxes, is mainly done in-house. The operator said that a factory system with direct supervision of workers is necessary to maintain the quality standard required by his customer.

This firm relied solely on one foreign buyer, with an office in Makati, Metro Manila (and its headquarters in Dallas, Texas). This buyer sends the company's inspectors to the factory to check the quality of products for export at the final packaging stage. This final check by the buyer is done on products that have passed an inspection by nine in-house quality control workers.

Although this firm relies on orders from a single buyer, it has a strong product development capability, with five employees specializing in product design and sample making. Thus product development is a collaborative effort between the buyer and the contractor, which underlies their stable, long-term trade relationship. However, this contractor does not receive trade credits and guarantees from the buyer, except that 10 per cent to 20 per cent of product value is advanced when the contract is closed on each order. Production to shipment takes one month or more and the final payment is normally a week after shipment, while payments for wages and purchasing materials must be made every two weeks. The operator thus considers the mobilization of working capital to be the most crucial element in management. He relies mainly on commercial bank loans, with interest rates around 25 per cent. However, this credit line is not easy to expand because of lack of sufficient collateral (his factory building is not owned but rented).

At the time of interview, the operator considered that labour management did not pose much of a problem. However, he thinks it not wise to expand his workshop further under the labour regulations that prohibit the use of workers paid less than the official minimum wage and prevent flexible employment (that is, lay-offs in cases of reduced orders). Thus he considers it necessary to utilize subcontracting even for the final processes of production in order to expand his business. At the same time, he thinks it is not easy to develop a reliable subcontract relationship that assures high product quality and precise delivery dates.

Complete Contracting-out

A diametrically opposed case to the modern factory model is found in the southern part of Metro Manila, near Quezon City. In terms of total sales, this firm does not seem so very different from the previous example based on the factory system. However, it only employs about ten workers, including two quality inspectors. The operation of this firm is mainly based on subcontracting, with more than seventy rural producers.

The most interesting aspect of this company is its use of the 'inside contract' system. This firm has its own workshop, where more than fifty workers produce not only metal objects but are also involved in plastic, paper and wood crafts. However, they are not employed by the firm but are employed by leaders of groups, each consisting of about ten workers. The firm pays the leaders at piece rates upon delivery of their products. This is the system that was practised in the early stages of industrialization in the Western world and Japan but disappeared later to be replaced by the manager/foreman/labour hierarchy (Okazaki and Okuno-Fujiwara, 1998). Thus it was like seeing a living fossil to find the inside contract system being practised in this firm. The merit of this system is said to be the reduction of the burden on the firm's management to monitor labourers' work efforts, while checks on product quality and delivery dates can be done throughout the production process. This advantage is especially beneficial to the small-lot production of complicated products requiring artisan skill.

In fact, it appears that the average lot size of orders received by this firm is relatively small. Unlike the factory based on the system that relies on one large buyer, this export contractor receives orders from about fifty buyers, through such media as international trade fairs and industrial shows. Its products, especially those produced within its workshop, such as model ships and locomotives, are rather complicated and obviously require artisan skill and dexterity. The organization of this firm may be efficient for mass production (though not in a very large lots) of the commodities requiring traditional artisan skills in response to a sudden increase in demand from abroad.

Towards Modern Subcontracting

The third type of export contractor is based in a middle-sized city near the north-eastern edge of Metro Manila. In terms of total sale value, this firm appears to be significantly larger than the two previous cases discussed. Yet manual workers engaged for the final modifications and finishing inside its own workshop are fewer than fifty in number, and the supply of the commodities in semi-final and even final forms is contracted out to nearly a hundred subcontractors. In order to maintain and improve the quality of the products, about twenty employees travel around rural-based subcontractors and give them technical guidance. Also, almost the same number are employed on product design and development. In total, the number of white-collar staff is larger than the number of blue-collar workers. The product quality of this firm is therefore high enough to meet the demand from the middle- to upper-middle-class population in high-income economies, whereas most other export contractors are geared to the demand from the lower-middle-class and below.

This strategy of concentrating in-house resources to product development and contracting out mass-production process as much as possible to small and medium enterprises, while strengthening their production capabilities through technical assistance and other measures, is the strategy also commonly adopted by Japanese firms over a wide range of industries, including textiles and electronics. This firm had been successful in obtaining orders from as many as seventy buyers all over the world. Some of the orders are acquired through participation in trade fairs in Tokyo and other places abroad.

The major problem confronted by this firm is how to develop trusting relationships with subcontractors. In fact, this is a problem shared by all the export contractors. Even in this firm, which has been making major efforts to provide technical guidance and other assistance, it occasionally happens that delivery is delayed, or that the delivered commodities are lower in quality than the sample products, resulting in crises in the firm's relationships with foreign customers. Thus the operator considers it better to reduce rather than to increase the number of subcontractors, and increase the capabilities of a smaller number of dependable subcontractors. In fact, this is the basic strategy of the major automobile manufacturers in Japan.

PROSPECTS FOR RURAL ENTREPRENEURS

Exploration of the metalwork industry from East Laguna Village to Metro Manila leaves little doubt about the great potential of labour-intensive industries to raise incomes and living standards among rural people, especially the landless poor in developing economies. Manufacturing of this type is very well suited to being a rural industry in the Philippines, because of the small capital requirement relative to the large absorption of labour with little skill. But, more importantly, it can exploit the potential of rural entrepreneurship that is relatively abundant in villages and local towns in the Philippines. Sharply rising wage rates in Asian NIEs followed by some ASEAN neighbours created a niche for entrepreneurs in the Philippines in the 1990s. Recovery from the country's political crisis, together with progress in liberalization and deregulation in trade, foreign exchange and foreign direct investment since the late 1980s, has opened the door for rural entrepreneurs to fill the niche. The opportunity has rapidly been exploited through the formation of subcontracting networks from the metropolis to rural villages.

A major question is whether the current surge of rural industrialization can be sustained. For the time being, there seems to be substantial scope to sustain momentum. Labour is still substantially cheaper in villages than in the metropolis and, more importantly, entrepreneurship and educated man-power are relatively abundant in the rural sector of the Philippines, with a large pool of potential entrepreneurs. Competition that has underlain the rapid development of rural industries will continue to be strong. Export contractors are eager to develop mutually beneficial trust relationships with conscientious and capable rural entrepreneurs. Many operators of rural factories are motivated to advance to the status of export contractors, and there is ample evidence that their wish is not an unattainable goal.

The active competition underlying the rapid development of this indus-try will be further promoted by the government's technical extension, including advice on product design and the provision of marketing oppor-tunities by such means as trade fairs and industrial shows. The activities of the DTI in those aspects have had a significant impact on promoting the industry. Such government support will have to (and is likely to) increase sharply to advance the Philippines beyond only being suppliers of cheap crafts to lower-income classes in high-income economies. Such a shift will be necessary to sustain the industry in view of growing competition from lower-wage economies such as China, Vietnam and South Asia.

At the time of writing, the government's support services stop at the local town level and do not reach small cottage industries in villages. However, this may not cause too much concern. Present efforts of the export contractors to foster relatively small, dependable subcontractors, coupled with government support, will strengthen the 'rural factories' as we have defined them. As their scale of operation expands, they will increasingly contract out their production process to the 'cottage indus-tries', as they have already begun to do. The rural factories will provide technical guidance and other forms of assistance as the requirement for product quality from export contractors will continue to rise. In this way, a multi-layered subcontracting structure may be created. This is the system typically used in the Japanese automobile industry (Asanuma, 1985; Wada, 1991). At the same time, public investment in transportation, communications and electrification in rural areas, which are vital for the inclusion of rural areas in the industrialization process, will continue to increase beyond the recovery from the slump of the 1980s.

Thus, barring the resurgence of political instability, the spread of labour-intensive manufacturing into rural areas is likely to continue until the Philippines catches up to its newly industrializing ASEAN neighbours such as Malaysia and Thailand, provided that demands for labour-intensive consumption goods from high-income economies will not be greatly curtailed. What will be the fate of rural entrepreneurs when the Philippines advances further to a high-income stage? As has been observed in the case of metalcraft manufacturing, recent rural industrialization in the Philippines is based on a decentralized hierarchy of many self-employed informal agents tied by customary trade practices and informal contracts, where vertical integration is weak. This was the organization that supported the rural-based development of the Japanese economy in the early period of modernization following the Meiji restoration in 1868 (Smith, 1988). In fact, until the turn of the twentieth century, or even later, up to about the time of the First World War, the growth of the national economy was, to a large extent, supported by the activities of rural entrepreneurs (Rosovsky and Ohkawa, 1961; Tussing, 1966).

In the low-income stage of economic development, a decentralized complex of small rural entrepreneurs is efficient in economizing the use of scarce capital and management input while making intensive use of labour, having a low opportunity cost. This system's efficiency depends, to a large extent, on the dualistic structure characterized by differentials in wage and interest rates across firm sizes. Will this system become inefficient and be replaced by vertically integrated large corporations when the economy advances to a stage at which factor market dualism is eliminated?

The experience of the Japanese economy since the 1960s may shed some light on this question. Within a decade of the beginning of high economic growth from the mid-1950s, the dualistic structure was largely eliminated (Minami, 1973). Yet, small-scale family enterprises have survived and have even been strengthened (Kiyonari, 1980; Patrick and Rohlen, 1987). Advantages of small- and medium-scale enterprises, such as high incentives for entrepreneurs and flexibility in employment and staffing, have increased in tandem with the increased need for small-lot production of differentiated products, as the Japanese economy has advanced to a stage characterized by high per capita income and diversified consumer demands. Large corporations in Japan continue to prefer subcontracting to vertical integration. Co-ordination between a parent company and small/medium firms has been developed with such precision that the subcontracting system is integrated inseparably within the automobile company, Toyota's famous *kanban* (just-in-time) system. In this system subcontractors deliver supplies of parts and materials to the assemblers exactly at the time when the parts are to be used, so that no inventory accumulates in the assembling plant even for the small lot-production of many differentiated products. This subcontracting system is now considered to be a major organizational innovation that underlies the strength of Japanese industries, especially the automobile industry (Abegglen and Stalk, 1985; Asanuma, 1985, 1989; Wada, 1991).

Is there any strong reason to doubt whether entrepreneurial and managerial skills now being learned in the countryside of the Philippines will provide the basis of a modern subcontracting system and thereby support the advancement of the Philippine economy to a higher level of development? Are there insurmountable cultural and social barriers for rural entrepreneurs in the Philippines in following the development of their Japanese counterparts?

10 Income Growth and Distributional Change

So far we have traced, one by one, the influences of various modernizing forces on East Laguna Village. We now examine whether, as a result of all those forces, the income level of villagers has increased or decreased, and how income distribution among households has changed over time.

A RECAPITULATION

Before proceeding to quantitative assessments on income growth and distributional change, it will be useful to recapitulate on the nature and timing of the major forces that have affected the economy of East Laguna Village.

East Laguna Village was first settled in the 1880s. In a marshy lowland area adjacent to Laguna de Bay, initial settlers cleared the land and practised rainfed rice monoculture under sharecropping contracts with landlords who lived in local towns. Because of their specialization in rice with no alternative crop being suitable for the marshy lowland, together with the nature of the colonial Philippine economy based on the export of primary commodities, villagers were involved in market transactions from the beginning, though their income came mainly from rice cultivation with virtually no cottage industries and few non-farm employment opportunities available. Villagers were poor as they had to give half of their rice harvest to the landlords, but they were a largely homogeneous group, with no significant class differentiation within the village.

The most fundamental and sustained force to bring about change in such a community structure was population growth. In this village, opportunity to clear new land for cultivation was closed by the late 1950s, but the population continued to increase at rates higher than 3 per cent per year. This explosive population growth was the result of high natural increases augmented by immigration from upland villages in the surrounding hills and mountains. The availability of rice fields per capita decreased rapidly and it became progressively more difficult for children of farmers in the village, and more so for migrants from other villages, to acquire land to establish themselves as farmers. Thus a class segmentation between farm operators and agricultural labourers began to emerge in the hitherto homogeneous village community.

The impoverishing effect of increased land scarcity was counteracted to some extent by the extension of a national irrigation system to this village in 1958 that converted rice production from rainfed single-cropping to irrigated double-cropping. Based on this infrastructure, the dramatic arrival of modern, high-yielding varieties of rice, and an associated increased application of fertilizers took place between the late 1960s and early 1980s. This technological innovation contributed significantly to an increase in incomes and employment in East Laguna Village. Concurrently, land reform programmes extended to this area in the early 1970s resulted in major income transfer from landlords in towns to tenant farmers in the village, primarily by means of conversion from sharecropping to leasehold tenancy, with land rents fixed at lower-than-market rates. New leaseholders' income continued to increase in parallel with increased rice yields under fixed land rents.

This benefit of land reform, however, was gained by tenant farmers alone, with no direct benefit accruing to landless agricultural labourers. Moreover, land reform regulations resulted in an inactive land-rental market and closed opportunities for agricultural labourers to become farm operators. Thus, land reform, together with the new rice technology consolidated class segmentation between farmers and agricultural labourers.

Despite the sharply increased population of agricultural labourers, they were able to subsist because of the expansion in wage employment opportunities. First, employment increased in the early phase of the Green Revolution because of the labour-absorptive nature of the new rice technology. Later, as tenant farmers became affluent and their children were educated for urban occupations, hired labour was substituted for family labour. In this way the benefits of new rice technology and land reform that accrued disproportionately to farmers have spilled over to agricultural labourers. More importantly, non-farm employment opportunities for villagers have expanded, especially since the late 1970s when major improvements in the highway system were accomplished. Landless labourers were able to capture a large share of income from non-farm sources such as construction, transportation, petty trades and small manufacturing.

As the village became closely integrated with the urban economy, a new class of 'non-farm workers' was created in East Laguna Village. Typically, they commute from their homes within the village to permanent salaried jobs in nearby towns. This class of household began to increase in the 1980s, and by the mid-1990s comprised nearly 20 per cent of all village households.

What was the net result of the complex interactions of all these forces on income growth and distributional change in East Laguna Village?

GROWTH OF AGGREGATE INCOME

First, we look at the growth trend of aggregate income earned by all the households in East Laguna Village.

Although we conducted nine full-enumeration surveys, we were able to collect sufficiently comprehensive data to estimate the income of all the households in East Laguna Village for only six years (1974, 1976, 1980, 1983, 1987 and 1995). For those six years, we estimated the incomes of all the individual households by adding (a) incomes from self-employed activities, such as rice farming; (b) earnings from labour employment, capital and land rentals (including rent from sub-tenancy contracts); and (c) transfer incomes, such as remittances from family members living outside the village (minus transfers to outside areas). The incomes from self-employed activities were obtained by subtracting all the paid-out costs from the output values. The values of self-employed products used for home consumption were imputed by market prices and included in income, whereas those used for production purposes, such as seeds, feed and payments in kind to inputs, are deducted as costs. The incomes of individual households thus estimated are aggregated into a total village income. The estimated incomes are 'gross' in the sense that capital depreciations are not deducted.

It must be cautioned that our income data, calculated from one-point interview surveys, may involve underestimation, especially for low-income households, because minor subsistence products, including the collection of wild plants and catching fish, as well as small grants and tips from neighbours and relatives were unlikely to be fully enumerated. Our estimates are more relevant for identifying trends in income changes rather than absolute income levels, since there is no reason to doubt whether the degree of possible underestimation changed systematically over time.

Data are not available to apply the same estimation procedure before 1974. We have tried, however, to estimate the village income in 1965/6 (1965/6 dry season and 1966 wet season), mainly based on the data of rice income shares prepared in Chapter 4 (see Table 4.6 on page 90). First, villagers' income from rice farming per hectare is calculated as the sum of the farmers' and hired labourers' income shares in value added in rice production. This average income per hectare is multiplied by the total rice farming area to produce an estimate of total rice income accruing to villagers. Total village income is calculated by adding to this rice income the income from non-rice sources. Non-rice income is estimated as 8 per cent of total village income for 1965/6. This percentage was obtained through extrapolation based on the growth rate between 1974 and 1995. It must be cautioned that the village income thus estimated for 1965/6 is much less reliable than the estimates for later years that were based on comprehensive household surveys.

Although we have relatively reliable data for six survey years, a major problem in ascertaining the trend of real income growth from the surveys over such a small number of years is the influence of weather and other ecological variations on rice yields that resulted in major fluctuations in rice income. In order to mitigate the effects of these random shocks, we based our comparisons over time on the averages of 1974 and 1976 data, and of 1980 and 1983 data. For 1995, we take the averages of rice income for 1995 and 1996, and add them to the non-rice income for 1995, because the 1996 survey covered farmers' households only. Such averaging is, admittedly, *ad hoc*. Yet, we think that readers will grasp the trend of real income growth better with the use of averaged data rather than single-year data.

Another problem was, which deflator to use for the conversion of nominal to real income. As a measure of the economic welfare enjoyed by the villagers, the consumer price index (CPI) outside Manila, prepared by the National Statistics Office (formerly the National Census and Statistics Office), may be relevant. As a measure of product or value added by village factors, however, the farm-gate price of rough rice might be a more appropriate deflator, considering the dominant weight of rice production in the economy of East Laguna Village, particularly in the earlier years. The problem is that the movements in CPI and the price of rice were very different, and therefore the trends of real income growth significantly diverge, depending on the choice of deflator.

Table 10.1 summarizes the estimates of total income from all sources for 1965/6 (sum of the 1965/6 dry season and the 1966 wet season); 1974/6 (average of 1974 and 1976); 1980/3 (average of 1980 and 1983); and 1995/6 (average of 1995 and 1996) in terms of total village aggregates, averages per household and averages per capita of population. The growth rate of total village income was faster than that of average household income, to the extent that the number of households increased. The growth rate of per capita income was faster than that of individual household income, to the extent that the average family size decreased. Average per capita income in this village in 1995/6 was 12 200 pesos (about US$ 470 at a nominal exchange rate of 26 pesos per dollar in 1995), about 40 per cent of the average GNP per capita in the Philippines.

As evident from the estimates given in Table 10.1, real income growth rates are very different when using the price of rice and CPI as deflators. For the whole period from 1965/6 to 1995/6, the growth rate of CPI-deflated per capita income was lower than that deflated by the price of

Table 10.1 Total village, average household, and per capita income per year, East Laguna Village, 1965–96, 1995 prices

	Deflated by rice price[a]			Deflated by CPI[b]			Rice price deflated by CPI
	Village total	Average per household	Average per capita	Village total	Average per household	Average per capita	
Real income (P000s/year)							
1965/6[c]	1 440	21.8	3.7	4 077	61.8	10.4	20.5
1974/6[d]	3 700	36.3	6.2	5 926	58.1	10.0	11.6
1980/3[e]	7 429	59.2	10.3	6 697	53.4	9.3	6.5
1995/6[f]	13 630	56.3	12.2	13 630	56.3	12.2	7.2
Growth rate (%/year)							
1966 to 1974/6	11.1	5.8	6.1	4.2	−0.7	−0.4	−6.1
1974/6 to 1980/3	11.3	7.8	8.0	1.9	−1.3	−1.1	−8.5
1980/3 to 1995/6	4.4	−0.4	1.3	5.2	0.4	2.0	0.7
1965/6 to 1995/6	7.9	3.3	4.2	4.2	−0.3	0.6	−3.5
1974/6 to 1995/6	6.6	2.2	3.3	4.1	−0.2	1.0	−2.3

Notes: [a] Farm-gate price of rough rice.
[b] Consumer price index outside Manila (1995 = 100).
[c] 1965 dry and 1966 wet seasons.
[d] Average of 1974 and 1976.
[e] Average of 1980 and 1983.
[f] Average of 1995 and 1996 for rice income and 1995 for non-rice income.

rice, by 3.6 percentage points. This difference resulted from the equivalent decline in the price of rice relative to CPI. According to the series deflated by the price of rice, fairly rapid rates of real income growth were recorded – 7.9 per cent per year for the village total; 3.3 per cent for the household average; and 4.2 per cent for per capita average – whereas the growth rate of household income was nearly zero and that of per capita income only 0.6 per cent for the whole period, if CPI deflation is used. Despite such major differences, one important conclusion we can draw from the data in Table 10.1 is that East Laguna Village was in someway able to overcome strong population pressure on limited land resources to prevent per capita real income from decreasing since the late 1960s. Essentially the same conclusion can be drawn for comparisons between 1974/6 and 1995/6, based on more reliable survey data. It is likely that the economic welfare of villagers improved more than the CPI-deflated per capita income data show, because the weight of rice in their consumption expenditure is higher than the average for households outside Manila, including not only rural but also urban areas.

It is somewhat surprising to find that during the heyday of the Green Revolution, CPI-deflated income per capita did not show a significant increase. Its growth rate was almost zero during 1965/6–1974/6 and decreased at a rate of 1.1 per cent during 1974/6–1980/3, whereas deflation by the price of rice resulted in a very fast increase in per capita income of the order of 6–8 per cent per year. This difference was created by a sharp decline in the price of rice relative to CPI under the pressure of increased rice supply as a result of the successful diffusion of modern, high-yielding varieties and related technologies. This implies that major gains in productivity from the adoption of new rice technology during the Green Revolution period were more than fully transferred from producers to consumers through deterioration in the terms of trade against the rice sector.

The negative effect of the terms of trade was not limited to rice farmers, however. It also fell on agricultural labourers because a significant share of labour wages from rice production was paid in kind. Figure 10.1 shows that the agricultural wage rate in East Laguna Village remained stable throughout the 1960s and the 1970s if deflated by the price of rice, but decreased significantly if deflated by CPI, corresponding to the relative decline in the price of rice. An interesting finding is that the industrial wage rate in Metro Manila deflated by CPI moved in parallel with the agricultural wage rate, indicating the integration of rural villages with the urban labour market.

However, there is no denying that the greater share of income loss caused by the rice price decline was shouldered by large farmers whose

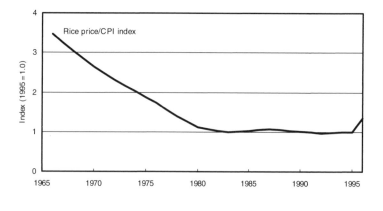

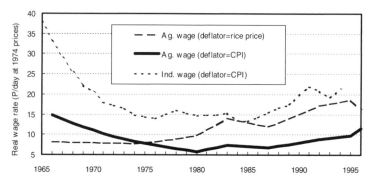

Figure 10.1   Rice price–CPI ratio and real wage rates in rice farming (transplanting), East Laguna Village, and in the industrial sector, Metro Manila,
1966–96

Source: Wage in the industrial sector from Department of Labour and Employment (various issues); CPI outside Metro Manila from National Statistical
Coordi-nation Board (various issues).

marketable surplus was large relative to home consumption (Hayami and
Herdt, 1977).

INCOME GROWTH BY HOUSEHOLD TYPE AND
INCOME SOURCE

How did relative income positions change across different classes of household? Table 10.2 shows the estimates of average income per household
and per capita for the four categories of household for 1974/6–1995/6.

Table 10.2   Average household and per capita income by type of household, East Laguna Village, 1974–96, deflated by CPI outside Manila (1995 = 100)

	Household income				Per capita income			
	Farmer		Agri-cultural labourer	Non-farm worker	Farmer		Agri-cultural labourer	Non-farm worker
	Large (2 ha and above)	Small (below 2 ha)			Large (2 ha and above)	Small (below 2 ha)		
Real income (000s pesos/year)[a]								
1974/6	127	55	29	n/a	16.5	9.4	5.8	n/a
	(100)	(43)	(23)		(100)	(57)	(35)	
1980/3	130	54	35	78	20.2	9.1	6.2	11.5
	(100)	(42)	(27)	(60)	(100)	(45)	(31)	(57)
1995/6	149	81	36	71	33.2	18.4	7.7	17.5
	(100)	(54)	(24)	(48)	(100)	(55)	(23)	(53)
Growth rate (%/year)								
1974/6 to 1980/3	0.4	−0.3	2.9	...[b]	3.2	−0.5	1.0	...
1980/3 to 1995/6	1.0	2.9	0.2	−0.7	3.6	5.2	1.5	3.0
1974/6 to 1995/6	0.8	1.9	1.1	...	3.5	3.3	1.4	...

Notes: [a] Percentages relative to large farmers' incomes are shown in parentheses.
[b] ...stands for 'undefined'.

Unfortunately, comparable data are not available before 1974. The comparisons based on CPI deflation alone are presented in Table 10.2 because our discussions here are focused on the relative welfare positions of the four social classes in the village.

According to the data in Table 10.2, the average income per household of agricultural labourers increased slightly faster than that of large farmers, though significantly slower than that of small farmers, during the two decades 1974/6 to 1995/6. Agricultural labourers' household income relative to large farmers' changed little, from 23 per cent to 24 per cent. However, because the number of family members in farmers' households decreased significantly faster than in those of agricultural labourers (see Table 3.6 on page 58), the latter's per capita income declined, from 35 per cent of the farmers' in 1974/6 to 23 per cent in 1995/6. These changes reflect the tendency that increased investment in children's education by farmers who received a disproportionately large benefit from land reform and new rice technology (although the benefits also spilled over to the agricultural labourers through increasing employment of hired labour) magnified income inequality in the long run through the children's migration to high-income urban occupations (Chapter 3).

Yet it is rather surprising to find that, despite the sharply increased population of agricultural labourers competing for employment over a limited farmland area, they were able to increase their average income by more than 30 per cent (1.4 per cent per year) between 1974/6 and 1995/6. Incidentally, it may appear anomalous to see that the per capita income growth rates of the three classes of households listed in Table 10.2 were higher than the average rate (1.0 per cent per year) of all the households listed in Table 10.1. This apparent anomaly resulted from the very large increase in the share of relatively poor agricultural labourers in the total number of village households, which pulled down the average per capita income growth rate of all the households to below the rate of agricultural labourers.

Also, it seems to be a rather remarkable achievement by agricultural labourers to match the speed of their household income growth with that of the farmers, considering the strong forces that operated to depress their income relative to the farmers' (see Chapters 3, 4 and 5). How were agricultural labourers able to achieve such increases in their income, both absolutely and relatively, under seemingly very unfavourable conditions? An answer can be found in the relative expansion in income from non-farm sources as well as earnings from hired employment (see Table 10.3). Indeed, the income of farm origin (an aggregate of self-employed farm income and earnings from hired farm employment) increased much more

Table 10.3   Average household income per year by source, East Laguna Village, 1974–96, deflated by CPI outside Manila (1995 = 100)

	Total	*Farm origin*	*Non-farm origin*
Real income (P000s/year)			
1974/6	58 (100)[a]	50 (87)	8 (13)
1980/3	53 (100)	33 (62)	20 (38)
1995/6	56 (100)	20 (36)	36 (64)
Growth rate (%/year)			
1974/6 to 80/3	− 1.3	− 6.3	15.9
1980/3 to 95/6	0.4	− 3.4	4.2
1974/6 to 95/6	− 0.2	− 4.3	7.7
Share of self employed (%)			
1974/6	73	79	31
1980/3	54	74	22
1995/6	43	59	35

Note: [a] Percentage composition shown in parentheses.

slowly than the income of non-farm origin, so that the share of the latter in average household income increased from 13 per cent in 1974/6 to 64 per cent in 1995/6. This expansion in the share of income from non-farm sources was associated with a reduction in the share of self-employed income from 73 per cent in 1974/6 to 43 per cent in 1995/6, because the income of non-farm origin, in which the share of self-employed income was lower, increased faster than the income of farm origin (see Table 10.3 and Figure 10.2). The share of self-employed income was lower in the income of non-farm origin because the latter consisted mainly of earnings from non-farm labour employment. Another factor underlying the relative shrinkage of self-employed income in total household income was the decrease in the share of self-employed income in the income of farm origin; this reflects the behaviour of relatively well-to-do beneficiaries from land reform, who increasingly replaced family labour by hired labour in farm work, which corresponded to their income increase.

Altogether, the income from hired employment increased much faster than the income from self-employment. Since the agricultural labourers' income depended more heavily on hired wage earnings than did the farmers' (see Table 10.4), reductions in the share of self-employed income in the average household income (lower part of Table 10.3) imply that the share of agricultural labourers in total village income increased at the expense of the farmers' share. Thus, despite a major expansion in the share

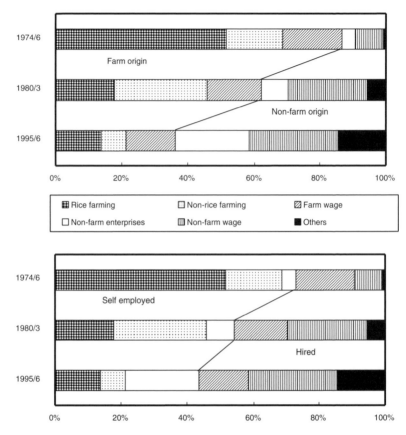

Figure 10.2   Percentage composition of average household income, East Laguna
Village, 1974–96

of agricultural labourers in the village population, they were able to keep
up with farmers in the growth of household income.

While the well-to-do farmers' retreat from manual farm work was not
an insignificant factor in increasing the employment of agricultural
labourers, their earnings from hired farm employment decreased rather
than increased, by 21 per cent between 1974/6 and 1995/6 (see Table
10.5), partly because of absolute reductions in labour input in rice production because of mechanization after the 1970s, and partly because of
depreciation in the value of farm wages received in rice relative to CPI. In
contrast, non-farm wage earnings increased by as much as 470 per cent,
while 'other', consisting mainly of remittances from family members

Table 10.4   Percentage composition of household income, by source and by type of household, East Laguna Village, 1974–96

		Self-employed					Hired wage earning			Other	Total	Farm origin total	Self-employed total
		Farming		Non-farm enterprise			Farm wage	Non-farm wage					
		Rice	Non-rice	Com-merce	Manu-facturing	Trans-port		Casual	Salaried				
1974/6	Large farmer	73	8	2	0	1	2	0	13	1	100	83	84
	Small farmer	55	25	4	1	1	11	1	2	0	100	91	86
	Ag. labourer	0	27	5	0	0	59	6	0	3	100	86	32
	All households	51	17	3	1	0	18	2	7	1	100	86	72
1980/3	Large farmer	36	27	3	0	2	2	4	18	8	100	65	68
	Small farmer	25	28	8	2	3	9	11	7	7	100	62	66
	Ag. labourer	0	33	3	1	3	35	17	5	3	100	68	40
	Non-farm worker	0	5	16	0	0	0	23	56	0	100	5	21
	All households	18	28	5	1	2	16	12	12	6	100	62	54
1995/6	Large farmer	43	7	8	1	1	0	1	22	17	100	50	60
	Small farmer	24	6	2	10	7	5	11	11	24	100	35	49
	Ag. labourer	1	11	4	11	4	35	21	7	6	100	47	30
	Non-farm worker	1	3	7	28	5	1	11	24	20	100	5	44
	All households	14	8	5	12	4	15	13	14	15	100	36	43

Table 10.5 Average household income per year of agricultural labourers, by source, East Laguna Village, 1974/6 and 1995/6, deflated by CPI outside Manila (1995 = 100)

	1974/6		*1995/6*		*Rate of change*
	(000s pesos) *(1)*	*(%)*	*(000s pesos)* *(2)*	*(%)*	*(%)* *((2)−(1))/(1)*
Self-employed					
Non-rice farm	7.8	27	4.3	12	−45
Non-farm enterprise					
Commerce	1.3	5	1.6	4	23
Manufacturing			3.8	11	
Transport			1.2	3	
Total	1.3	5	6.6	18	408
Hired wage earning					
Farm wage	17.0	59	13.4	37	−21
Non-farm wage					
Casual	1.7	6	7.3	20	329
Salaried			2.4	7	
Total	1.7	6	9.7	27	471
Other	0.8	3	2.1	6	163
Grand Total	28.6	100	36.1	100	26
Average income per capita	5.8		7.7		33

working away from home (including overseas contract work), increased by about 160 per cent. In addition, agricultural labourers' self-employed income from non-farm activities, such as petty trades and tricycle driving, also recorded a major gain, of about 400 per cent. Clearly, significant increases in these non-farm income-earning opportunities were the basic force underlying an increase in the average per capita income of agricultural labourers by more than 30 per cent, despite very rapid increases in their population under the limited land resources available in East Laguna Village.

The increased integration of East Laguna Village with the urban labour markets was especially evident with the emergence of non-farm workers as a new social class from the 1980s. Their average household income, earned mainly from permanent salaried jobs in local towns, was about the same as that of small farmers and more than twice as large than that of agricultural labourers, whose earnings were based mainly on casual daily-wage employment. These non-farm workers and small farmers together composed a middle class in the village, comprising about a third of population and earning nearly half of the total income in the village in 1995/6.

CHANGES IN INCOME DISTRIBUTION
AND POVERTY INCIDENCE

How did the distribution of income change across the households in the village? Table 10.6 compares the distribution of household income and operational land holding in terms of the shares of income and land area held by the quintile groups of households that are classified according to the ranks of household income and farm size, for the six years for which data are available. Judging from the quintile income share, the income distribution in East Laguna Village was already highly skewed by 1974 – as much as 56 per cent of total village income accrued to the richest 20 per cent of households, and only 4 per cent was received by the poorest 20 per cent, implying that average household income in the top quintile was more than ten times higher than that of the bottom quintile. This high degree of income inequality was reflected in the Gini coefficient of 0.49, although this might be somewhat overestimated because minor subsistence products, small grants and tips, which could be relatively more important in poorer households, may not have been fully recorded in our survey data.

It is important to note in Table 10.6 that the Gini coefficient has not risen significantly since the 1970s. Indeed, changes in the Lorenz curve drawn from the household income data are barely discernible over the years 1974, 1983 and 1995 (see Figure 10.3). One may wonder if these household income data tend to exaggerate inequality in income distribution, because the family size of large farmers was significantly higher than that of small farmers and agricultural labourers in the early period, so that the differences in per capita income were not as large as in household income. However, adjustments for family size differences under the assumption that members in each household receive a similar income share, as shown in parentheses, do not alter the basic conclusion.

In this respect, movements in income distribution represent a sharp contrast to those in the distribution of land holdings. The Gini coefficient of land holdings in 1966 calculated from the Umehara survey data and modified by our family reconstitution data suggests that the degree of land concentration in that year is not much different from that of household income in 1974. This affinity suggests that, so long as East Laguna Village remained a pure agrarian community based mainly on rice production (as was the situation in 1966), the major determinant of income distribution across households was the distribution of operational landholdings. However, as non-farm income-earning opportunities increased, the power of land distribution to bind income distribution was progressively weakened; this is likely to be the main reason why the Gini coefficient of income inequality was

Table 10.6   Size distribution of household income and operational land holdings,
all households, East Laguna Village, 1966–95

	Share of income (%)						
	1966	*1974*	*1976*	*1980*	*1983*	*1987*	*1995*
I (Top 20%)	n/a	56	50	51	55	52	56
II	n/a	21	22	22	20	21	21
III	n/a	13	14	14	13	14	12
IV	n/a	7	9	9	9	9	8
V (Bottom 20%)	n/a	4	5	4	4	5	4
Gini coefficient[a]	n/a	0.49	0.45	0.46	0.45	0.47	(0.51)
		(0.47)	(0.41)	(0.44)	(0.41)	(0.44)	(0.51)
Poverty incidence[b]	n/a	68	69	59	67	69	56
	Share of land (%)						
	1966	*1974*	*1976*	*1980*	*1983*	*1987*	*1995*
I (Top 20%)	51	62	66	77	80	84	99
II	28	28	27	23	20	16	1
III	17	9	7	0	0	0	0
IV	4	0	0	0	0	0	0
V (Bottom 20%)	0	0	0	0	0	0	0
Gini coefficient	0.54	0.62	0.71	0.76	0.77	0.79	0.89

Notes: [a] Gini coefficients calculated for income distribution across households are
shown outside parentheses, whereas those shown inside parentheses
are calculated across individuals' incomes under the assumption that a
household income was distributed equally among the members of the
household.
[b] Percentage of population having incomes below the poverty line. The
poverty line is defined as an annual per capita income required to satisfy
basic nutritional requirements (2000 calories) and other basic needs. The
poverty line in the survey years is estimated by deflating the 1994 poverty
line estimated by the National Statistical Co-ordination Board (1996) for
the rural sector of the Philippines.

prevented from rising significantly, despite sharp increases in the Gini coefficient of land concentration from 0.54 in 1966 to as high as 0.89 in 1995.

Like other rural villages in the Philippines as well as other developing
economies, East Laguna Village is characterized by a high incidence
of poverty. The percentage of the population living below the poverty line,
(calculated by the National Statistical Co-ordination Board (1996) as an
income barely sufficient to purchase basic food requirements (2000 calories)
together with other basic needs) was 56 per cent in East Laguna Village

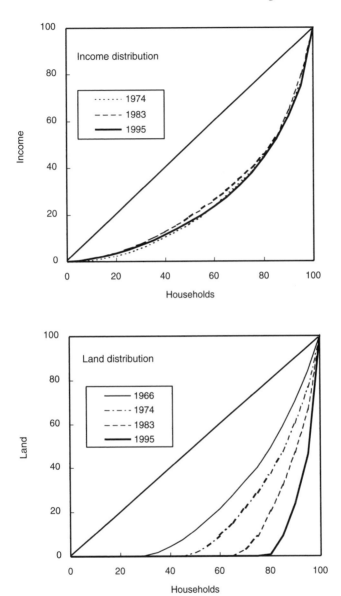

Figure 10.3   Changes in land and income distribution, East Laguna Village,
1966–95

in 1995, compared to the rural sector of the Philippines overall, which was 53 per cent in 1994 (28 per cent in the urban sector). This calculation is likely to involve an overestimation of the incidence of poverty in East Laguna Village because we consider that our income data are subject to underestimation, especially for low-income households, as explained earlier. Yet it seems safe to infer that nearly a half of the villagers lived at a subsistence minimum or even less. The incidence of poverty, however, has not increased since the 1970s. According to our data, the percentage of the population living below the poverty line in East Laguna Village was as high as 68 per cent in 1974, was about the same in 1987, and decreased to 56 per cent by 1995, corresponding to increased non-farm employment opportunities in the 1990s (see 'Poverty incidence' in Table 10.6).

It must be recalled that, although the basic factor underlying the increased inequality in the distribution of landholdings was strong population pressure on the limited land for cultivation, a more immediate cause was the land reform regulations that made the land-rental market inactive, thereby removing the opportunity for landless agricultural labourers to rent lands for their own cultivation. Ironically, the land reform programmes that aimed at achieving greater equity in the rural sector contributed to greater inequality within the village community, although the programmes were able to achieve the intended goal of transferring income from rich landlords living in towns to poor tenants living in villages. By this process, the lot of the landless poor was prevented from worsening, first because of increased employment opportunities in rice production in the 1970s through new rice technology as well as the retreat of well-to-do land reform beneficiaries from farm work, and later, and more decisively, because of increased employment in non-farm economic activities which became available to villagers through the closer integration of the village economy with wider markets.

Thus, in this village case, the market has proven to be an effective mechanism of trickling down a significant benefit from urban-based economic development. However, it must be clearly recognized that this trickling-down mechanism was critically supported by investment in public infrastructure, such as roads and schools, which increased villagers' opportunity to access the market and their ability to exploit this opportunity. Throughout our long association with East Laguna, we are convinced of the villagers' capacity in handling the market so as to make major advancements in their economic well-being if such infrastructure support are provided adequately.

From Thomas More's *Utopia* to Russian Narodniks and US Populists in the nineteenth century, and further to the recent 'moral economy school'

(Scott, 1976), a popular belief has repeatedly been asserted, that the encroachment of the market into traditional agrarian communities tends to result in greater inequality and misery among the rural poor. Such a view does not seem to find support in the history of East Laguna Village over the past several decades, however. Instead, the experience of East Laguna Village since the 1960s suggests strongly that the misery of the poor would have been magnified further by rapid population growth with closed land frontiers, if the village had continued to rely on traditional agriculture in isolation from urban market activities.

Epilogue: Will the Village Remain a Village?

Mrs Captain who had been so helpful throughout our study in this village died unexpectedly on 4 February 1997 from a heart attack at the age of 71. Masao Kikuchi and I heard the news in Japan and were able to visit the Philippines to attend a memorial ceremony on the thirtieth day of her 'departure'.

The Captains' house used to be a solid but ordinary wooden house commonly found in rural areas of the Philippines but it was rebuilt as an urban-style concrete house paid for by a daughter who had been employed in the Middle East as a nurse. As we entered the house, a group of old ladies were reciting prayers. Outside, men were being served with beer and palm liquour together with barbecued chicken and pork. Mr Captain was as calm and reserved as usual. He said none but only smiled while receiving our condolences. However, he looked very much older. My former assistant, who had married his son, expressed her concern that Mr Captain had become too dependent on alcohol since the tragedy.

It was not easy to refuse the offer of drinks from old acquaintances, and a few drinks in the tropical heat soon made me feel drowsy. I escaped the feast and took a walk. The village looked as peaceful as ever under the shade of coconut trees, but the major changes since my first visit were very obvious. Houses had become much more dense, while trees had become thinner. The village road on which I was walking had been paved since three years ago, and urban-style houses based on remittances from overseas employment were no longer exceptional, with the result that the main street of the village looked rather like a newly-developed, low-class suburb of Manila. I heard that there was a plan to develop a housing subdivision within the village for sale to urban dwellers. With a sigh I said to myself, 'How long will this remain a rural village?' Suddenly, the lively smile of Mrs Captain when I had first met her a quarter of century before flashed into my mind.

YUJIRO HAYAMI

Appendix A

Table A1 Demographic changes in East Laguna Village estimated by family reconstitution, 1917–97

Year	Population at end of year	Number				Percentage rate[a]			
		Birth	Death	Migrated		Birth	Death	Immigration	Emigration
				In	Out				
1917	43								
1918	47	1	1	4	0	2.33	2.33	9.30	0.00
1919	49	2	2	2	0	4.26	4.26	4.26	0.00
1920	51	2	2	2	0	4.08	4.08	4.08	0.00
1921	55	2	1	3	0	3.92	1.96	5.88	0.00
1922	55	3	2	0	1	5.45	3.64	0.00	1.82
1923	55	1	2	1	0	1.82	3.64	1.82	0.00
1924	56	2	2	2	1	3.64	3.64	3.64	1.82
1925	58	1	0	1	0	1.79	0.00	1.79	0.00
1926	60	3	1	0	0	5.17	1.72	0.00	0.00
1927	69	5	1	6	1	8.33	1.67	10.00	1.67
1928	71	3	1	0	0	4.35	1.45	0.00	0.00
1929	76	5	4	4	0	7.04	5.63	5.63	0.00
1930	82	7	1	0	0	9.21	1.32	0.00	0.00
1931	85	2	2	4	1	2.44	2.44	4.88	1.22
1932	90	4	1	2	0	4.71	1.18	2.35	0.00
1933	92	5	3	0	0	5.56	3.33	0.00	0.00
1934	92	3	2	1	2	3.26	2.17	1.09	2.17
1935	97	4	1	2	0	4.35	1.09	2.17	0.00
1936	107	6	3	7	0	6.19	3.09	7.22	0.00
1937	113	5	0	1	0	4.67	0.00	0.93	0.00
1938	116	3	4	5	1	2.65	3.54	4.42	0.88
1939	121	8	2	0	1	6.90	1.72	0.00	0.86
1940	131	6	2	6	0	4.96	1.65	4.96	0.00
1941	132	3	1	0	1	2.29	0.76	0.00	0.76
1942	149	8	2	11	0	6.06	1.52	8.33	0.00
1943	156	9	3	1	0	6.04	2.01	0.67	0.00
1944	177	7	4	18	0	4.49	2.56	11.54	0.00
1945	181	11	6	0	1	6.21	3.39	0.00	0.56
1946	176	7	4	2	10	3.87	2.21	1.10	5.52
1947	183	3	2	9	3	1.70	1.14	5.11	1.70
1948	193	10	1	2	1	5.46	0.55	1.09	0.55
1949	199	7	4	3	0	3.63	2.07	1.55	0.00

Table A1 *(Continued)*

Year	Population at end of year	Number				Percentage rate[a]			
		Birth	Death	Migrated		Birth	Death	Immigration	Emigration
				In	Out				
1950	204	9	3	0	1	4.52	1.51	0.00	0.50
1951	211	8	2	2	1	3.92	0.98	0.98	0.49
1952	226	16	2	5	4	7.58	0.95	2.37	1.90
1953	238	14	1	2	3	6.19	0.44	0.88	1.33
1954	241	16	3	1	11	6.72	1.26	0.42	4.62
1955	247	10	1	2	5	4.15	0.41	0.83	2.07
1956	258	16	5	4	4	6.48	2.02	1.62	1.62
1957	272	23	5	0	4	8.91	1.94	0.00	1.55
1958	286	19	2	1	4	6.99	0.74	0.37	1.47
1959	292	11	1	2	6	3.85	0.35	0.70	2.10
1960	305	13	3	3	0	4.45	1.03	1.03	0.00
1961	318	18	6	3	2	5.90	1.97	0.98	0.66
1962	334	11	4	11	2	3.46	1.26	3.46	0.63
1963	358	20	5	11	2	5.99	1.50	3.29	0.60
1964	376	14	3	9	2	3.91	0.84	2.51	0.56
1965	389	18	3	2	4	4.79	0.80	0.53	1.06
1966	399	17	6	9	10	4.37	1.54	2.31	2.57
1967	407	19	8	11	14	4.76	2.01	2.76	3.51
1968	415	18	7	6	9	4.42	1.72	1.47	2.21
1969	437	21	5	7	1	5.06	1.20	1.69	0.24
1970	460	20	4	10	3	4.58	0.92	2.29	0.69
1971	478	19	5	6	2	4.13	1.09	1.30	0.43
1972	498	17	4	19	12	3.56	0.84	3.97	2.51
1973	523	21	3	27	20	4.22	0.60	5.42	4.02
1974	548	22	5	17	9	4.21	0.96	3.25	1.72
1975	593	31	1	39	24	5.66	0.18	7.12	4.38
1976	639	35	6	32	15	5.90	1.01	5.40	2.53
1977	646	24	3	9	23	3.76	0.47	1.41	3.60
1978	671	34	5	14	18	5.26	0.77	2.17	2.79
1979	676	26	4	10	27	3.87	0.60	1.49	4.02
1980	707	36	12	34	27	5.33	1.78	5.03	3.99
1981	722	23	6	26	28	3.25	0.85	3.68	3.96
1982	746	24	6	26	20	3.32	0.83	3.60	2.77
1983	739	17	10	28	42	2.28	1.34	3.75	5.63
1984	764	18	1	32	24	2.44	0.14	4.33	3.25
1985	792	23	4	36	27	3.01	0.52	4.71	3.53
1986	826	20	4	37	19	2.53	0.51	4.67	2.40

Table A1   (*Continued*)

Year	Population at end of year	Number				Percentage rate[a]			
		Birth	Death	Migrated		Birth	Death	Immigration	Emigration
				In	Out				
1987	871	28	3	41	21	3.39	0.36	4.96	2.54
1988	889	25	2	18	23	2.87	0.23	2.07	2.64
1989	928	22	6	41	18	2.47	0.67	4.61	2.02
1990	964	26	5	48	33	2.80	0.54	5.17	3.56
1991	991	27	4	35	31	2.80	0.41	3.63	3.22
1992	1042	27	9	60	27	2.72	0.91	6.05	2.72
1993	1052	30	8	27	39	2.88	0.77	2.59	3.74
1994	1077	32	5	44	46	3.04	0.48	4.18	4.37
1995	1184	30	3	114	34	2.79	0.28	10.58	3.16
1996	1199	30	14	54	55	2.53	1.18	4.56	4.65
1997[b]	1209	22	5	55	62	1.83	0.42	4.59	5.17

Notes: [a] Relative to the population at the end of the previous year.
          [b] Data are until October.

Appendix B

Table B1 Migratory flows to and from East Laguna Village, 1918–97[a]

| | Immigration to the village | | | | | Emigration from the village | | | | |
| | Rural | | Urban | | | Rural | | Urban | | |
	Lowland rice area	Upland area[b]	Formal	Informal	Total	Lowland rice area	Upland area[b]	Formal	Informal	Total
1918–39										
Large farmer	7	27	0	0	34	7	0	1	0	8
Small farmer	5	8	0	0	13	0	0	0	0	0
Ag. labourer	0	0	0	0	0	0	0	0	0	0
Total	12	35	0	0	47	7	0.	1	0	8
1940–59										
Large farmer	29	14	7	1	51	21	6	9	0	36
Small farmer	4	8	0	0	12	11	12	0	0	23
Ag. labourer	6	2	0	0	8	0	0	0	0	
Total	39	24	7	1	71	32	18	9	0	59
1960–9										
Large farmer	2	11	0	0	13	8	4	8	0	20
Small farmer	14	19	0	1	34	9	2	1	0	12
Ag. labourer	8	13	0	4	25	3	10	0	1	14
Total	24	43	0	5	72	20	16	9	1	46

1970–9

Large farmer	1	3	16	6	26	15	21	25	6	67
Small farmer	19	8	1	5	33	28	1	9	10	48
Ag. labourer	21	75	0	27	123	10	11	4	13	38
Non-farm	0	0	1	0	1	0	0	0	0	0
Total	41	86	18	38	183	53	33	38	29	153

1980–9

Large farmer	1	6	13	7	27	4	1	15	0	20
Small farmer	15	21	5	2	43	5	14	25	4	48
Ag. labourer	64	79	20	34	197	49	56	37	48	190
Non-farm	0	0	19	0	19	0	0	3	5	8
Total	80	106	57	43	286	58	71	80	57	266

1990–7

Large farmer	1	0	8	0	9	1	6	17	0	24
Small farmer	0	8	29	4	41	15	8	47	3	73
Ag. labourer	93	89	22	79	283	39	24	63	62	188
Non-farm	2	8	46	52	108	0	3	44	19	66
Total	96	105	105	135	441	55	41	171	84	351

Notes: [a] Data are from the family reconstitution of the village. The accuracy of family reconstitution is higher for 1918–79 than for 1980–97. For the latter period, particularly for the 1980s, the destinations or origins of a substantial number of migration cases remain unknown; these unknown cases are allocated to each destination/origin according to the percentage shares of the known cases. Number of migrants in the flows includes family members. [b] Include fishing villages.

Notes and References

3 Population Growth and the Evolution of Households

1. An attempt to extend the family reconstitution to earlier years using parish registers was not feasible. Parish registers from around 1900 are available with village (*barrio*) identifications in numbers, but no record is available to relate these identification numbers to the names of villages.
2. Adjustments in the age of marriage to employment opportunities and wage rates was a major variable to control population growth rates in pre-modern agrarian societies underlying Malthus's theory of population (Hayami, 1997, pp. 62–3).
3. According to the 1986 Contraceptive Prevalence Survey (Commission on Population, 1992), the total fertility rate in rural areas of the Philippines was 5.65 per cent in 1980, compared to 3.98 per cent in urban areas.
4. According to the life tables estimated for the village using the data for the periods 1920–49 and 1950–80 (Kikuchi *et al.*, 1982), declines in the mortality rate between these two periods occurred for almost all the age groups. For males, the factor that contributed most to the increase in the life expectancy at birth from 48.5 to 59.1 years old was the reduction in infant mortality rate from 97 to 53 per 1000. For females, for whom life expectancy at birth increased from 53.6 to 65.5 years, the infant mortality rate did not decline significantly, but the mortality rates of child-bearing age groups were reduced significantly. For example, the mortality rate for the 20–29 age group declined from 51 to 7 per 1000.
5. An anthropological comparison between Japan and Thailand by Embree (1950) suggests a hypothesis that the loose definition of village borders might be a common characteristic of South-east Asia, in contrast with the clear and tight definition in North-east Asia.
6. They say that in the past some large farmers employed young boys as permanent farm helpers (*kasugpong*). However, this form of labour employment was rarely practised in this village. For *kasugpong*, see Hayami, Quisumbing and Adriano (1990, ch. 4).
7. Another significant change in the occupational pattern of villagers is the increase in the number of villagers who find job opportunities overseas. These overseas contract workers are not included in Table 3.7, since the table summarizes the major occupations of villagers normally residing in the village.
8. The numbers of immigrants to and emigrants from the village increased suddenly during and immediately after the Second World War (see Appendix B). These migration flows were created by the evacuation of town dwellers to the village, and their repatriation after the war.

4 Agrarian Structure and Land Reform

1. This section draws heavily on Hayami and Kikuchi (1981, ch. 4) and Hayami, Marciano and Kikuchi (1998).

2. Some scholars assume a nobility class in addition to the chiefs, and some do not distinguish two categories in the dependent class (Larkin, 1972; McLennan, 1969; Phelan, 1959). Our exposition follows Ikehata (1971) and Umehara (1976). There must have existed considerable variation in *barangay* organizations across regions.

3. It was a common practice for tenants to sign detailed written contracts with *haciendas*, while written contracts were rare outside *haciendas* before land reform. For the hacienda tenancy contract, see Umehara (1974).

4. The accession of Corazon C. Aquino to the presidency in February 1986 created great expectations that land reform would become more comprehensive and drastic. However, the Comprehensive Agrarian Law (RA 6657) of 1988 was a compromise between the massive popular demand, especially from intellectuals comprising the urban middle class, and the resistance of the landlord bloc in the congress. This law appears to represent a break from the traditional pattern of Philippine land reform legislation as its coverage expanded from tenanted rice and corn lands to all the agricultural lands, regardless of tenure arrangements and types of crop produced. This expanded coverage necessarily involved much greater complexity in administrative and legal procedures. Under the weak administrative and financial capability of the Aquino government, the law was largely a dead letter, beyond a modest after-care of the Marcos programmes. For procedures and accomplishments of various past reform programmes, see Hayami, Quisumbing and Adriano (1990, ch. 3).

5. In fact, it was estimated that the average rent on new leasehold land was 21.3 per cent in 1976, while the average rent on old leasehold land was 15.6 per cent. See Hayami and Kikuchi (1981, p. 112).

6. They say that the compensation payment before land reform was not limited to leasehold tenants; it was also applied sometimes to share tenants. It is possible that land rents from the customary 50:50 sharecropping contracts also exceeded economic returns to land, especially in the case of fertile land, even before the introduction of new rice technology.

7. In the case where the ownership of land on which a farmer has held cultivation rights is sold to someone else, the landlord pays compensation to the former tenant, either in cash or in ownership of a part of the land. The increase in the number of paddy fields owned by villagers, as observed in Table 4.1, resulted partly from such compensations.

8. Legally, inheritance is equal among heirs, but it is varied and flexible in practice. It is often the case that a child who continues to live with and take care of parents receives a major share of the farm, as explained in Chapter 1. In recent years, cases have been increasing in number in which children cultivate the inherited land in rotation without subdividing it into individual units of operation; this tends to disguise the influence of population pressure on average farm size.

9. Even if the benefits from the reform were not so different initially between large and small farmers on a per capita basis, large ones were in a better position to mobilize absolutely larger benefits for the purchase of indivisible capital items such as tractors and threshers, which became a significant source of cash income from the use for custom services beyond operating in their own fields. Their advantage in this regard was often extended to investing in starting non-farm businesses and, more importantly, to human capital formation in

        providing higher education for the bright ones among their children. Through this process the difference in per capita gains between large and small farmers tended to increase over time.

10.   Such results are found rather commonly in many yield comparisons conducted world-wide (Hayami and Otsuka, 1993, p. 93).

5   Diffusion of New Rice Technology

1.   This chapter draws heavily on Hayami and Kikuchi (1999).
2.   Short and sturdy stems prevent rice plants from lodging under the weight of heavy grain, and erect, pointed leaves facilitate the acceptance of solar energy. Non-photo-period sensitivity means that the flowering of rice plants does not depend on day length. Traditional rice varieties in tropical Asia had their flowering induced by shortened day length, and therefore ripened for harvest in dry months (late November to December) after the rainy season. This was a convenient characteristic for single cropping under rainfed condition. However, as double cropping began to be practised with the development of irrigation systems, earlier harvests before the monsoon rains became necessary. Non-photo-period sensitivity was thus developed as a necessary trait of MV for irrigated rice production. For more details, see Yoshida (1981).
3.   Paddy of traditional varieties such as Intan, Binato and Malagkit commanded higher prices than IR8 for better eating qualities and smaller percentages of grain breakage in the milling process.
4.   Since 1990, new rice varieties bred at IRRI, as well as those bred at the Philippine Rice Research Institute and other national institutes in the country, have been released through the Philippine Seed Board under the series name of PSB-RC (abbreviated as RC).
5.   The yield in the 1966 wet season thus estimated is in close conformity with that reported by Umehara (1967). His 1965 dry season yield, however, is higher than our estimate for the 1965 dry season by about one ton per hectare. Judging from the 1959 average yield per hectare in Pila of 1.8 tons reported in the 1960 Agriculture Census, it is likely that rice yield was exceptionally high in the'1965 dry season.
6.   During this period the price of fertilizer relative to the consumer price index (CPI) declined rapidly. However, it did not decrease relative to the price of rice, because rice prices in the Philippines, deflated by the CPI, went down equally fast, corresponding to major increases in rice supply as a result of the very success of the Green Revolution. The decline in real rice prices had crucial implications for villagers' incomes, which will be examined in detail in Chapter 10. Here we concentrate on changes in input prices paid by farmers relative to the price of rice they received.
7.   Though data are not available, it is almost certain that the substitution of hired to family labour was paralleled by increases in the share of agricultural labourers in hired wage employment on farms, which had traditionally occupied neighbouring farmers and their family members to a large extent.
8.   Changes in factor shares are produced not only by biases in technological progress but also by changes in relative factor prices if the elasticity of substitution is not 1 (one). For the relationship between factor shares and technological change, see Hayami (1997, pp. 151–61).

6 Community and State in Irrigation Management

1. This chapter draws heavily on Kikuchi, Fujita, Marciano and Hayami (1999).
2. In the jargon of economics, local commons, alternatively called 'common-pool resources' or 'common-property resources' can be defined as the resources that are strong in the attribute of non-excludability but weak in the attribute of non-rivalness. They are a part of 'local public goods', of which the use is *de facto* limited to people living in a certain location.
3. In particular, if a rural community, such as a village, is largely self-sufficient with little exposure to urban market activities, the expectation should be strong for its members to continue their collective actions indefinitely; this is akin to the situation of infinitely repeating games for sustaining positive-sum co-operative games (Bardhan, 1993; Seabright, 1993; Ostrom *et al.*, 1994).
4. This classification does not coincide exactly with the geographical demarcation by the highway. In the service area of Lateral E, for example, three villages are located above the highway, of which only the one closest to the main canal did not experience water shortage and, was therefore classified into the upper reach, while the remaining two villages were classified in the lower reach.
5. The NIA was established in 1963 as a government-owned and controlled corporation by the Republic Act 3601: 'An Act Creating the National Irrigation Administration'. A revision of the Act in 1974, required the NIA to be autonomous in financing its current expenditure, with a limit to the government subsidy of six million pesos. By the 1980 revision, the government subsidy was removed, but the NIA was allowed to receive 5 per cent of the project fund for new construction and major rehabilitation as a set-aside for administrative overhead costs. In addition to irrigation fees, the NIA raises revenues from such activities as the rental of bulldozers and machinery, see Fujita (1998).
6. The NIA has rarely allocated IDOs for institutional development in existing systems, but has often assigned them for the development of newly constructed systems with generous external support.
7. Such a failure is not unique to this system, and it can be found in many other systems: for example, a system in Central Luzon studied by Oorthuizen and Kloezen (1995).

7 Community and Market in Labour Relations

1. This chapter draws heavily on Hayami (1998, 1999) and Kikuchi and Hayami (1999).
2. Increased dependency on hired labour may be explained, to some extent, by increased disutility of labour for enriched land reform beneficiaries. However, that was not the response of land reform beneficiaries in Japan, Korea and Taiwan.
3. A cultural norm is here distinguished from a social norm; the former is defined as a standard of belief, and the latter defined as a standard of conduct in society. For details of the classification of norms, see Hayami (1998a).
4. In Central Luzon, north of Manila, where large *haciendas* prevailed, rice harvesting was done on a daily wage contract and threshing was performed by large threshing machines called *tilyadora*, mainly for the purpose of the accurate

measurement of sharecroppers' rice outputs, and hence the collection of due share rents by *hacienda* management. In contrast, in Laguna and its surroundings, where small and medium-scale landownership was traditionally dominant, landlords were able to rely on mutual trust relationships with tenants for the collection of share rents (Hayami and Kikuchi, 1981, ch. 4).

5. This new *hunusan* contract was practised from the mid-1970s, with the traditional share rate of one-sixth in exceptional low-yielding plots, where the one-sixth of output was barely sufficient to cover the cost of harvesting at a rate of renumeration to labour comparable to the market wage rate. Also, in the 1970s it began to be observed that marginal farmers cultivating very small plots harvested their fields by family labour, corresponding to an increased subdivision of farms under strong population pressure.

6. Threshing machines introduced earlier were not equipped with blowers, so winnowing by blowers was contracted out separately. Charges to the custom services of threshing and winnowing were typically 6 per cent and 2 per cent, respectively. Later, as threshers with blowers attached were developed, 8 per cent to 10 per cent of output was allocated to the combined services of threshing and winnowing. Paddy received for the custom service was shared between machine owners and operators: two-thirds to owners and one-third to operators initially, and later shared 50 : 50.

8   Farmers and Middlemen in Rice Marketing

1. This chapter draws heavily on Hayami, Kikuchi and Marciano (1999).
2. Interest rates for formal credit in the Philippines range from 10 per cent to 40 per cent per annum. At the lower end, loans are available with subsidized interest rates of 10 per cent to 20 per cent per annum from government-controlled banks, such as the Land Bank. Depending on the credit-worthiness of borrowers, the banks' lending rate can become high. According to our observations, in the mid-1990s, the interest rate for private bank loans available to farmers and small entrepreneurs in rural areas was around 25 per cent per year.

9   Emergence of Rural-based Industries

1. This chapter draws heavily on Hayami, Kikuchi and Marciano (1998).

Bibliography

Abegglen, J. C. and Stalk, G. Jr (1985) *Kaisha: The Japanese Corporation* (New York: Basic Books).

Akerlof, G. A. (1984) *An Economic Theorist's Book of Tales* (Cambridge University Press).

Anderson, J. N. (1964) 'Land and Society in a Pangasinan Society', in S. C. Espiritu and C. L. Hunt (eds), *Social Foundations of Community Development* (Manila: R. M. Garcia) pp. 71–93.

Asanuma, B. (1985) 'Organization of Parts Purchases in the Japanese Automobile Industry', *Japanese Economic Studies*, vol. 13 (Summer) pp. 32–53.

Asanuma, B. (1989) 'Manufacturer–Supplier Relationships in Japan in the Concept of Relation-Specific Skill', *Journal of the Japanese and International Economies*, vol. 3 (March) pp. 1–30.

Asian Development Bank (various issues) *Key Indicators of Developing Asian and Pacific Countries* (Manila: Asian Development Bank).

Baland, J. M. and Platteau, J. P. (1996) *Halting Degradation of Natural Resources: Is there a Role for Rural Communities?* (Oxford University Press).

Bardhan, P. (1993) 'Symposium on Management of Local Commons', *Journal of Economic Perspectives*, vol. 7 (Fall) pp. 87–92.

Barker, R. and Herdt, R. W., with Rose, B. (1985) *The Rice Economy of Asia* (Washington DC: Resources for the Future).

Barker, R., Meyers, W. H., Crisostomo, C. and Duff, B. (1972) 'Employment and Technological Change in Philippine Agriculture', *International Labor Review*, vol. 106 (August–September) pp. 111–39.

Bauer, P. T. (1964) *West African Trade: A Study of Competition, Oligopoly, and Monopoly in a Changing Economy* (Cambridge University Press).

Becker, G. S. (1974) 'A Theory of Social Interactions', *Journal of Political Economy*, vol. 82 (November–December) pp. 1063–93.

Benedict, R. (1946) *The Chrysanthemum and the Sword: Patterns of Japanese Culture* (Boston, Mass.: Houghton Mifflin).

Binswanger, H. P. and Rosenzweig, M. R. (1986) 'Behavioural and Material Determinants of Production Relations in Agriculture', *Journal of Development Studies*, vol. 22 (April) pp. 503–39.

Brewster, J. M. (1950) 'The Machine Process in Agriculture and Industry', *Journal of Farm Economics*, vol. 32 (February) pp. 69–81.

Bureau of Agricultural Statistics (various issues) *Rice and Corn Survey* (Quezon City, Philippines: Department of Agriculture).

Chambers, R. (1988) *Managing Canal Irrigation* (New Delhi: Oxford & IBH Publishing).

Chandler, R. F. (1982) *An Adventure in Applied Science: A History of the International Rice Research Institute* (Los Baños, Philippines: International Rice Research Institute).

Chayanov, A. V. (1966) *The Theory of Peasant Economy* (ed. D. Thorner *et al.*), first publ. 1925 (Homewood, Ill.: Richard D. Irwin).

255

Commission on Population (1992) *Population and Development in the '90s: The Philippines* (Quezon City, Philippines: Commission on Population in co-ordination with US Agency for International Development).

Corpuz, O. D. (1997) *An Economic History of the Philippines* (Quezon City: University of the Philippines Press).

Dalisay, A. M. (1937) 'Types of Tenancy Contracts on Rice Farms of Nueva Ecija', *Philippine Agriculturist*, vol. 26 (July) pp. 159–98.

David, C. and Otsuka, K. (eds) (1994) *Modern Rice Technology and Income Distribution in Asia* (Boulder, Col.: Lynne Rienner).

de los Reyes, B. N. (1972) 'Can Land Reform Succeed?', *Philippine Sociological Review*, vol. 20 (January–April) pp. 79–92.

Department of Labor and Employment (various issues) *Yearbook of Labor Statistics* (Manila: Department of Labor and Employment).

Dewey, A. G. (1962) *Peasant Marketing in Java* (New York: Free Press).

Embree, J. F. (1950) 'Thailand – A Loosely Structured Social System', *American Anthropologist*, vol. 52 (April–June) pp. 181–193.

Feeny, D., Berkes, F., McCay, B. J. and Acheson, J. M. (1990) 'The Tragedy of the Commons: Twenty-Two Years Later', *Human Ecology*, vol. 18, no. 1, pp. 1–19.

Fujita, M. (1998) *Tojokoku Kangai System ni okeru Seifuto Kyodotai* (Government and Community in the Management of Irrigation Systems in Developing Countries: A Case of the Philippines) Ph.D. thesis submitted to Aoyama-Gakuin University, Tokyo.

Fürer-Haimendorf, C. U. (1980) *A Himalayan Tribe: From Cattle to Cash* (Berkeley, Calif.: University of California Press).

Geertz, C. (1963) *Agricultural Involution: The Process of Ecological Change in Indonesia* (Berkeley, Calif.: University of California Press).

Gorospe, V. R. (1966) 'Christian Renewal of Filipino Values', *Philippine Studies*, vol. 14 (April) pp. 191–227.

Greif, A. (1994) 'Cultural Beliefs and the Organization of Society: A Historical and Theoretical Reflection on Collectivist and Individualist Societies', *Journal of Political Economy*, vol. 102, pp. 912–50.

Griffin, K. (1974) *The Political Economy of Agrarian Change: An Essay on the Green Revolution* (Cambridge, Mass.: Harvard University Press).

Hardie, R. S. (1952) *Philippine Land Tenure Reform: Analysis and Recommendations* (Manila: Special Technical and Economic Mission, United States Mutual Security Agency).

Hardin, G. (1968) 'The Tragedy of the Commons', *Science*, vol. 162, pp. 1243–8.

Harris, J. R. and Todaro, M. P. (1970) 'Migration, Unemployment and Development: A Two-Sector Analysis', *American Economic Review*, vol. 60 (March) pp. 126–42.

Hayami, A. (1973) *Kinsei Noson no Rekishi Jinko Gakuteki Kenkyu* (A Study on the Demographic History of Rural Villages in the Late Medieval Era) (Tokyo: Toyokeizaishimposha).

Hayami, Y. (1992) 'Agricultural Innovation, Economic Growth and Equity: A Critique of Michael Lipton', *Southeast Asian Journal of Agricultural Economics*, vol. 1 (June) pp. 1–9.

Hayami, Y. (1994) 'Peasant and Plantation in Asia', in G. M. Meier (ed.), *From Classical Economics to Development Economics* (New York: St Martin's Press) pp. 121–34.

Hayami, Y. (1996) 'The Peasant in Economic Modernization', *American Journal of Agricultural Economics*, vol. 78 (December) pp. 1157–67.

Hayami, Y. (1997) *Development Economics: From the Poverty to the Wealth of Nations* (Oxford University Press).

Hayami, Y. (1998) 'Norms and Rationality in the Evolution of Economic Systems: A View from Asian Villages', *Japanese Economic Review*, vol. 49 (February) pp. 36–53.

Hayami, Y. (1999) 'Community Mechanism of Employment and Wage Determination: Classical or Neoclassical', in G. Saxonhouse and T. N. Srinivasan (eds), *Development, Duality and International Economic Regime* (Ann Arbor, Mich.: University of Michigan Press) pp. 85–106.

Hayami, Y., in association with Kikuchi, M., Moya, P. F., Bambo, L. and Marciano, E. B. (1978) *Anatomy of a Peasant Economy: A Rice Village in the Philippines* (Los Baños, Philippines: International Rice Research Institute).

Hayami, Y. and Herdt, R. W. (1977) 'Market Price Effects of Technological Change on Income Distribution in Semisubsistence Agriculture', *American Journal of Agricultural Economics*, vol. 59 (May) pp. 245–56.

Hayami, Y. and Kawagoe, T. (1993) *The Agrarian Origins of Commerce and Industry: A Study of Peasant Marketing in Indonesia* (London: Macmillan).

Hayami, Y. and Kikuchi, M. (1981) *Asian Village Economy at the Crossroads: An Economic Approach to Institutional Change* (Tokyo: University of Tokyo Press; Baltimore and London: Johns Hopkins University Press).

Hayami, Y. and Kikuchi, M. (1999) 'Three Decades of Green Revolution in a Philippine Village,' *Japanese Journal of Agricultural Economics*. vol. 1 (in press).

Hayami, Y. and Otsuka, K. (1993) *The Economics of Contract Choice* (Oxford University Press).

Hayami, Y. and Otsuka, K. (1994) 'Beyond the Green Revolution: Agricultural Strategy into the New Century', in J. A. Anderson (ed.), *Agricultural Technology: Policy Issues for the International Community* (Wallingford, Surrey: CAB International) pp. 15–42.

Hayami, Y., Kikuchi, M., Bambo, L. and Marciano, E. B. (1990) *Transformation of a Laguna Village in the Two Decades of Green Revolution,* IRRI Research Paper No. 142 (Los Baños, Philippines: International Rice Research Institute).

Hayami, Y., Kikuchi, M. and Marciano, E. B. (1998) 'Structure of Rural-based Industrialization: Metal Craft Manufacturing in the Outskirts of Greater Manila, the Philippines', *Developing Economies*, vol. 36 (June) pp. 133–54.

Hayami, Y., Kikuchi, M. and Marciano, E. B. (1999) 'Middlemen and Peasants in Rice Marketing in the Philippines', *Agricultural Economics*, vol. 20 (March), pp. 79–93.

Hayami, Y. and Ruttan, V. W. (1985) *Agricultural Development: An International Perspective* (Baltimore: Johns Hopkins University Press).

Hayami, Y., Marciano, E. B. and Kikuchi, M. (1998) 'Did Philippine Land Reform Reduce Inequality? A Perspective from a Laguna Village', *Journal of Agricultural Economics and Development*, vol. 26 (January–July) pp. 13–37.

Hayami, Y., Quisumbing, M. A. R. and Adriano, L. S. (1990) *Toward An Alternative Land Reform Paradigm: A Philippine Perspective* (Quezon City, Philippines: Ateneo de Manila University Press).

Hester, E. D. and Mabbun, P. (1924) 'Some Economic and Social Aspects of Philippine Tenancies', *Philippine Agriculturist*, vol. 12 (February) pp. 367–444.

Hirschman, A. O. (1970) *Exit, Voice and Loyalty: Responses to Decline in Firms, Organizations and States* (Cambridge, Mass.: Harvard University Press).

Hopper, W. D. (1965). 'Allocation Efficiency in a Traditional Indian Agriculture', *Journal of Farm Economics*, vol. 47 (August) pp. 611–24.

Ikehata, S. (1971) *'Tonan Ajia Kiso Shakai no Ichi Keitai: Philippine no Barangai Shakai ni Tsuite'* (A Contribution to South-east Asian Infrastructure: An Analysis of Pre-Spanish Philippine Society) *The Memoirs of the Institute of Oriental Culture* (University of Tokyo), vol. 54 (March) pp. 83–163.

International Rice Research Institute (1978) *Economic Consequences of New Rice Technology* (Los Baños, Philippines: International Rice Research Institute).

International Rice Research Institute (1995) *World Rice Statistics 1993–94* (Los Baños, Philippines: International Rice Research Institute).

Ishikawa, S. (1967) *Economic Development in Asian Perspective* (Tokyo: Kinokuniya).

Japan Ministry of Agriculture and Forestry (1974) *Norinsho Keizal Ruinen Tokeihyo* (Historical Statistics of Agricultural Economy), vol. 4 (Tokyo: Norin Tokei Kyokai).

Jones, W. O. (1972) *Marketing Staple Food Crops in Tropical Africa* (Ithaca, NY and London: Cornell University Press).

Jorgenson, D. W. (1961) 'The Development of a Dual Economy', *Economic Journal*, vol. 71 (June) pp. 309–34.

Kerkvliet, B. J. (1971) 'Peasant Society and Unrest Prior to the Huk Revolution in the Philippines', *Asian Studies*, vol. 9 (August) pp. 164–213.

Kerkvliet, B. J. (1977) *The Huk Rebellion: A Study of Peasant Revolt in the Philippines* (Berkeley, Calif.: University of California Press).

Kikuchi, M. (1998) 'Export-Oriented Garment Industries in Rural Philippines', in Y. Hayami (ed.), *Toward the Rural-based Development of Commerce and Industry: Selected Experiences in East Asia* (Washington, DC: World Bank Economic Development Institute) pp. 89–129.

Kikuchi, M., Fujita, M., Marciano, E. B. and Hayami, Y. (1999) 'State and Community in the Deterioration in a National Irrigation System', Paper presented at the World Bank-EDI Conference on Community and Market in Economic Development', held in Stanford University, 5–6 February 1999.

Kikuchi, M. and Hayami, Y. (1980) 'Technology and Labor Contract: Two Systems of Rice Harvesting in the Philippines', *Journal of Comparative Economics*, vol. 4 (December) pp. 357–77.

Kikuchi, M. and Hayami, Y. (1983) 'New Rice Technology, Intrarural Migration, and Institutional Innovation in the Philippines', *Population and Development Review*, vol. 9 (June) pp. 247–57.

Kikuchi, M. and Hayami, Y. (1999) 'Technology, Market and Community in Contract Choice: Rice Harvesting in the Philippines', *Economic Development and Cultural Change*, 47 (January) pp. 371–86.

Kikuchi, M. and Opeña, C. (1983) 'Migration and Wage Differentials: A Note on Rural–Urban Labor Market Segmentation in Southern Tagalog, Philippines', Agricultural Economics Department Paper, No. 83–01 (Los Baños, Philippines: IRRI).

Kikuchi, M., Bambo, L., Fortuna, N. and Opeña, C. (1982) 'Estimations of Life Tables and True Rates of Birth, Death and Natural Increase of Population for a Rural Village in Southern Tagalog, Philippines, 1920–49 and 1950–80',

Agricultural Economics Department Paper, No. 82–24 (Los Baños, Philippines IRRI).

Kiyonari, T. (1980) *Chusho Kigyo Dokuhon* (Textbook of Small and Medium-sized Industries) (Tokyo: Toyo Keizai Shinposha).

Larkin, J. A. (1972) *The Pampangans: Colonial Society in a Philippine Province* (Berkeley, Calif., Los Angeles and London: University of California Press).

Lele, U. J. (1971) *Food Grain Marketing in India* (Ithaca, NY, and London: Cornell University Press).

Lewis, A. W. (1954) 'Economic Development with Unlimited Supplies of Labour', *Manchester School of Economics and Social Studies*, vol. 22 (May) pp. 139–91.

Lipton, M., with Longhurst, R. (1989) *New Seeds and Poor People* (London: Unwin and Hyman).

Marx, K. (1953) *Grundrisse der Kritik der Politischen Ökonomie, 1857–1858* (Foundations of the Critique of Political Economy), first publ. 1939/41 (Berlin: Dietz).

Massell, B. F. (1967) Farm Management in Peasant Agriculture: An Empirical Study', *Food Research Institute Studies*, vol. 7, no. 2, pp. 205–15.

McLennan, M. S. (1969) 'Land and Tenancy in the Central Luzon Plain', *Philippine Studies*, vol. 17 (October) pp. 651–82.

Mears, L. A. (1974) *Rice Economy of the Philippines* (Quezon City, Philippines: University of the Philippines Press).

Mears, L. A. (1981) *The New Rice Economy of Indonesia* (Yogyakarta, Indonesia: Gadjah Mada University Press).

Minami, R. (1973) *The Turning Point in Economic Development: Japan's Experience* (Tokyo: Kinokuniya).

Murray, F. J. (1972) 'Land Reform in the Philippines: An Overview', *Philippine Sociological Review*, vol. 20 (January–April) pp. 151–68.

Myint, H. (1965) *The Economics of The Developing Countries* (New York: Praeger).

National Statistical Coordination Board (1996) *Philippine Poverty Statistics* (Makati, Philippines: National Statistical Coordination Board).

National Statistical Coordination Board (various issues) *Philippine Statistical Yearbook* (Makati, Philippines: National Statistical Coordination Board).

North, D. C. (1990) *Institutions, Institutional Change and Economic Performance* (Cambridge University Press).

North, D. C. (1994) 'Economic Performance Through Time', *American Economic Review*, vol. 84 (June) pp. 359–68.

North, D. C. and Thomas, R. T. (1973) *The Rise of the Western World: A New Economic History* (Cambridge University Press).

Ohkama, K. and Kikuchi, M. (1996) *'Farmers' Participation in Development Projects: A Case Study of a Village in Meiji Japan'*, in S. Hirashima and W. Gooneratne (eds), *State and Community in Local Resource Management: The Asian Experience* (New Delhi: Har-Anand Publications) pp. 41–93.

Okazaki, T. and Okuno-Fujiwara, M. (1998) 'Evolution of Economic Systems: The Case of Japan', in Y. Hayami and M. Aoki (eds), *The Institutional Foundation of Economic Development in East Asia* (London: Macmillan) pp. 482–521.

Olson, M. (1965) *The Logic of Collective Action* (Cambridge, Mass.: Harvard University Press).

Oorthuizen, J. and Kloezen, W. H. (1995) 'The Other Side of the Coin: A Case Study on the Impact of Financial Autonomy on Irrigation Performance in the Philippines', *Irrigation and Drainage Systems*, vol. 9, pp. 15–37.

Ostrom, E. (1990) *Governing the Commons* (New York: Cambridge University Press).

Ostrom, E. (1992) *Crafting Institutions for Self-Governing Irrigation Systems* (San Francisco: Institute for Contemporary Studies Press).

Ostrom, E., Gardner, R. and Walker, J. (1994) *Rules, Games, and Common-Pool Resources* (Ann Arbor, Mich.: University of Michigan Press).

Paglin, M. (1965) 'Surplus Agricultural Labor and Development: Facts and Theories', *American Economic Review*, vol. 55 (September) pp. 815–34.

Patrick, H. R. and Rohlen, T. P. (1987) 'Small-scale Family Enterprises', in K. Yamamura and Y. Yasuba (eds), *The Political Economy of Japan*, vol. 1: *The Domestic Transformation* (Palo Alto, Calif.: Stanford University Press) pp. 331–84.

Pelzer, K. J. (1945) *Pioneer Settlement in the Asiatic Tropics* (New York: American Geographical Society).

Phelan, J. L. (1959) *The Hispanization of the Philippines: Spanish and Filipino Responses, 1565–1700* (Madison, Wisc.: University of Wisconsin Press).

Pingali, P. L., Hossain, M. and Gerpacio, R. V. (1997) *Asian Rice Bowls: The Returning Crisis?* (Wallingford, UK: CAB International, in association with International Rice Research Institute, Philippines).

Popkin, S. L. (1979) *The Rational Peasant* (Berkeley, Calif., Los Angeles and London: University of California Press).

Putnam, R. D. (1993) *Making Democracy Work: Civic Traditions in Modern Italy* (Princeton, NJ: Princeton University).

Putzel, J. (1992) *Captive Land: The Politics of Agrarian Reform in the Philippines* (New York: Monthly Review Press).

Ranis, G. and Fei, J. C. H. (1961) 'A Theory of Economic Development', *American Economic Review*, vol. 51 (September) pp. 533–65.

Resnick, S. A. (1970) 'The Decline in Rural Industry under Export Expansion: A Comparison among Burma, Philippines and Thailand, 1870–1938', *Journal of Economic History*, vol. 30 (March) pp. 51–73.

Riedinger, J. M. (1995) *Agrarian Reform in the Philippines: Democratic Transitions and Redistributive Reform* (Palo Alto, Calif.: Stanford University Press).

Rivera, G. E. and McMillan, R. T. (1954) *An Economic and Social Survey of Rural Households in Central Luzon* (Manila: Cooperative Research Project of the Philippine Council for United States Aid and the United States of America Operations Mission to the Philippines).

Rosenzweig, M. R. (1988a) 'Risk, Private Information, and the Family', *American Economic Review*, vol. 78 (May) pp. 245–50.

Rosenzweig, M. R. (1988b) 'Risk, Implicit Contracts and the Family in Rural Areas of Low Income Countries', *Economic Journal*, vol. 98 (December) pp. 1148–70.

Rosovsky, H. and Ohkawa, K. (1961) 'The Indigenous Components in the Modern Japanese Economy', *Economic Development and Cultural Change*, vol. 9 (April) pp. 476–501.

Ruttan, V. W. (1964) 'Equity and Productivity Objectives in Agrarian Reform Legislation: Perspectives on the New Philippine Land Reform Code', *Indian Journal of Agricultural Economics*, vol. 19 (July–December) pp. 115–30.

Ruttan, V. W. (1969) 'Agricultural Product and Factor Market in Southeast Asia', *Economic Development and Cultural Change*, vol. 17 (July) pp. 501–19.

Schultz, T. W. (1964) *Transforming Traditional Agriculture* (New Haven, Conn.: Yale University Press).

Scott, J. C. (1972) 'The Erosion of Patron–Client Bonds and Social Change in Rural Southeast Asia', *Journal of Asian Studies*, vol. 32 (November) pp. 5–37.

Scott, J. C. (1976) *The Moral Economy of the Peasant* (New Haven, Conn. and London: Yale University Press).

Seabright, P. (1993) 'Managing Local Commons: Theoretical Issues in Incentive Design', *Journal of Economic Perspectives*, vol. 7 (Fall) pp. 113–34.

Small, S. E. and Carruthers, I. (1991) *Farmer-Financed Irrigation: The Economics of Reform* (Cambridge University Press).

Smith, T. C. (1988) *Native Sources of Japanese Industrialization, 1750–1920* (Berkeley, Calif.: University of California Press).

Spillman, W. J. (1919) 'The Agricultural Ladder', *American Economic Review*, vol. 9 (1-Supplement) pp. 170–9.

Srinivas, M. N. (1976) *The Remembered Village* (Berkeley, Calif.: University of California Press).

Stark, O. and Lucas, R. E. B. (1988) 'Migration, Remittance, and the Family', *Economic Development and Cultural Change*, vol. 36 (April) pp. 465–81.

Svendsen, M. (1993) 'The Impact of Financial Autonomy on Irrigation System Performance in the Philippines', *World Development*, vol. 21, no. 6, pp. 989–1005.

Takahashi, A. (1969) *Land and Peasants in Central Luzon: Socio-economic Structure of Bulacan Village* (Tokyo: Institute of Developing Economies).

Takahashi, A. (1972) 'Philippine no Kachi Taikei' (Value Structure in the Philippines), in N. Ogiwara and A. Takahashi, *Tonan Aija no Kachi Taikei* (Value Structure in South-east Asia), vol. 4 (Tokyo: Gendai Ajia Shuppan-kai) pp. 117–212.

Takigawa, T. (1976) *Sengo Philippine Nochi Kaikaku Ron* (Treatise on Post-war Philippine Land Reform) (Tokyo: Institute of Developing Economies).

Takigawa, T. (1994) *Tonan Ajia Nogyo Mondai Ron* (Treatise on Agrarian Problems in South-east Asia) (Tokyo: Keiso Shobo).

Tamaki, T. (1983) *Mizushakai no Kozo* (Structure of Hydraulic Society) (Tokyo: Ronsosha).

Tamaki, T. and Hatate, I. (1974) *Hudo: Daichi to Ningen no Rekishi* (Environment: History of Land and Man) (Tokyo: Heibonsha).

Timmer, C. P. (1973) 'Choice of Technique in Rice Milling in Java', *Bulletin of Indonesian Economic Studies*, vol. 9 (July) pp. 57–76.

Tönnies, F. (1922) *Gemeinschaft und Gesellschaft: Grundbegriffe der reinen Soziologie* (Community and Society: Basic Concepts in Pure Sociology) first publ. 1887 (Berlin: K. Curtius).

Toquero, Z. F. and Duff, B. (1985) *Physical Losses and Quality Deterioration in Rice Post Production Systems*, IRRI Research Paper Series No. 107 (Los Baños, Philippines: International Rice Research Institute).

Tussing, A. (1966) 'The Labor Force in Meiji Economic Growth: A Quantitative Study of Yamanashi Prefecture', *Journal of Economic History*, vol. 26 (March) pp. 59–92.

Umehara, H. (1967) 'Philippine no Beisaku Noson' (A Rice Village in the Phillipines), in T. Takigawa and H. Saito (eds), *Ajia no Tochi Seido to Noson*

Shakai Kozo (Land Tenure System and Rural Social Structure in Asia) (Tokyo: Institute of Developing Economies).

Umehara, H. (1974) *A Hacienda Barrio in Central Luzon: A Case Study of a Philippine Village* (Tokyo: The Institute of Developing Economies).

Umehara, H. (1976) 'Philippine ni okeru Shiteki Tochi Shoyuken Tenkai ni Kansuru Ichi Kosatsu' (A Study on the Development of Private Land Ownership in the Philippines), in H. Saito (ed.), *Ajia Tochi Seisakuron Josetsu* (Introduction to Land Tenure Systems in Asia) (Tokyo: Institute of Developing Economies) pp. 317–44.

Umehara, H. (1992) *Philippine no Noson: Sono Kozo to Henka* (Rural Villages in the Philippines: Their Structure and Change) (Tokyo: Kokon Shoin).

Umehara, H. (1997) *Sonraku Level de Miru Philippine Nochi Kaikaku no Tenmatsu* (Outcomes of Land Reform in the Philippines Observed at a Village Level), in H. Mizuno and S. Shigetomi (eds), *Tonan Ajia no Keizai Kaihatsu to Tochi Seido* (Economic Development and Land Systems in South-east Asia) (Tokyo: Institute of Developing Economies) pp. 153–98.

Uphoff, N. (1986) *Improving International Irrigation Management with Farmers' Participation: Getting the Process Right* (Boulder, Col. and London: Westview Press).

Wada, K. (1991) 'The Development of Tiered Inter-firm Relationships in the Automobile Industry: A Case Study of Toyota Motor Corporation'. *Japanese Yearbook of Business History* (August) pp. 23–47.

Wade, R. (1990) *Village Republics: Economic Conditions for Collective Action in South India* (Cambridge, UK and New York: Cambridge University Press).

Weber, M. (1924) 'Agrarverhältnisse im Altertum' (Agrarian Relations of Ancient Civilizations), in M. Weber, *Gesammelte Aufsätze zur Sozial und Wirtschaftgeschichte*, first publ. 1909 (Tübingen: J. C. B. Mohr), pp. 1–288.

Wiser, W. H. and Wiser, C. V. (1963) *Behind Mud Walls, 1930–1960* (Berkeley, Calif.: University of California Press).

Wrigley, E. A. and Schofield, R. S. (1981) *The Population History of England 1541–1871* (Cambridge, Mass.: Harvard University Press).

Wurfel, D. (1958) 'Philippine Agrarian Reform under Magsaysay', *Far Eastern Survey*, vol. 27 (January and February) pp. 7–15 and 23–30.

Yoshida, S. (1981) *Fundamentals of Rice Crop Science* (Los Baños, Philippines: International Rice Research Institute).

Yotopoulos, P. A. (1968) 'On the Efficiency of Resource Utilization in Subsistence Agriculture', *Food Research Institute Studies*, vol. 8, no. 2, pp. 125–35.

Glossary

aliping namamhay	Serfs or peons in the pre-Hispanic and early Hispanic Philippine communities
aliping saguiguilid (saguiguilid)	Slaves in pre-Hispanic and early Hispanic Philippine communities
barangay	Communities in pre-Hispanic and Hispanic Philippines, coming from the Malayan term meaning 'boat'; used now to designate the lowest unit of government administration, village or *barrio*, below municipality (town)
barangay captain	Village headman
barrio	See *barangay*
bayanihan	Mutual help through labour exchange
canon	Leasehold arrangement practised in the Inner Central Luzon during the early phase of land development
carabao	Water buffalo
casique	Indigenous elite or leading family in Spanish period
cavan	Sack for carrying and storing grain; for paddy, one *cavan* contains 40–50 kg
commadre	The relationship between the godmother of a daughter/son and the mother of the daughter/son
compadre	The relationship between the godfather of a daughter/son and the father of the daughter/son
cono	A rice milling machine equipped with an iron disc-sheller and a cone polisher
dapog	A type of seedbed preparation on dry ground
datu	Chief or chieftain of a *barangay*
encargado	Farm manager/overseer
gama	Literally means 'weed'; a type of labour contract in rice farming in which hired labourers do weeding. They do not receive a wage but establish a right to harvest paddy on the weeded fields and receive a share of output in lieu of wages
hacienda	Large agricultural estate
haciendero	*Hacienda* owner
hunusan	A traditional rice harvest in which anyone can join and receive a certain share of the harvested crop (*hunus*)

263

inquilino (inquilinato)	Agricultural entrepreneur who leased land for rice and sugar cultivation from monastic orders in Central Luzon in Spanish times; later their land turned to *haciendas*
jeepney	Informal mini-bus
kabisilya	Foreman (forewoman) of a labour gang working on, in the case of rice farming, transplanting
kapilya	Small chapel
karapatan	Tenancy right
kasama	Share-cropping arrangement, originating from the meaning of 'partnership'
kasugpong	Permanent farm labourer
katiwala	Farm overseer
kiskisan	An old type of rice milling machine with a steel huller
maharlica (timagua)	Freemen in pre-Hispanic and early Hispanic Philippine communities
mestizo	a person of mixed foreign (mostly Chinese and Spanish) and native Filipino stock
milled rice	Husked and polished rice ready for cooking. A standard conversion factor from dry paddy to milled rice in the Philippines is 0.65
pacto de retroventa	A money-lending arrangement in which the lender secured control of the land as a mortgage for the loan; during the loan period, the borrower continued to cultivate the land as a sharecropper of the creditor
paddy	Unhusked rice grain
peso (P)	The unit of Philippine local currency; US$1 was equivalent to P3.90 in 1966 and P26.22 in 1996
poblacion	Urban district of town (municipality)
principalia	Local land-owning class during the Spanish period, formed through intermarriage between Spanish/Chinese *mestizos* and *casiques*
pulot	Rice panicle fallen to the ground in the harvesting process
punla	A type of rice seedbed preparation in a wet paddy field
realenga	Grant or purchase of the royal domain in Spanish period
rough rice	Same as paddy
sari-sari	Small grocery store selling a variety of daily needs

suki	Continuous mutual-trust relationship between a buyer and a seller which is lasting, long and close
tricycle	Petty-cab motorcycle with a sidecar; a major means of short-distance transportation in rural areas, such as between a village and its nearest town
tilyadora	Large threshing machine
upahan	A labour hiring contract with daily cash wage
utang na loob	Sense of gratitude or indebtedness, literally means 'debt deep inside'
walang hiya	'Shameless', a person who violates social rules and norms is considered to be *walang hiya*
white rice	Same as milled rice

Name Index

Subject Index